# Close-up

## COMPANION A2

Liz Gardiner

NATIONAL
GEOGRAPHIC
L E A R N I N G

Australia · Brazil · Mexico · Singapore · United Kingdom · United States

**Close-up A2 Companion**
Liz Gardiner

Publisher: Gavin McLean

Editorial Manager: Claire Merchant

Commissioning Editor: Kayleigh Buller

Editor: Nicola Foufouti-Kraia

Head of Production: Celia Jones

Content Project Manager: Melissa Beavis

Manufacturing Manager: Eyvett Davis

Cover designer: MPS Limited

Compositor: Wild Apple Design

For product information and technology assistance, contact us at
**Cengage Learning Customer & Sales Support, cengage.com/contact**

For permission to use material from this text or product,
submit all requests online at **cengage.com/permissions**
Further permissions questions can be emailed to
**permissionrequest@cengage.com**

ISBN: 978-1-4080-9693-2

**National Geographic Learning**
Cheriton House, North Way, Andover, Hampshire, SP10 5BE
United Kingdom

National Geographic Learning, a Cengage Learning Company, has a mission to bring the world to the classroom and the classroom to life. With our English language programs, students learn about their world by experiencing it. Through our partnerships with National Geographic and TED Talks, they develop the language and skills they need to be successful global citizens and leaders.

Locate your local office at **international.cengage.com/region**

Visit National Geographic Learning online at **NGL.Cengage.com/ELT**
Visit our corporate website at **www.cengage.com**

**Photo credits**
**Cover image:** © Karen Gowlett-Holmes/Getty Images

**Student Access:** to access the Close-up A2 Companion audio, please visit the Student Online Zone at NGL.Cengage.com/closeup

**Teacher Access:** to access the Grammar and Vocabulary Answer Keys, please visit the Teacher Online Zone at NGL.Cengage.com/closeup and use the password provided in the Teacher's Book

Printed in the United Kingdom by CPI Antony Rowe
Print Number 02      Print Year 2019

# Contents

# Note to Teachers

*Close-up A2 Companion* provides students with everything they need to understand the vocabulary and grammar in the *Close-up A2 Student's Book*.

In the vocabulary section, words and phrases are listed in order of appearance together with their parts of speech and IPA. Each entry includes a clear explanation of the headword, an example sentence, derivatives (appropriate for the level) and the Greek translation of the word or phrase as it is used in the context of the Student's Book. For some entries there are special notes. These include antonyms, synonyms and expressions. At the end of the word lists for most sections, there are word sets that help students learn related words or phrases more easily. There are also *Look!* boxes with notes on usage. The vocabulary section ends with a variety of tasks that practise many of the new words and phrases of that unit.

In the grammar section, there are comprehensive grammar explanations in Greek with plenty of topic-related example sentences. The grammar section ends with tasks that practise the grammar of that unit.

At the back of the book, there is a complete list of all the words and phrases in the companion in alphabetical order with their entry number. This helps teachers and students to locate words easily, for example, if they want to refer to a word they learnt in another unit, or if they come across any difficulties.

Finally, *Close-up A2 Companion* is accompanied by audio, which contains the accurate pronunciation of each headword. You can find the audio here: ngl.cengage.com

## Terms & Abbreviations

| Terms / Abbreviations | | Όροι / Συντομεύσεις |
|---|---|---|
| n | noun | ουσιαστικό |
| v | verb | ρήμα |
| phr v | phrasal verb | περιφραστικό ρήμα |
| adj | adjective | επίθετο |
| adv | adverb | επίρρημα |
| det | determiner | προσδιοριστικό |
| pron | pronoun | αντωνυμία |
| prep | preposition | πρόθεση |
| conj | conjunction | σύνδεσμος |
| expr | expression | έκφραση |
| excl | exclamation | επιφώνημα |
| Opp | opposite | αντίθετο |
| Syn | synonym | συνώνυμο |
| abbr | abbreviation | συντόμευση |

## Key to pronunciation and phonetic symbols

| Consonants | | | | | |
|---|---|---|---|---|---|
| p | pen | /pen/ | tʃ | chain | /tʃeɪn/ |
| b | bad | /bæd/ | dʒ | jam | /dʒæm/ |
| t | tea | /tiː/ | f | fall | /fɔːl/ |
| d | did | /dɪd/ | v | van | /væn/ |
| k | cat | /kæt/ | θ | thin | /θɪn/ |
| g | get | /get/ | ð | this | /ðɪs/ |

| Vowels and diphthongs | | | | | |
|---|---|---|---|---|---|
| iː | see | /siː/ | ɜː | fur | /fɜː/ |
| i | happy | /ˈhæpi/ | ə | about | /əˈbaʊt/ |
| ɪ | sit | /sɪt/ | eɪ | say | /seɪ/ |
| e | ten | /ten/ | əʊ | go | /gəʊ/ |
| æ | cat | /kæt/ | aɪ | my | /maɪ/ |
| ɑː | father | /ˈfɑːðə/ | ɔɪ | boy | /bɔɪ/ |
| ɒ | got | /gɒt/ | aʊ | now | /naʊ/ |
| ɔː | saw | /sɔː/ | ɪə | near | /nɪə/ |
| ʊ | put | /pʊt/ | eə | hair | /heə/ |
| u | actual | /ˈæktʃuəl/ | ʊə | pure | /pjʊə/ |
| uː | too | /tuː/ | ʌ | cup | /kʌp/ |

# 1 Who Am I?

**1.1** **present** (v) /prɪˈzent/
show sth to sb ● *We presented our project to the class.* ❖ παρουσιάζω

**1.2** **ink** (n) /ɪŋk/
coloured liquid usually in a pen ● *Write the answers with a pen that has blue ink.* ❖ μελάνι

**1.3** **thumb** (n) /θʌm/
the short thick finger on the side of your hand that helps you pick things up ● *Bob held up his thumb to tell us everything was okay.* ❖ αντίχειρας

**1.4** **general election** (n) /ˈdʒenrəl ɪˈlekʃn/
an event when everyone in the country chooses a new government ● *They're having a general election in Russia to choose a new president.* ❖ βουλευτικές εκλογές

## Reading

**1.5** **activity** (n) /ækˈtɪvəti/
something that you do to have fun ● *My favourite activity is playing tennis.* ➤ act (v), active (adj), actively (adv) ❖ δραστηριότητα

**1.6** **photography** (n) /fəˈtɒɡrəfi/
the activity of taking photos ● *My aunt is good at photography. She takes photos of animals.* ➤ photograph (v, n), photo (n), photographer (n) ❖ φωτογράφηση, φωτογραφία

**1.7** **cricket** (n) /ˈkrɪkɪt/
a game played by two teams of eleven players who score points by hitting a hard ball with a wooden bat, then running between two sets of wooden sticks ● *Children in India like playing cricket in the park.* ➤ cricketer (n) ❖ κρίκετ

**1.8** **play in a band** (phr) /pleɪ ɪn ə bænd/
play music together in small group of other people ● *My sister plays the guitar in the school band.* ❖ παίζω σε συγκρότημα

**1.9** **swimming** (n) /ˈswɪmɪŋ/
the activity of moving through water by moving your arms and legs ● *Eleni goes swimming in the sea in summer.* ➤ swim (v), swimmer (n) ❖ κολύμπι

**1.10** **online** (adj) /ˌɒnˈlaɪn/
that you can use on the internet ● *Do you play online games on your computer?* ➤ online (adv) ❖ διαδικτυακός, μέσω διαδικτύου ✎ Opp: offline

**1.11** **profile** (n) /ˈprəʊfaɪl/
a short description of who a person is, what they like, etc. ● *Mum put a photo of our cat on her online profile.* ❖ προφίλ

**1.12** **hobby** (n) /ˈhɒbi/
an activity that sb does for fun ● *Lesley's hobbies are playing the piano and swimming.* ❖ χόμπυ

**1.13** **country** (n) /ˈkʌntri/
an area of land that has its own government, laws and way of life ● *Which country is Miguel from? Spain or Italy?* ❖ χώρα

**1.14** **pet** (n) /pet/
an animal that lives with you in your home ● *Sylvia's pets are two rabbits and three fish.* ❖ κατοικίδιο ζώο

**1.15** **New Zealand** (n) /ˌnjuː ˈziːlənd/
❖ Νέα Ζηλανδία

**1.16** **travel** (v) /ˈtrævl/
go from one place to another ● *I travel to school by bus every day.* ➤ travelling (n), traveller (n) ❖ ταξιδεύω

**1.17** **information** (n) /ˌɪnfəˈmeɪʃn/
facts about sb or sth ● *You can find some information about photography online.* ➤ inform (v) ❖ πληροφορία

### Look!

Το ρήμα **play** χρησιμοποιείται σε πολλές εκφράσεις για αθλήματα, για παιχνίδια και για μουσική. Θυμηθείτε ότι για τα αθλήματα δεν βάζουμε το άρθρο **the** ή **a/an** μετά από το ρήμα **play**.

| | |
|---|---|
| play basketball | play in a band |
| play cricket | play the piano |
| play football | play the guitar |
| play tennis | play a game |
| play volleyball | |

## Word Focus

**1.18** **nature** (n) /ˈneɪtʃə(r)/
all the wild things like plants, animals, rocks, etc.● *I enjoy going for walks near the lake to be close to nature.* ➤ natural (adj), naturally (adv) ❖ φύση

**1.19** **forest** (n) /ˈfɒrɪst/
a large group of trees ● *Monkeys live in the big green forest next to the river.* ❖ δάσος

**1.20** **area** (n) /ˈeəriə/
a part of a country ● *There aren't many houses in this area.* ❖ περιοχή

**1.21** **land** (n) /lænd/
a piece of ground ● *The land next to our house is Mr Smith's garden.* ❖ γη, έδαφος

**1.22** **hang out (together)** (phr v) /hæŋ aʊt (təˈgeðə(r))/
spend a lot of free time (together) somewhere
• *George and his friends hang out together at the café after school.* ❖ κάνω παρέα (με)

**1.23** **street market** (n) /striːt ˈmɑːkɪt/
a place where you can go to buy or sell things in the street • *People buy fruit and vegetables at the street market here on Tuesdays.* ❖ λαϊκή αγορά

**1.24** **souvenir** (n) /ˌsuːvəˈnɪə(r)/
sth you buy to remember a place you're visiting • *His T-shirt with the Eiffel Tower on it is a souvenir from Paris.* ❖ αναμνηστικό, σουβενίρ

**1.25** **remember** (v) /rɪˈmembə(r)/
not forget sth; to keep sth in your mind
• *Can you remember your phone number?* ❖ θυμάμαι

# Reading
Page 7

**1.26** **high school** (n) /haɪ skuːl/
school for students from about 11 to 18 years old • *Eva is twelve and she's in her first year at high school.* ❖ λύκειο, γυμνάσιο
✎ Syn: secondary school

**1.27** **student** (n) /ˈstjuːdnt/
a person who studies at a school, university, etc. • *There are twenty-five students in our class.* ➢ study (v) ❖ μαθητής, φοιτητής

**1.28** **brilliant** (adj) /ˈbrɪliənt/
very good or clever • *I can't ride a horse, but my sister is brilliant at riding.* ❖ άριστος, υπέροχος

**1.29** **well-known** (adj) /ˌwel ˈnəʊn/
that a lot of people know about • *One Direction is a well-known band.* ❖ διάσημος, γνωστός

**1.30** **artist** (n) /ˈɑːtɪst/
a person who does painting, drawing or other kinds of art • *Leonardo Da Vinci was a brilliant artist.* ➢ art (n), artistic (adj) ❖ ζωγράφος

**1.31** **future** (n) /ˈfjuːtʃə(r)/
the time after now • *In the future, Ted wants to be a teacher.* ❖ μέλλον

**1.32** **incredible** (adj) /ɪnˈkredəbl/
not easy to believe • *This song is incredible! Listen to it.* ❖ απίστευτος

**1.33** **close** (adj) /kləʊs/
that you know very well and like very much
• *Kate and Pauline are close friends and they go everywhere together.* ➢ closely (adv) ❖ στενός, καλός (για φίλους)

**1.34** **busy** (adj) /ˈbɪzi/
having a lot of things to do • *Mum is busy at work, so Dad's cooking dinner.* ➢ απασχολημένος

**1.35** **spend time** (phr) /spend taɪm/
use your time • *I like spending time with my dog Fred.* ❖ περνώ την ώρα

**1.36** **summer** (n) /ˈsʌmə(r)/
the hottest three-month period of the year between spring and autumn • *It's hot here in summer and we go swimming in the sea.* ❖ καλοκαίρι

**1.37** **sport** (n) /spɔːt/
sth you do for fun and to be strong that often has rules • *We don't have sport every day at school.* ➢ sporty (adj) ❖ σπορ, γυμναστική

**1.38** **winter** (n) /ˈwɪntə(r)/
the coldest three-month period of the year between autumn and spring • *It snows a lot in Germany in winter.* ❖ χειμώνας

**1.39** **popular** (adj) /ˈpɒpjələ(r)/
liked by many people • *Is tennis a popular sport in your country?* ➢ popularity (n) ❖ δημοφιλής
✎ Opp: unpopular

**1.40** **South Africa** (n) /saʊθ ˈæfrɪkə/
➢ South African (adj, n) ❖ Νότια Αφρική

**1.41** **England** (n) /ˈɪŋglənd/
➢ English (adj, n) ❖ Αγγλία

**1.42** **Australia** (n) /ɒˈstreɪliə/
➢ Australian (adj, n) ❖ Αυστραλία

**1.43** **India** (n) /ˌɪndiə/
➢ Indian (adj, n) ❖ Ινδία

**1.44** **European** (adj) /ˌjʊərəˈpiːən/
➢ Europe (n), European (n) ❖ ευρωπαϊκός

**1.45** **also** (adv) /ˈɔːlsəʊ/
too; as well • *I love football, but I also play cricket.* ❖ επίσης

**1.46** **too** (adv) /tuː/
also; as well • *Megan paints pictures of the sea and the mountains, too.* ❖ επίσης

**1.47** **always** (adv) /ˈɔːlweɪz/
all the time • *I always go to school by bus.* ❖ πάντα

**1.48** **make sure** (phr) /meɪk ʃʊə(r)/
do sth so that you know sth will happen or sth is true • *Phone Tom to make sure he knows about the basketball game.* ❖ διασφαλίζω

**1.49** **crowded** (adj) /ˈkraʊdɪd/
with a lot of people • *The bus is very crowded and we can't sit down.* ➢ crowd (n) ❖ πολυσύχναστος, γεμάτος με κόσμο

**1.50** **tourist** (n) /ˈtʊərɪst/
a person who goes to a place for a holiday
• *Hundreds of tourists visit the Acropolis every day.* ➢ tourism (n) ❖ τουρίστας

**1.51** **famous** (adj) /ˈfeɪməs/
very well-known • *Andy Murray is a famous tennis player.* ➢ fame (n) ❖ διάσημος

**1.52** **gallery** (n) /ˈgæləri/
a building where you can see a lot of paintings or other art • *The artist's paintings are in a gallery in London.* ❖ πινακοθήκη, γκαλερί

**1.53** **around** (prep) /əˈraʊnd/
in many parts of a place • *I've got lots of friends from all around the world.* ❖ γύρω

**1.54** **excellent** (adj) /ˈeksələnt/
very good • *This shop sells excellent souvenirs. You should try it.* ❖ άριστος, εξαιρετικός

**1.55** **rich** (adj) /rɪtʃ/
with a lot of money • *Tracy wants to be rich so she can buy a big house one day.* ❖ πλούσιος

**1.56** **amazing** (adj) /əˈmeɪzɪŋ/
surprising; wonderful • *Your holiday photos are amazing. What a beautiful place.* ➢ amaze (v), amazed (adj) ❖ καταπληκτικός

**1.57** **colourful** (adj) /ˈkʌləfl/
with many colours • *Dora is wearing a colourful dress.* ➢ colour (v, n) ❖ πολύχρωμος

**1.58** **well-liked** (adj) /ˌwel laɪkt/
liked by many people • *Kevin is well-liked by everybody in the class because he's very friendly.* ❖ δημοφιλής

**1.59** **unusual** (adj) /ʌnˈjuːʒuəl/
not usual; different • *It's unusual to see people playing cricket in Greece.* ❖ ασυνήθιστος
✎ Opp: usual

**1.60** **noisy** (adj) /ˈnɔɪzi/
with a lot of noise • *The teacher isn't happy because the students are so noisy.* ➢ noise (n) ❖ θορυβώδης

**1.61** **busy** (adj) /ˈbɪzi/
with many people • *The shops are always busy on Saturdays.* ❖ πολυσύχναστος

**1.62** **better** (adj) /ˈbetə(r)/
more than good • *Is it better to go to a café or to go for a walk?* ❖ καλύτερος

**1.63** **creative** (adj) /kriˈeɪtɪv/
with a lot of skill and imagination • *Cheryl is creative and she writes unusual stories.* ➢ create (v), creation (n) ❖ δημιουργικός

### Adjectives

| | | |
|---|---|---|
| amazing | crowded | popular |
| better | excellent | rich |
| brilliant | famous | unusual |
| busy | incredible | well-known |
| colourful | national | well-liked |
| creative | noisy | |

# Vocabulary

**1.64** **date** (n) /deɪt/
the day when sth happens • *What's the date today? Is it the fifth or the sixth?* ❖ ημερομηνία

**1.65** **national** (adj) /ˈnæʃnəl/
relating to all parts of one country • *The first of January is a national holiday in the UK.* ➢ nationality (n) ❖ εθνικός

**1.66** **June** (n) /dʒuːn/
the month between May and July ❖ Ιούνιος

**1.67** **twenty-fifth** (number) /ˈtwenti fɪfθ/
the number 25th ❖ εικοστός πέμπτος

**1.68** **March** (n) /maːrtʃ/
the month between February and April ❖ Μάρτιος

**1.69** **twelfth** (number) /twelfθ/
the number 12th ❖ δωδέκατος

**1.70** **October** (n) /aːkˈtoʊbər/
the month between September and November ❖ Οκτώβριος

**1.71** **July** (n) /dʒuˈlaɪ/
the month between June and August ❖ Ιούλιος

**1.72** **February** (n) /ˈfebrueri/
the month between January and March ❖ Φεβρουάριος

**1.73** **twenty-first** (number) /ˈtwenti fɜːst/
the number 21st ❖ εικοστός πρώτος

**1.74** **September** (n) /sepˈtembər/
the month between August and October ❖ Σεπτέμβριος

**1.75** **December** (n) /dɪˈsembər/
the month between November and January ❖ Δεκέμβριος

**1.76** **May** (n) /meɪ/
the month between April and June ❖ Μάιος

**1.77** **August** (n) /ɔːˈgʌst/
the month between July and September ❖ Αύγουστος

**1.78** **twenty-eighth** (number) /ˈtwenti eɪtθ/
the number 28th ❖ εικοστός όγδοος

**1.79** **November** (n) /noʊˈvembər/
the month between October and December ❖ Νοέμβριος

**1.80** **Italy** (n) /ˈɪtəli/
➢ Italian (adj, n) ❖ Ιταλία

**1.81** **Greece** (n) /griːs/
➢ Greek (adj, n) ❖ Ελλάδα

**1.82** **Spain** (n) /speɪn/
➢ Spanish (adj, n) ❖ Ισπανία

**1.83** **France** (n) /fraːns/
➢ French (adj, n) ❖ Γαλλία

**1.84** **Serbia** (n) /ˈsɜːbiə/
➢ Serbian (adj, n) ❖ Σερβία

**1.85**  **Malta** (n) /ˈmɔltə/
➢ Maltese (adj, n) ❖ Μάλτα

**1.86**  **Portugal** (n) /ˈpɔːtʃʊgl/
➢ Portuguese (adj, n) ❖ Πορτογαλία

**1.87**  **Poland** (n) /ˈpəʊlənd/
➢ Polish (adj, n) ❖ Πολωνία

**1.88**  **Switzerland** (n) /ˈswɪtsələnd/
➢ Swiss (adj, n) ❖ Ελβετία

**1.89**  **Albania** (n) /ælˈbeɪniə/
➢ Albanian (adj, n) ❖ Αλβανία

**1.90**  **January** (n) /ˈdʒænjueri/
the month between December and February
❖ Ιανουάριος

**1.91**  **April** (n) /ˈeɪprəl/
the month between March and May
❖ Απρίλιος

### Dates, Months & Seasons

| Dates | Months | Seasons |
|---|---|---|
| the twenty-first | January | spring |
| the twenty-second | February | summer |
| the twenty-third | March | autumn |
| the twenty-fourth | April | winter |
| the twenty-fifth | May | |
| the twenty-sixth | June | |
| the twenty-seventh | July | |
| the twenty-eighth | August | |
| the twenty-ninth | September | |
| the thirtieth | October | |
| the thirty-first | November | |
| | December | |

**1.92**  **Chinese** (adj) /ˌtʃaɪˈniːz/
➢ China (n) ❖ κινέζικος, Κινέζος

**1.93**  **dragon** (n) /ˈdrægən/
an imaginary animal like a big lizard that
breathes fire • In China, people often make
colourful paper dragons for the New Year.
❖ δράκος

**1.94**  **spaghetti** (n) /spəˈgeti/
a kind of pasta in long thin pieces • Do you
want some spaghetti with tomato sauce?
❖ σπαγκέτι, μακαρόνια

**1.95**  **dancer** (n) /ˈdɑːnsə(r)/
a person who dances • Margaret is a ballet
dancer. ➢ dance (v), dancing (n) ❖ χορευτής

**1.96**  **symbol** (n) /ˈsɪmbl/
a letter or a sign that means sth • I can't read
Russian symbols. ➢ symbolise (v), symbolic
(adj) ❖ σύμβολο

**1.97**  **bulldog** (n) /ˈbʊldɒg/
a short dog with a big head and thick neck
• Bessie has got two small French bulldogs.
❖ μπουλντόγκ

**1.98**  **cuckoo clock** (n) /ˈkʊkuː klɒk/
a wooden clock with a small wooden bird in
the middle, which comes out and makes a
noise every hour • Granny has got an old
cuckoo clock and it's very noisy. ❖ ελβετικό
ρολόι με κούκο

**1.99**  **Dutch** (adj) /dʌtʃ/
❖ ολλανδικός, Ολλανδός

**1.100**  **the Netherlands** (n) /ðə ˈneðələndz/
❖ Ολλανδία

**1.101**  **tulip** (n) /ˈtjuːlɪp/
a plant with a big cup-shaped flower that
usually grows in spring • In February, we've
got lovely red and yellow tulips in our garden.
❖ τουλίπα

### Countries & Nationalities

| | | | |
|---|---|---|---|
| Albania | Albanian | Italy | Italian |
| Australia | Australian | Poland | Polish |
| Canada | Canadian | Portugal | Portuguese |
| China | Chinese | Serbia | Serbian |
| Cyprus | Cypriot | South Africa | South African |
| England | English | | |
| France | French | Spain | Spanish |
| Greece | Greek | Switzerland | Swiss |
| India | Indian | the Netherlands | Dutch |

**1.102**  **granny** (n) /ˈgræni/
grandma; grandmother • My granny in Sparta
is my dad's mother. ❖ γιαγιά

**1.103**  **grandad** (n) /ˈgrændæd/
grandpa; grandfather • We sometimes visit
our grandad in Glasgow at the weekend.
❖ παππούς

**1.104**  **parent** (n) /ˈpeərənt/
a mother or father • Gina's parents are from
Crete. ❖ γονιός

**1.105**  **grandparent** (n) /ˈgrænpeərənt/
the mother or father of one of your parents
• My grandparents live near us so I see them
often. ❖ παππούς, γιαγιά

**1.106**  **grandchild** (n) /ˈgræntʃaɪld/
the son or daughter of sb's son or daughter
• My grandad has got six grandchildren – me
and my five cousins. ❖ εγγονός, εγγονή

**1.107**  **granddaughter** (n) /ˈgrændɔːtə(r)/
the daughter of sb's son or daughter • Lynn's
granddaughter comes to her house after
school because Lynn's daughter and her
husband are working. ❖ εγγονή

**1.108**  **married** (adj) /ˈmærid/
not single; having a husband or a wife • Uncle
Rick is married to my Aunt Jane. ➢ marriage
(n) ❖ παντρεμένος

**1.109 surname** (n) /ˈsɜːneɪm/
your family name; your last name • *Write your name and surname on the front page of your test.* ❖ επίθετο, επώνυμο

**1.110 twin** (n) /twɪn/
a child born at the same time as his/her brother or sister with the same mother • *Robert and David are twins and they look the same as each other.* ❖ δίδυμος

**1.111 altogether** (adv) /ˌɔːltəˈgeðə(r)/
as a total • *Altogether, I've got five cousins – Aunt Helen's two sons and Aunt Beth's three daughters.* ❖ συνολικά

**1.112 favourite** (n) /ˈfeɪvərɪt/
the thing or person you like best • *Sally has got a lot of hobbies, but reading is her favourite.* ➣ favourite (adj) ❖ αγαπημένος

**1.113 same** (adj) /seɪm/
not different • *The twins have got the same colour of eyes and hair.* ❖ ίδιος

**1.114 past** (n) /pɑːst/
the time before now • *The life I have now is better than my grandparent's life in the past.* ➣ past (adj) ❖ παρελθόν

**Family**

| | |
|---|---|
| daughter | granny |
| grandad | married |
| grandchild | parent |
| granddaughter | son |
| grandparent | twin |

# Grammar

**Pages 10-11**

**1.115 Cyprus** (n) /ˈsaɪprəs/
➣ Cypriot (adj, n) ❖ Κύπρος

**1.116 freeze** (v) /friːz/
get cold and turn to ice • *When it's very cold in winter, the lake freezes.* ➣ frozen (adj), freezing (adj), freezer (n), frost (n) ❖ παγώνω

**1.117 fact** (n) /fækt/
sth that is true • *It's a fact that summer is hot in Greece.* ❖ γεγονός

**1.118 routine** (adj) /ruːˈtiːn/
usual • *Eating and sleeping are routine activities.* ➣ routine (n) ❖ ρουτίνα

**1.119 Lucky you!** (phr) /ˈlʌki juː/
used to say that sb is lucky • *Lucky you! You're in your school band, but we don't play music at our school.* ❖ Τυχερέ!/Τυχερή!

**1.120 cycle** (v) /ˈsaɪkl/
ride a bicycle • *Dad and I cycle in the park sometimes.* ➣ cycling (n), cyclist (n) ❖ κάνω ποδήλατο, πηγαίνω με ποδήλατο

**1.121 often** (adv) /ˈɒfn/
a lot of times; many times • *How often do you go swimming?* ❖ συχνά

**1.122 late** (adv) /leɪt/
• *The school bus is never late. It's always here at 7.30.* ❖ αργά

**1.123 never** (adv) /ˈnevə(r)/
not at any time • *Daisie doesn't like football, so she never watches it on TV.* ❖ ποτέ

**1.124 lazy** (adj) /ˈleɪzi/
not wanting to do activities or work • *Lisa doesn't like cycling because she's lazy.* ➣ laziness (n) ❖ τεμπέλης

**1.125 usually** (adv) /ˈjuːʒuəli/
as a usual routine • *We usually walk to school, but today we're going in Mum's car.* ➣ usual (adj) ❖ συνήθως

**1.126 cry** (v) /kraɪ/
have tears coming from your eyes usually because you are sad • *Don't cry. Everything will be okay.* ❖ κλαίω

**1.127 sometimes** (adv) /ˈsʌmtaɪmz/
not always • *Sometimes Harry meets his friends after school, but not every day.* ❖ μερικές φορές, καμιά φορά

**1.128 hardly ever** (adv) /ˈhɑːdli ˈevə(r)/
not very often; almost never • *I hardly ever see Uncle Joe because he lives in New Zealand.* ❖ σχεδόν ποτέ

**1.129 pupil** (n) /ˈpjuːpl/
a student in primary school • *There are thirty pupils in Mr Johnson's class – 18 girls and 12 boys.* ❖ μαθητής (δημοτικού)

**1.130 exam** (n) /ɪgˈzæm/
a school test • *I can't go out this evening because I've got an English exam tomorrow.* ➣ examine (v), examination (n), examiner (n) ❖ εξέταση, διαγώνισμα

**1.131 invite** (v) /ɪnˈvaɪt/
ask sb to come to an event • *I want to invite all my friends to my party.* ➣ invitation (n) ❖ προσκαλώ

**1.132 specific** (adj) /spəˈsɪfɪk/
particular; exact • *I know that the game is on Saturday, but I don't know the specific time.* ❖ συγκεκριμένος

**1.133 reason** (n) /ˈriːzn/
the fact or event that makes sth happen • *The reason why Tina is happy is that she is going on holiday.* ❖ αιτία, λόγος

**1.134 come from** (phr v) /kʌm frəm/
be from the place where you were born • *Where do you come from? Are you Chinese?* ❖ κατάγομαι, προέρχομαι

**1.135 Canadian** (adj) /kəˈneɪdiən/
➣ Canada (n), Canadian (n) ❖ καναδικός, Καναδός

**1.136** **pasta** (n) /ˈpæstə/
noodles, spaghetti, etc. • *Italy is famous for its pasta with cheese or tomato sauce.* ❖ ζυμαρικά

**1.137** **break** (n) /breɪk/
a time to relax between lessons at school • *I like chatting with my school friends in the break.* ➢ break (v) ❖ διάλειμμα

**1.138** **classmate** (n) /ˈklɑːsmeɪt/
people in the same class at school • *Derek is in a new school and he doesn't know his new classmates.* ❖ συμμαθητής

**1.139** **soon** (adv) /suːn/
after a short time • *Don't stop cycling now. We can have a break soon.* ❖ σύντομα

**1.140** **until** (prep) /ənˈtɪl/
up to a certain time • *I'm staying with my granny until August.* ❖ μέχρι

**1.141** **lie** (v) /laɪ/
put yourself in a flat position • *Andrew is lying on the sofa and reading a book.* ❖ ξαπλώνω

**1.142** **Arabic** (n) /ˈærəbɪk/
➢ Arabian (adj), Arab (n), Arabia (n) ❖ αραβικά

**1.143** **right now** (adv) /raɪt naʊ/
exactly at this moment • *Can I ask you something or are you busy right now?* ❖ αμέσως

**1.144** **action** (n) /ˈækʃn/
sth that sb does • *Write four sentences about actions you do every day.* ➢ act (v, n), active (adj), actively (adv), actor (n) ❖ πράξη

**1.145** **happen** (v) /ˈhæpən/
take place • *What's happening out there? The street is very noisy.* ❖ συμβαίνω

**1.146** **temporary** (adj) /ˈtempərəri/
happening only for a short time • *Dan has got a temporary job in a café just for the summer.* ❖ προσωρινός

**1.147** **situation** (n) /ˌsɪtʃuˈeɪʃn/
the things that are happening at a specific time and place • *The country is in a difficult situation.* ❖ κατάσταση, περίσταση

**1.148** **homework** (n) /ˈhəʊmwɜːk/
school work to do at home • *I always do my homework in my bedroom after school.* ❖ μαθήματα, εργασία για το σπίτι

**1.149** **bus stop** (n) /bʌs stɒp/
a place in the street where buses stop for people to get on or off • *There's a bus stop outside the cinema.* ❖ στάση λεωφορείων

**1.150** **take a break** (phr) /teɪk ə breɪk/
stop working or studying for a short time • *I'm hungry. It's time to take a break for lunch.* ❖ κάνω διάλειμμα

**1.151** **answer the phone** (phr) /ˈɑːnsə(r) ðə fəʊn/
pick up the phone when sb calls • *Don't answer the phone! It's just somebody selling something again.* ❖ σηκώνω/απαντάω το τηλέφωνο

**1.152** **chat** (v) /tʃæt/
talk (or send texts) in a friendly way • *Mum is chatting to her friend on the phone.* ➢ chat (n) ❖ κουβεντιάζω

**1.153** **feel** (v) /fiːl/
have a certain feeling • *Carol is feeling better today, so she's going to school.* ➢ feeling (n) ❖ αισθάνομαι, νιώθω

**1.154** **make sense** (phr) /meɪk sens/
be logical • *Dad doesn't like that book because the story doesn't make sense.* ❖ βγάζω νόημα

**1.155** **make a guess** (phr) /meɪk ə ges/
say or write an answer without being sure if it is right • *I don't know what my present is, but I can make a guess.* ❖ μαντεύω

**1.156** **hospital** (n) /ˈhɒspɪtl/
a place where sick people go to get help from doctors, etc. • *Stephanie is a doctor and she works in the children's hospital.* ❖ νοσοκομείο

**1.157** **hope** (v) /həʊp/
wish that sth good is possible • *I hope Grandad likes his present.* ➢ hope (n) ❖ ελπίζω

**1.158** **get well** (phr) /get wel/
stop feeling ill • *Get well soon! We need you in the basketball team.* ❖ γίνομαι καλά

**1.159** **have a great time** (phr) /hæv ə greɪt taɪm/
have a lot of fun; to enjoy yourself • *The children are having a great time playing with their friends.* ❖ περνάω πολύ καλά

**1.160** **best friend** (n) /best frend/
the friend that you like spending time with most • *I know many people, but George is my best friend. We go everywhere together.* ❖ καλύτερος φίλος

**1.161** **really** (adv) /ˈriːəli/
very much • *It's really hot in here. Please open the window.* ➢ real (adj) ❖ πάρα πολύ, πραγματικά

**1.162** **cool** (adj) /kuːl/
fashionable and fun • *Paul is wearing his cool new trainers to the party.* ❖ πρώτος, φοβερός

**1.163** **take photos** (phr) /teɪk ˈfəʊtəʊz/
take pictures with a camera • *Liz loves taking photos of her friends.* ❖ βγάζω/τραβάω φωτογραφίες

**1.164** **mobile** (n) /ˈməʊbaɪl/
a small phone that you can carry everywhere • *Phone me on my mobile if I'm not at home.* ❖ κινητό (τηλέφωνο)

**Time**

| Adverbs | Nouns |
|---|---|
| always | past |
| hardly ever | present |
| late | future |
| never | |
| often | **Phrases** |
| right now | free time |
| sometimes | have a great time |
| usually | spend time |

# Listening
Page 12

**1.165** **price** (n) /praɪs/
the money you need to buy sth • *What price are the art lessons?* ❖ τιμή

**1.166** **begin** (v) /bɪˈgɪn/
start • *What time does the lesson begin?*
➢ beginning (n) ❖ αρχίζω

**1.167** **cost** (v) /kɒst/
need a certain amount of money to buy it • *How much does the book cost?* ➢ cost (n), costly (adv) ❖ στοιχίζω, κοστίζω

**1.168** **teach** (v) /tiːtʃ/
explain and show sb how to do sth • *Mum is teaching me how to take photos.* ➢ teacher (n), teaching (n) ❖ διδάσκω

**1.169** **course** (n) /kɔːs/
a group of lessons on one subject • *My sister is doing a one-year course to learn Chinese.* ❖ σειρά μαθημάτων

**1.170** **club** (n) /klʌb/
a group of people who meet to do a particular activity together • *Charles is in a club which meets every week to talk about photography.* ❖ όμιλος

# Speaking
Page 13

**1.171** **apartment** (n) /əˈpɑːtmənt/
a home on one floor of a building that has other homes in it • *Our apartment is on the third floor.* ❖ διαμέρισμα
✎ Syn: flat

**1.172** **share** (v) /ʃeə(r)/
use sth together with other people • *Mum and Dad have got only one car, so they share it to go to work.* ➢ share (n) ❖ μοιράζομαι

**1.173** **learn** (v) /lɜːn/
find out about and understand sth • *I want to learn to ride a horse.* ❖ μαθαίνω

**1.174** **watch TV** (phr) /wɒtʃ ˌtiː ˈviː/
see films and other shows on TV • *How often do you watch TV?* ❖ βλέπω τηλεόραση

**1.175** **subject** (n) /ˈsʌbdʒɪkt/
a lesson you study at school • *My favourite subject at school is maths.* ❖ μάθημα, θέμα

**1.176** **free time** (n) /friː taɪm/
the time when you don't need to study or work, etc. • *In my free time, I often play games with my sister.* ❖ ελεύθερος χρόνος

**School**

| Nouns | Verbs |
|---|---|
| art | learn |
| break | study |
| classmate | teach |
| course | |
| homework | |
| pupil | |
| sport | |
| student | |
| subject | |

## Look!

Θυμηθείτε ότι το ρήμα **learn** σημαίνει *μαθαίνω*, ενώ το ρήμα **teach** σημαίνει *διδάσκω*.

*Martha and Daniel are students. They're **learning** Spanish.*

*Mr Wilson is our teacher. He **teaches** Spanish to high school students.*

# Writing
Pages 14-15

**1.177** **accuracy** (n) /ˈækjərəsi/
the state of being completely correct • *Read your answers again to check the accuracy before you send the form.* ➢ accurate (adj), accurately (adv) ❖ ακρίβεια

**1.178** **complete** (v) /kəmˈpliːt/
write information needed on a form, test paper, etc. • *Make sure you complete all the answers in the test.* ➢ complete (adj), completely (adv) ❖ συμπληρώνω

**1.179** **form** (n) /fɔːm/
a paper with questions and spaces for answers on it • *Write your name, age and address on the form to join our club.* ❖ αίτηση, φόρμα

**1.180** **title** (n) /ˈtaɪtl/
a word or letters in front of your name that show a certain job or if you are married • *Patrick's title is Dr because he's a doctor.* ❖ τίτλος

**1.181** **date of birth** (phr) /deɪt əv bɜːθ/
the day you first come into the world as a baby • *My sister Denise's date of birth is the same day as mine because we're twins.* ❖ ημερομηνία γέννησης
✎ short form = DOB

**1.182** **address** (n) /əˈdres/
your house number and street name, etc. that shows where you live • *Write your address at the top of your letter.* ❖ διεύθυνση

**1.183** **interest** (n) /ˈɪntrəst/
sth that you enjoy doing or want to know more about • *Tracy and I have the same interests – we both like dancing and art.* ➢ interest (v), interesting (adj), interested (adj) ❖ χόμπυ, ενδιαφέρον

**1.184** **application** (n) /ˌæplɪˈkeɪʃn/
a form you write on to give your personal details needed for a certain reason • *Keith is sending an application for a job in Australia.* ➢ apply (v), applicant (n) ❖ αίτηση

**1.185** **passport** (n) /ˈpɑːspɔːt/
a small official book that shows who you are and where you come from when you travel to another country • *We must show our passports at the airport.* ❖ διαβατήριο

**1.186** **membership** (n) /ˈmembəʃɪp/
the state of belonging to a group, club, etc. • *My membership for the sports club is from January to December.* ➢ member (n) ❖ ιδιότητα μέλους, συνδρομή

**1.187** **enter a competition** (phr) /ˈentə(r) ə ˌkɒmpəˈtɪʃn/
say you want to take part in an event to try to win sth • *Our band is entering the singing competition.* ❖ δηλώνω συμμετοχή σε αγώνα

**1.188** **landline** (n) /ˈlændlaɪn/
a phone that you can only use in one house, office, etc. because it isn't a mobile • *I can't hear you on the mobile, phone me on my landline.* ❖ σταθερό τηλέφωνο

**1.189** **signature** (n) /ˈsɪgnətʃə(r)/
your name the way you write it by hand at the end of a letter, etc. • *Don't forget to write your signature on the form.* ➢ sign (v) ❖ υπογραφή

**1.190** **order** (v) /ˈɔːdə/
say what you would like to buy or eat • *Mum is ordering some books for me online.* ➢ order (n) ❖ παραγγέλνω

**1.191** **monthly** (adj) /ˈmʌnθli/
that you can get once a month • *Dad gets a monthly ticket for the bus to go to work.* ➢ month (n) ❖ μηνιαίος

**1.192** **magazine** (n) /ˌmægəˈziːn/
a thin book that you can buy once a week/ month/etc. with articles, pictures and information about different things • *My favourite monthly magazine is about travelling.* ❖ περιοδικό

**1.193** **personal** (adj) /ˈpɜːsənl/
belonging to one person • *I never give all my personal details on Facebook.* ➢ personally (adj), personality (n) ❖ προσωπικός

**Personal Information**

| | |
|---|---|
| address | signature |
| date of birth | surname |
| nationality | title |

**1.194** **especially** (adv) /ɪˈspeʃəli/
more than other things • *I love art, especially drawing people.* ➢ special (adj) ❖ ιδίως

**1.195** **computer geek** (n) /kəmˈpjuːtə(r) giːk/
sb who knows a lot about using computers • *Sylvia can teach you about the internet because she's a computer geek.* ❖ κομπιουτεράκιας

**1.196** **gossip** (n) /ˈgɒsɪp/
things people say about sb that aren't always true or nice • *This magazine has lots of gossip about famous people.* ➢ gossip (v) ❖ κουτσομπολιό

**1.197** **cooking** (n) /ˈkʊkɪŋ/
making food ready to eat • *Christina is really good at cooking Greek food.* ➢ cook (v, n), cooker (n) ❖ μαγείρεμα, μαγειρική

**1.198** **variety** (n) /vəˈraɪəti/
many different kinds of one thing • *The shop sells a variety of souvenir T-shirts for people of all ages.* ➢ vary (v) ❖ ποικιλία

**1.199** **expression** (n) /ɪkˈspreʃn/
a phrase • *We are learning some useful expressions in our English lessons.* ➢ express (v) ❖ έκφραση

**1.200** **prize** (n) /praɪz/
sth you win for being the best at sth • *What's the first prize in the swimming competition?* ❖ βραβείο

**1.201** **strange** (adj) /streɪndʒ/
surprising or different from usual • *The band always wear strange clothes when they are playing.* ➢ stranger (n) ❖ περίεργος

**1.202** **epic** (adj) /ˈepɪk/
especially good • *The football final was an epic game.* ❖ επικός

**1.203** **headphones** (n pl) /ˈhedfəʊnz/
sth you wear over your ears to listen to music without other people hearing it • *Vincent wears headphones when he's playing computer games.* ❖ ακουστικά

**1.204** **perfume** (n) /ˈpɜːfjuːm/
sth that you put on your skin or clothes to smell nice • *Mum is giving Granny some nice French perfume for her birthday.* ❖ άρωμα

**1.205** **announce** (v) /əˈnaʊns/
to tell people an important plan or decision
• *I hope they announce the competition winner soon.* ➢ announcement (n), announcer (n) ❖ ανακοινώνω

**1.206** **issue** (n) /ˈɪʃuː/
one of a series of magazines, etc. • *In this month's issue of Geek Games, there's a free CD.* ➢ issue (v) ❖ τεύχος

# Video 1
# Animal Families   Page 16

**1.207** **group** (n) /gruːp/
people, animals or things that are together for some reason • *Many groups of tourists visit the island every year.* ❖ ομάδα, συλλογή

**1.208** **team** (n) /tiːm/
a group that work together or play a sport against other teams • *I'm in the school basketball team.* ❖ ομάδα

**1.209** **female** (n) /ˈfiːmeɪl/
a female animal; a girl or woman • *A female cat usually stays close to her children.* ➢ female (adj) ❖ θηλυκό

**1.210** **male** (n) /meɪl/
a male animal; a boy or man • *Male lions have long hair around their head.* ➢ male (adj) ❖ αρσενικός

**1.211** **meerkat** (n) /ˈmɪəkæt/
a small animal that lives in southern Africa and has a very long tail • *Meerkats look very funny when they sit up on their back legs.* ❖ σουρικάτα, μίρκατ

**1.212** **alpha pair** (n) /ˈælfə peə(r)/
the mother and father of all the animals in one family, e.g. meerkats • *In a meerkat family, the alpha pair are the mum and dad of up to 30 children.* ❖ κυρίαρχο ζευγάρι

**1.213** **silver** (adj) /ˈsɪlvə(r)/
with a shiny light grey colour • *My grandparents have all got silver hair.* ➢ silver (n) ❖ ασημένιος

**1.214** **back** (n) /bæk/
the back part of the top of your body • *You can sit on the elephant's back and go for a ride.* ➢ back (adj) ❖ πλάτη

**1.215** **front** (n) /frʌnt/
the front part of the top of your body
• *A female kangaroo has got a pocket on her front.* ➢ front (adj) ❖ μπροστινό μέρος

**1.216** **leader** (n) /ˈliːdə(r)/
a person or animal who shows the others in a group what to do • *Janice is the leader of our school band. She writes and sings all the songs.* ➢ lead (v) ❖ αρχηγός

**1.217** **gorilla** (n) /gəˈrɪlə/
a big African animal like a really large monkey
• *Gorillas are big and strong animals and they don't eat meat.* ❖ γορίλας

**1.218** **alone** (adv) /əˈləʊn/
without any other person • *Don't walk in the forest alone.* ❖ μόνος

**1.219** **daughter** (n) /ˈdɔːtə(r)/
a girl child • *The Smiths' daughter Sharon is doing her homework.* ❖ κόρη

**1.220** **handsome** (adj) /ˈhænsəm/
nice looking • *David looks really handsome in his new clothes.* ❖ όμορφος

**1.221** **son** (n) /sʌn/
a boy child • *Tom and Mary's son is a really handsome boy.* ❖ γιός

# Vocabulary Exercises

**A** Write the nationalities.

1 China _____
2 Spain _____
3 Greece _____
4 Switzerland _____
5 England _____
6 the Netherlands _____
7 France _____
8 Portugal _____
9 Italy _____
10 Australia _____

**B**  Match.

| | | | |
|---|---|---|---|
| 1 | free | ☐ | **a** geek |
| 2 | best | ☐ | **b** clock |
| 3 | high | ☐ | **c** time |
| 4 | street | ☐ | **d** school |
| 5 | computer | ☐ | **e** pair |
| 6 | cuckoo | ☐ | **f** friend |
| 7 | alpha | ☐ | **g** election |
| 8 | general | ☐ | **h** market |

**C**  Circle the correct words.

1  A(n) **incredible / creative** number of people visit the Greek islands in summer.
2  This song is **famous / popular** with teenagers because they like dancing to it.
3  Always make **sense / sure** you complete all the information on the form.
4  I'm too **busy / crowded** to go to the sports club today.
5  Do you like my photo on my online **profile / symbol**?
6  We live near a forest because we like being close to **country / nature**.
7  Where do you **come from / hang out** with your friends at weekends?
8  Remember to take your **passport / souvenir** to show your nationality at the airport.
9  My teacher's **daughter / son** is a really nice girl.
10  The twins are five years old and their **granny / grandchild** lives in Scotland.

**D**  Complete the sentences with words formed from the words in bold.

1  Mike's favourite _____ is playing football.                       **ACT**
2  Write your _____ information on the front of the form.             **PERSON**
3  Peter is a _____ in second year at high school.                    **STUDY**
4  Mum isn't _____ in watching cricket on TV.                         **INTEREST**
5  What _____ is Gloria?                                              **NATIONAL**
6  I would like to be a _____ in the future.                          **PHOTOGRAPH**
7  Bruce reads a _____ magazine about sport.                          **MONTH**
8  Dad's mother and father are my _____ .                             **PARENT**

**E** Complete the months. Find out Grandad's nationality.

Grandad's nationality is __ __ __ __ __   __ __ __ __ __ __ __ .

# 1 Grammar

## 1.1 Present Simple

| Κατάφαση |
|---|
| I/we/you/they play<br>he/she/it play**s** |
| **Άρνηση** |
| I/we/you/they **don't** play<br>he/she/it **doesn't** play |
| **Ερώτηση** |
| **Do** I/we/you/they play?<br>**Does** he/she/it play? |

| Σύντομες απαντήσεις | |
|---|---|
| **Yes**, I/we/you/they **do**.<br>**Yes**, he/she/it **does**. | **No**, I/we/you/they **don't**.<br>**No**, he/she/it **doesn't**. |

Χρησιμοποιούμε **Present Simple** για:
γεγονότα.
→ *Gorillas **live** in family groups.*
ρουτίνα ή συνήθειες (συχνά με επιρρήματα συχνότητας).
→ *We **sometimes watch** TV in the evening.*
μόνιμες καταστάσεις.
→ *My grandad **works** in a hospital.*
**Σημείωση:** Χρονικές εκφράσεις που αφορούν **επαναλαμβανόμενες πράξεις** χρησιμοποιούνται συχνά με Present Simple. Για παράδειγμα, *every day/week/month, once a week, twice a year, at night, at weekends, in the morning/afternoon/evening,* κλπ.
→ *I go to an island **every summer**.*

## 1.2 Adverbs of frequency

Χρησιμοποιούμε **adverbs of frequency** για να πούμε πόσο συχνά συμβαίνει κάτι. Μπαίνουν πριν από το κύριο ρήμα, αλλά μετά από το ρήμα *be*.
→ *We **often visit** our grandparents at weekends.*
→ *Our grandparents **are always** happy to see us.*
Συνηθισμένα adverbs of frequency είναι: *always, usually, often, sometimes, rarely, never.*

## 1.3 Present Continuous

| Κατάφαση |
|---|
| I **am ('m)** play**ing**<br>he/she/it **is ('s)** play**ing**<br>we/you/they **are ('re)** play**ing** |
| **Άρνηση** |
| I **am ('m) not** playing<br>he/she/it **is not (isn't)** playing<br>we/you/they **are not (aren't)** playing |
| **Ερώτηση** |
| **Am** I play**ing**?<br>**Is** he/she/it play**ing**?<br>**Are** we/you/they play**ing**? |

| Σύντομες απαντήσεις | |
|---|---|
| **Yes**, I **am**.<br>**Yes**, he/she/it **is**.<br>**Yes**, we/you/they **are**. | **No**, I'm not.<br>**No**, he/she/it **isn't**.<br>**No**, we/you/they **aren't**. |

**Ορθογραφία:** live → living  run → running  cry → crying

Χρησιμοποιούμε **Present Continuous** για:

πράξεις που συμβαίνουν την ώρα που μιλάμε.

→ They **are watching** a video about families.

πράξεις που συμβαίνουν περίπου την ώρα που μιλάμε.

→ My dad **is teaching** me to ride a bike.

προσωρινές καταστάσεις.

→ She **is living** with her grandparents this summer.

**Σημείωση:** Χρησιμοποιούμε αυτές τις συνηθισμένες χρονικές εκφράσεις με Present Continuous: *at the moment, now, right now, for the time being, at present, this morning/afternoon/evening/week/month/year, today,* κλπ.

**Σημείωση:** Τα stative verbs που περιγράφουν καταστάσεις (states) π.χ. *like, love, believe, know, think,* δεν χρησιμοποιούνται στους χρόνους διαρκείας (continuous tenses).

# Grammar Exercises

## A Match.

1 Does your brother speak Italian?  ☐
2 Are the twins studying English?  ☐
3 Do you meet your friends on Sundays?  ☐
4 Is your dad an artist?  ☐
5 Do your parents come from Cyprus?  ☐
6 Are you in the school football team?  ☐

a  Yes, he is.
b  No, we aren't.
c  Yes, they do.
d  No, he doesn't.
e  Yes, they are.
f  No, I don't.

## B Write the words in the correct order to make sentences.

1 always / school / walks / she / to

_____

2 to / aren't / listening / right now / they / the teacher

_____

3 for / is / late / never / football games / he

_____

4 friends / to / we / home / often / our / invite

_____

5 ? / lesson / time / does / what / begin / English / the

_____

6 arrive / hardly ever / for / I / lessons / late

_____

7 ? / students / do / usually / lunch / where / the / have

_____

8 at / brilliant / always / writing / are / you

_____

# 1 Grammar

**C** **Complete the dialogue using the Present Simple or Present Continuous of the verbs in brackets.**

**Ann:** Hi Sam! What [1] _____ you _____ (do)? [2] _____ (be) you busy?

**Sam:** Hi Ann! Yes, I [3] _____ (be) really busy. Right now I [4] _____ (help) the twins. They [5] _____ (play) in their band in a competition tonight. You know I always [6] _____ (write) their songs.

**Ann:** What? I can't hear you. [7] _____ you _____ (listen) to music?

**Sam:** No. My brother [8] _____ (sing) next to me. Hey, Thomas! We [9] _____ (talk) on the phone. Ann, [10] _____ you _____ (want) to come with us to watch the competition?

**Ann:** Okay, I can hear you now. Yes, I'd like to come. We [11] _____ (not go) out often. I'll ask Mum first. She [12] _____ (clean) the car at the moment.

**Sam:** Great! Phone me back soon.

# 2 Look At Me!

**2.1** **bride** (n) /braɪd/
a woman who is about to get married or
has just got married • *I went to a wedding
yesterday and the bride was so beautiful!*
❖ νύφη

**2.2** **traditional** (adj) /trəˈdɪʃənl/
done in the same way for many years
• *It's traditional to eat lamb at Easter in
Greece.* ➣ tradition (n), traditionally (adv)
❖ παραδοσιακός

**2.3** **dress** (n) /dres/
a piece of clothing for women or girls that
covers the top half of the body and hangs
down over the legs • *The girl wore a beautiful
red dress at her birthday party.* ➣ dress (v)
❖ φόρεμα

## Reading Page 18

**2.4** **Congratulations!** (excl) /kənˌgrætʃuˈleɪʃn/
We say this to sb to say we are happy about
a happy event or when they did sth well.
• *Congratulations! You got the first prize.*
➣ congratulate (v) ❖ Συγχαρητήρια!

**2.5** **bored** (adj) /bɔːd/
tired because you're not interested • *Ken
never gets bored at work because he meets
new people every day.* ➣ bore (v, n), boring
(adj), boredom (n) ❖ βαριεστημένος

**2.6** **surprised** (adj) /səˈpraɪzd/
how you feel when sth happens that you don't
expect • *I'm very surprised that you're moving
to Canada. It's so cold there!* ➣ surprise (v, n),
surprising (adj) ❖ ξαφνιασμένος

**2.7** **scared** (adj) /skeəd/
afraid • *My cousin is scared of snakes.*
➣ scare (v), scary (adj) ❖ τρομαγμένος

## Word Focus Page 18

**2.8** **Aboriginal Australian** (n) /ˌæbəˈrɪdʒənl
ɒˈstreɪliən/
the first people in Australia • *Andrew's
grandfather is an Aboriginal Australian.*
❖ ιθαγενής Αυστραλός

**2.9** **fringe** (n) /frɪndʒ/
the front part of your hair that is cut above your
eyes • *Your fringe is getting too long. How can
you see where you're going?* ❖ φράντζα

**2.10** **eyebrow** (n) /ˈaɪbraʊ/
one of the two lines of hair on your face
above your eyes • *Mandy's eyebrows lifted in
surprise when she saw us.* ❖ φρύδι

**2.11** **didgeridoo** (n) /ˌdɪdʒəriˈduː/
a long wooden musical instrument • *We
bought a small didgeridoo as a souvenir
from Australia.* ❖ είδος πνευστού μουσικού
οργάνου, ντινζεριντού

**2.12** **wooden** (adj) /ˈwʊdn/
made of wood • *The children are playing
with their colourful wooden toys.* ➣ wood (n)
❖ ξύλινος

**2.13** **instrument** (n) /ˈɪnstrəmənt/
an object used to make musical sounds • *The
band picked up their instruments and started
to play.* ❖ (μουσικό) όργανο

**2.14** **blow** (v) /bləʊ/
push air out from your mouth • *When you
blow across the top of an open bottle, it makes
a noise.* ❖ φυσώ

**2.15** **professional** (adj) /prəˈfeʃənl/
a job that needs training and experience
• *Frank is a professional football player.*
➣ profession (n) ❖ επαγγελματικός

**2.16** **job** (n) /dʒɒb/
the work that sb does to get money • *My
aunt has two jobs – she cleans houses in the
morning and works in a café in the evening.*
❖ δουλειά, επάγγελμα

**2.17** **culture** (n) /ˈkʌltʃə/
the beliefs, art and way of life in a country
• *We learnt a lot about Chinese food and
culture on our holiday in Beijing.* ➣ cultural
(adj) ❖ κουλτούρα

**2.18** **snack** (n) /snæk/
a small meal • *I usually take a snack to school
to eat in the break.* ❖ κολατσιό

**2.19** **tasty** (adj) /ˈteɪsti/
having a nice flavour • *These cheese pies are
really tasty.* ➣ taste (v) ❖ νόστιμος
✎ Opp: tasteless

**2.20** **meal** (n) /miːl/
the food you eat, e.g. lunch, dinner • *We have
a big meal in the evening when my parents
come home from work.* ❖ γεύμα

## Reading Pages 18-19

**2.21** **finish** (v) /ˈfɪnɪʃ/
complete • *Helen wants to be a teacher when
she finishes her English course.* ➣ finish (n)
❖ τελειώνω

**2.22** **business** (n) /ˈbɪznəs/
an organisation or company that makes or
sells things • *Katy has a business making
clothes for children.* ❖ επιχείρηση

**2.23** **sound** (v) /saʊnd/
if sth sounds a particular way, that is how it
seems to you when you hear it • *This music
sounds strange when you hear it for the first
time.* ➢ sound (n) ❖ ακούγομαι

**2.24** **weird** (adj) /wɪəd/
very strange • *We heard a weird noise from
outside, but it was only our cat.* ❖ περίεργος

**2.25** **design** (n) /dɪ'zaɪn/
the lines and shapes drawn to make sth
beautiful • *I love the design on the front
of your T-shirt.* ➢ design (v), designer (n)
❖ σχέδιο

**2.26** **surfer** (n) /'sɜːfə(r)/
sb who does surfing on water • *We sat on the
beach watching the surfers on the sea.* ➢ surf
(v), surfing (n) ❖ κάποιος που κάνει σερφ

**2.27** **ago** (n) /ə'gəʊ/
before a certain time in the past • *Jack went to
Italy two years ago.* ❖ πριν

**2.28** **take part in** (phr v) /teɪk pɑːt ɪn/
be involved in • *Our class is taking part in the
school sports day.* ❖ συμμετέχω

**2.29** **champion** (n) /'tʃæmpiən/
sb who wins a competition • *Serena Williams
was a world tennis champion in 2015.*
❖ πρωταθλητής

**2.30** **early** (adv) /'ɜːli/
before the usual time; at the start of a period
of time • *The school bus is hardly ever early –
it's often late.* ❖ νωρίς

**2.31** **fun** (n) /fʌn/
sth that you enjoy doing • *Going to the beach
in summer is good fun.* ➢ funny (adj) ❖ πλάκα,
διασκέδαση

**2.32** **watch out** (phr v) /wɒtʃ aʊt/
be careful • *Watch out! Don't fall into the river.*
❖ προσέχω

**2.33** **shark** (n) /ʃɑːk/
a very big fish with sharp teeth and a big fin on
its back • *We were scared to go surfing when
we saw the sharks.* ❖ καρχαρίας

**2.34** **so** (adv) /səʊ/
very • *Bill was so surprised when he won the
competition.* ❖ τόσο, πάρα πολύ

**2.35** **German Shepherd** (n) /'dʒɜːmən 'ʃepəd/
a kind of big dog often used to guard places
• *Our dog looks like a wolf, but he's a friendly
German Shepherd.* ❖ Γερμανικός Ποιμενικός,
λυκόσκυλο

**2.36** **train** (v) /treɪn/
teach sb/sth to do a job • *Chris had to train
his dog not to eat the furniture.* ➢ trainer (n),
training (n) ❖ εκπαιδεύω

**2.37** **police dog** (n) /pə'liːs dɒg/
a dog taught to help the police to catch or find
people • *The police dog found the thieves
from the smell of their shoes.* ❖ λαγωνικό της
αστυνομίας

**2.38** **quite** (adv) /kwaɪt/
really • *This dog looks scary, but he's quite
friendly with children.* ❖ αρκετά

**2.39** **smart** (adj) /smɑːt/
clever • *My cat is so smart that he knows how
to open the fridge.* ❖ έξυπνος

**2.40** **each one** (phr) /iːtʃ wʌn/
every one thing or person (of the same kind)
• *Lots of tourists came into our shop today
and each one bought souvenirs.* ❖ καθένας,
καθεμία

**2.41** **different** (adj) /'dɪfrənt/
not the same • *Your hair seems different
today. It looks very nice.* ➢ difference (n)
❖ διαφορετικός

**2.42** **like** (prep) /laɪk/
in the same way as sb • *Like his brother, Tim
plays cricket very well.* ❖ όπως, σαν

**2.43** **successful** (adj) /sək'sesfl/
very good at doing sth • *Laura became
a successful artist at an early age and
people around the world buy her paintings.*
➢ succeed (v), success (n) ❖ επιτυχημένος
✎ Opp: unsuccessful

---

**Work**

| Nouns | Adjectives |
|---|---|
| business | interesting |
| job | professional |
| | successful |
| **Verbs** | traditional |
| create | |
| decide | |
| design | |
| train | |

---

**2.44** **Labrador** (n) /'læbrədɔː(r)/
a kind of large dog that is yellow, black or
brown • *Most Labradors can swim very well
because they were trained as fishing dogs.*
❖ Λαμπραντόρ

**2.45** **look after** (phr v) /lʊk 'ɑːftə(r)/
take care of sth/sb • *Granny looks after our
pets when we go on holiday.* ❖ φροντίζω

**2.46** **ill** (adj) /ɪl/
sick; not well • *Our teacher wasn't at school
last week because she was ill.* ➢ illness (n)
❖ άρρωστος

**2.47** **unkind** (adj) /ˌʌn'kaɪnd/
not nice to others • *It's terrible to see people
being unkind to animals.* ❖ αγενής, σκληρός
✎ Opp: kind

**2.48** **choice** (n) /tʃɔɪs/
sth that you can choose out of different things
• It wasn't easy to make a choice about which dog to take home. They were all lovely. ➣ choose (v) ❖ επιλογή

**2.49** **decide** (v) /dɪˈsaɪd/
think about things, and then make a choice
• Greta decided to become a doctor. ➣ decision (n), decisive (adj) ❖ αποφασίζω

**2.50** **musical** (adj) /ˈmjuːzɪkl/
related to music • I love listening to the musical sounds of the sea. ➣ music (n), musician (n) ❖ μουσικός

**2.51** **Hawaii** (n) /həˈwaɪi/
Hawaiian (adj, n) ❖ Χαβάη

**2.52** **Brazil** (n) /brəˈzɪl/
Brazilian (adj, n) ❖ Βραζιλία

**2.53** **still** (adv) /stɪl/
not stopping up to a certain time • Dad's aunt is ninety and she still walks ten kilometres a day. ❖ ακόμα

**2.54** **policeman** (n) /pəˈliːsmən/
a man who is a police officer • Some policemen use German Shepherd dogs to find people or things that are lost. ❖ αστυνομικός
✎ Note: policewoman = female police officer

**2.55** **according to** (phr) /əˈkɔːˌdɪŋ tuː/
from what sb said • According to our English teacher, Australia has got beautiful beaches. ❖ σύμφωνα με

**2.56** **horrible** (adj) /ˈhɒrəbl/
very bad • There's a horrible noise from Theo's room because he's learning to play the violin. ❖ φρικτός

**2.57** **police officer** (n) /pəˈliːs ˌɒfɪsər/
a man or woman who works in the police force • Michelle described her lost bike to the police officers and they found it after two days. ❖ αστυνομικός

**2.58** **mean** (adj) /miːn/
not kind; very bad • My big brother is mean to me. He doesn't let me play with his computer. ❖ σκληρός, πολύ κακός

**2.59** **normal** (adj) /ˈnɔːml/
usual • Our lessons start at 8.30 on normal school days. ❖ κανονικός, νορμάλ

**2.60** **attractive** (adj) /əˈtræktɪv/
good-looking • These Aboriginal instruments have colourful attractive designs. ➣ attract (v), attraction (n) ❖ γοητευτικός
✎ Opp: unattractive

**2.61** **intelligent** (adj) /ɪnˈtelɪdʒənt/
able to learn and understand things quickly
• Dogs are intelligent animals – they can learn very quickly. ➣ intelligence (n) ❖ έξυπνος
✎ Syn: clever

# Vocabulary

**2.62** **short hair** (n) /ʃɔːt heə(r)/
hair that isn't long • Jane likes to have short hair because she swims a lot. ❖ κοντά μαλλιά

**2.63** **straight hair** (n) /streɪt heə(r)/
hair that isn't curly • My Scottish cousins have got short straight hair. ❖ ίσια μαλλιά

**2.64** **brown hair** (n) /braʊn heə(r)/
hair that is a brown colour • Grandad had brown hair when he was young, but now it's grey. ❖ καστανά μαλλιά

**2.65** **brown eyes** (n pl) /braʊn aɪz/
eyes that are a brown colour in the centre
• My Labrador has got big brown eyes. ❖ καστανά μάτια

**2.66** **Turkey** (n) /ˈtɜːki/
➣ Turk (n), Turkish (adj, n) ❖ Τουρκία

**2.67** **tan** (n) /tæn/
brown colour on your skin from the sun
• Alison has a tan on her arms because she was out walking in the sunshine. ➣ tan (v), tanned (adj) ❖ μαύρισμα

## Look!

Χρησιμοποιούμε τη λέξη **blond** (ξανθός) όταν μιλάμε για έναν άντρα ή ένα αγόρι, ενώ χρησιμοποιούμε **blonde** (ξανθιά) όταν μιλάμε για μια γυναίκα ή ένα κορίτσι με ξανθά μαλλιά.
Wendy and Susan have got **blonde** hair.
The boys' hair is **blond**.

**2.68** **red hair** (n) /red heə(r)/
hair that is an orange colour • Patrick is from Ireland and everyone in his family has got red hair. ❖ κόκκινα μαλλιά

**2.69** **freckles** (n pl) /ˈfreklz/
small brown spots on your skin • I've got lots of freckles on my face, so my skin goes red in the sun. ❖ φακίδες

**2.70** **skin** (n) /skɪn/
the outside cover of your body • Amal has dark skin because she's from Arabia. ❖ επιδερμίδα, δέρμα

**2.71** **braces** (n pl) /ˈbreɪsɪz/
a metal thing you wear on your teeth to change their position • My teeth are a funny shape, so I'm wearing braces to make them straight. ❖ σιδεράκια

**2.72** **long hair** (n) /lɒŋ heə(r)/
hair that is not short • Nearly all the girls in my class have got long hair. ❖ μακριά μαλλιά

**2.73** **wavy hair** (n) /ˈweɪvi heə(r)/
quite curly hair • Aunt Stephanie has silver wavy hair. ❖ σπαστά μαλλιά

**2.74** **blond/blonde hair** (n) /blɒnd heə(r)/
hair that is a light yellow colour • *Many north Europeans have blonde hair and blue eyes.*
❖ ξανθά μαλλιά

**2.75** **pale** (adj) /peɪl/
light coloured • *You look a bit pale. Do you feel okay?* ❖ χλωμός

**2.76** **suncream** (n) /ˈsʌnkriːm/
cream to protect your skin from the sun
• *Don't forget to put on your suncream before you go to the beach.* ❖ αντιηλιακό

**2.77** **curly hair** (n) /ˈkɜːli heə(r)/
hair that has lots of round curls • *Dad had curly hair when he was young, but now he hasn't got any.* ❖ σγουρά μαλλιά

**2.78** **beard** (n) /bɪəd/
hair that grows on a man's chin • *Grandad looks like Santa Claus with his long white beard.* ❖ γενιάδα

**2.79** **moustache** (n) /məˈstɑːʃ/
hair that grows on a man's face between his nose and his mouth • *My brother wants to grow a moustache to look like Johnny Depp.*
❖ μουστάκι

---

### Appearance

| Nouns | | Adjectives |
|---|---|---|
| blond/blonde hair | beard | attractive |
| | eyebrow | lovely |
| brown hair | freckles | pale |
| curly hair | fringe | tall |
| long hair | moustache | weird |
| red hair | skin | |
| short hair | tan | **Things you wear** |
| wavy hair | | braces |
| | | glasses |
| | | swimming costume |
| | | uniform |

---

**2.80** **shave** (v) /ʃeɪv/
cut hair off your skin • *David decided to shave off his beard to keep cool in summer.* ❖ ξυρίζω

**2.81** **Irish** (adj) /ˈaɪrɪʃ/
➢ Ireland ❖ ιρλανδικός

**2.82** **kind** (adj) /kaɪnd/
friendly and caring • *Maria is a kind person. She always helps others.* ➢ kindness (n)
❖ ευγενικός
✎ Opp: unkind

**2.83** **cheerful** (adj) /ˈtʃɪəfl/
happy and smiling • *Mark has a cheerful smile that makes everyone feel happy.* ➢ cheer (v, n), cheerfully (adv) ❖ χαρούμενος

**2.84** **shy** (adj) /ʃaɪ/
afraid or not comfortable about talking to other people • *My little sister is shy, so she stays close to Mum and doesn't talk much.*
➢ shyness (n) ❖ ντροπαλός

**2.85** **sociable** (adj) /ˈsəʊʃəbl/
enjoying being with other people • *Karen is very sociable and she likes making new friends.* ➢ socialise (v) ❖ κοινωνικός

**2.86** **silly** (adj) /ˈsɪli/
stupid • *Don't be silly. Dogs can't talk!*
❖ ανόητος

**2.87** **make sb laugh** (phr) /meɪk ˈsʌmbədi lɑːf/
do sth to cause sb to laugh • *Mike is so funny! He always makes me laugh.* ❖ κάνω κάποιον να γελάει

**2.88** **laugh** (v) /lɑːf/
make sounds to show that you think sth is funny • *The children laughed at the funny street performer.* ➢ laughter (n) ❖ γελώ

**2.89** **tell jokes** (phr) /tel dʒəʊks/
say funny stories • *My friend Sarah is good at telling jokes, but I can never remember them.*
❖ λέω ανέκδοτα/αστεία

**2.90** **hard** (adj) /hɑːd/
not easy • *It's hard for Tracy to go out on hot sunny days because she has very pale skin.*
❖ δύσκολος
✎ Syn: difficult

**2.91** **smile** (v) /smaɪl/
make a happy expression with your mouth
• *We smiled as the photographer took our photo.* ➢ smile (n), smiley (adj, n) ❖ χαμογελώ

**2.92** **annoyance** (n) /əˈnɔɪəns/
the feeling of being a bit angry • *Our teacher showed her annoyance by giving us more homework.* ➢ annoy (v), annoyed (adj), annoying (adj) ❖ ενόχληση

**2.93** **beauty** (n) /ˈbjuːti/
the quality of being beautiful • *Her photos showed the beauty of the island.* ➢ beautiful (adj) ❖ ομορφιά

**2.94** **care** (n) /keə(r)/
giving attention and looking after sth/sb
• *Parents have to give their children love and care.* ➢ care (v), caring (adj), careful (adj), careless (adj) ❖ έννοια, φροντίδα

**2.95** **love** (n) /lʌv/
the feeling of liking sb/sth very much
• *Magda's smile showed her love for her grandchildren when she saw them.* ➢ love (v), loving (adj), lover (n) ❖ αγάπη

**2.96** **shock** (n) /ʃɒk/
a feeling of surprise when sth bad happens suddenly • *I got a shock when I saw a snake in the garden.* ➢ shock (v), shocking (adj), shocked (adj) ❖ σοκ

**2.97**  **worry** (v) /ˈwʌri/
feel that sth bad might happen • *Don't worry. I can help with your homework.* ➤ worry (n), worried (adj) ❖ ανησυχώ, στεναχωριέμαι

**2.98**  **use** (v) /juːz/
do an action with sth for a certain purpose • *Use a pencil to complete the form.* ➤ use (n), useless (adj), useful (adj) ❖ χρησιμοποιώ

**2.99**  **neighbour** (n) /ˈneɪbə(r)/
sb who lives in a house next to yours • *My neighbours are a bit noisy sometimes and we can't hear our TV.* ❖ γείτονας

**2.100**  **terrible** (adj) /ˈterəbl/
really bad • *Please stop making that terrible noise! I'm doing my homework.* ❖ τρομερός, τρομακτικός

**2.101**  **news** (n) /njuːz/
a piece of information about sth new that happened • *I've got some good news. I won the surfing competition.* ❖ νέο, είδηση

**2.102**  **crash** (n) /kræʃ/
an event where sth, e.g. a car, bus, train or plane, hits sth else • *We saw a car crash in our street, but nobody was hurt.* ➤ crash (v) ❖ τρακάρισμα, σύγκρουση

**2.103**  **singer** (n) /ˈsɪŋə(r)/
sb who sings songs, usually as a job • *Is Adele your favourite female singer?* ➤ sing (v) ❖ τραγουδιστής

**2.104**  **call** (v) /kɔːl/
phone (sb) • *Maisie called her daughter to tell her the good news.* ➤ call (n) ❖ τηλεφωνώ, καλώ

**2.105**  **unhappy** (adj) /ʌnˈhæpi/
not happy • *Louise is unhappy because her friend didn't call her.* ➤ unhappiness (n) ❖ δυστυχισμένος
✎ Opp: happy

**Feelings**

| | | |
|---|---|---|
| annoyed | scared | unhappy |
| bored | shocked | worried |
| happier | surprised | |

**2.106**  **without** (prep) /wɪˈðaʊt/
not having sth • *Ted never goes out without his mobile.* ❖ χωρίς, δίχως

**2.107**  **younger** (adj) /ˈjʌŋɡə(r)/
not as old as sb; born after sb else • *Tina is three years younger than her brother.* ➤ young (adj) ❖ νεότερος, μικρότερος

**2.108**  **visit** (v) /ˈvɪzɪt/
go and see sb • *How often do you visit your cousins?* ➤ visit (n), visitor (n) ❖ επισκέπτομαι

**2.109**  **girlfriend** (n) /ˈɡɜːlfrend/
a close female friend • *My brother is going to the cinema with his girlfriend.* ❖ φιλενάδα, φίλη

**2.110**  **certainly** (adv) /ˈsɜːtnli/
for sure • *Our neighbours are certainly not rich. They have a very small house.* ➤ certain (adj) ❖ σίγουρα, βεβαίως

**2.111**  **lovely** (adj) /ˈlʌvli/
nice; nice-looking • *Rita is wearing a lovely blue dress.* ❖ χαριτωμένος

**2.112**  **friendly** (adj) /ˈfrendli/
kind and easy to make friends with • *Labradors are usually quite friendly dogs, so they're good with chidren.* ➤ friend (n), friendship (n) ❖ φιλικός
✎ Opp: unfriendly

**2.113**  **happier** (adj) /ˈhæpiə(r)/
more happy • *Ryan is happier now because he has a better job.* ➤ happy (adj), happiness (n) ❖ πιο ευτυχισμένος

**2.114**  **agree** (v) /əˈɡriː/
say you think the same as sb else about sth • *I think hairy spiders are horrible. Do you agree with me?* ❖ συμφωνώ
✎ Opp: disagree

**Personality**

| | | |
|---|---|---|
| annoying | horrible | shy |
| caring | intelligent | silly |
| cheerful | kind | sociable |
| friendly | mean | social |
| funny | | |

# *Grammar* Pages 22-23

**2.115**  **swimming costume** (n) /ˈswɪmɪŋ ˈkɒstjuːm/
clothes you wear for swimming • *You can put on your swimming costume in the room at the pool.* ❖ μαγιό

**2.116**  **message** (n) /ˈmesɪdʒ/
a note sent on a mobile phone • *Peter was waiting for his friends when he got a message on his phone.* ❖ μήνυμα

**2.117**  **background** (adj) /ˈbækɡraʊnd/
information to help readers understand where, when or how an event happened • *The story gives some background information about the history of Ireland where the action takes place.* ➤ background (n) ❖ πλαίσιο

**2.118**  **interrupt** (v) /ɪntəˈrʌpt/
make sb stop what they are doing or saying • *Dad's talking on the phone, so please don't interrupt him now.* ➤ interruption (n) ❖ διακόπτω

**2.119**  **shine** (v) /ʃaɪn/
be very bright • *The sun was shining on the sea.* ➤ shiny (adj) ❖ λάμπω

**2.120** **suddenly** (adv) /'sʌdənli/
quickly when you don't expect it • *We were watching TV, when suddenly we heard a noise outside.* ➢ sudden (adj) ❖ ξαφνικά

**2.121** **towards** (prep) /təˈwɔːdz/
nearer to sb/sth • *Paul was surprised when the large dog ran towards him.* ❖ προς

**2.122** **oven** (n) /'ʌvn/
the inside part of a cooker where food is cooked • *The cakes were still in the oven when we came home.* ❖ φούρνος (συσκευή)

**2.123** **heavy rock** (n) /'hevi rɒk/
a very loud kind of music played with electric guitars and drums, etc. • *My grandparents like listening to heavy rock bands from the 1970s, like Led Zeppelin.* ❖ ροκ μουσική

# Listening Page 24

**2.124** **tall** (adj) /tɔːl/
higher than usual height • *Both my parents are tall, but my grandparents are shorter.* ❖ ψηλός

**2.125** **glasses** (n) /'glɑːsɪz/
something that you wear over your eyes to help you see better • *Simon has to wear glasses when he's reading.* ❖ γυαλιά

**2.126** **uniform** (n) /'juːnɪfɔːm/
clothes sb wears for a certain job, school, etc. to look the same as others • *Our school uniform is a white shirt with blue trousers or a blue skirt.* ❖ στολή

**2.127** **identify** (v) /aɪˈdentɪfaɪ/
find or discover sb/sth • *The police officer asked me to identify the man in the photo.* ➢ identity, identification (n) ❖ αναγνωρίζω

**2.128** **option** (n) /'ɒpʃn/
choice • *I don't know what to wear to the party, but I think my red dress is the best option.* ➢ opt (v), optional (adj) ❖ επιλογή

**2.129** **incorrect** (adj) /ˌɪnkəˈrekt/
wrong; not correct • *Some of Jeff's answers were incorrect, so he got a B in the test.* ❖ λάθος
✎ Opp: correct

**2.130** **probably** (adv) /'prɒbəbli/
likely to be true; likely to happen • *Jill's probably not at home. She isn't answering her phone.* ➢ probable (adj), probability (n) ❖ πιθανότατα, μάλλον

**2.131** **little** (adj) /'lɪtl/
young • *Sometimes I help my little brother with his homework.* ❖ μικρός, νέος

# Speaking Page 25

**2.132** **role** (n) /rəʊl/
a part sb plays, e.g. in a play • *Daniel Radcliff played the role of Harry Potter in the films.* ❖ ρόλος

**2.133** **appearance** (n) /əˈpɪərəns/
how sb/sth looks • *Do you believe that personality is more important than appearance?* ➢ appear (v) ❖ εμφάνιση

**2.134** **look like** (phr v) /lʊk laɪk/
used to ask how sb/sth looks • *What does your dog look like? Has he got long or short hair?* ❖ φαίνομαι

**2.135** **similar** (adj) /'sɪmələ(r)/
like sb/sth but not the same • *My friend and I have got similar interests. We both love music and art.* ➢ similarity (n) ❖ παρόμοιος

**2.136** **each other** (pron) /iːtʃ ˈʌðə(r)/
used to show that two or more people do sth the same as the others in a pair/group • *The twins always wear the same clothes as each other.* ❖ ο ένας τον άλλον

**2.137** **nearly** (adv) /'nɪəli/
almost • *Nearly all my classmates have got brown hair. Only two are blond.* ➢ near (adj) ❖ σχεδόν

**2.138** **disagree** (v) /ˌdɪsəˈgriː/
say sth to show you think sth different from somebody else • *Mark thinks his jokes are funny, but Fiona disagrees.* ❖ διαφωνώ
✎ Opp: agree

**2.139** **discuss** (v) /dɪˈskʌs/
talk about • *Let's discuss the things we like doing.* ➢ discussion (n) ❖ συζητώ

**2.140** **swap** (v) /swɒp/
change sth for sth else • *When we finished the exercise, we swapped books to check each other's answers.* ➢ swap (n) ❖ ανταλλάσσω

**2.141** **describe** (v) /dɪˈskraɪb/
give details to say how sb/sth is • *Can you describe your clothes?* ➢ descriptive (adj), description (n) ❖ περιγράφω

**2.142** **likes** (n pl) /laɪks/
the things you like • *Molly's main likes are sports and shopping.* ➢ like (v), likeable (adj) ❖ πράγματα που μου αρέσουν, αρεσκίες

**2.143** **dislikes** (n pl) /dɪsˈlaɪks/
the things you don't like • *My only dislikes are homework and getting up early.* ➢ dislike (v) ❖ πράγματα που δεν μου αρέσουν

**2.144** **link** (v) /lɪŋk/
connect; join together • *We use words like 'and' and 'but' to link our ideas in a sentence.* ➢ link (v), linking (adj) ❖ συνδέω

**2.145** **problem** (n) /ˈprɒbləm/
a difficulty • *Cheryl always discusses her problems with her best friend.* ❖ πρόβλημα

**2.146** **volleyball** (n) /ˈvɒlibɔːl/
a sport in which two teams of players use their hands to hit a ball over a high net to score points • *We often play volleyball on the beach in summer.* ❖ βόλει

**2.147** **shopping** (n) /ˈʃɒpɪŋ/
buy things that you need, e.g. food, clothes • *Natalie enjoys shopping with her mum at weekends.* ➤ shop (v, n) ❖ ψώνια

## Speaking Verbs

| | | |
|---|---|---|
| agree | disagree | interrupt |
| believe | discuss | link |
| describe | identify | mention |

# Writing

**2.148** **quality** (n) /ˈkwɒləti/
how good or bad sth is • *The shoes in this shop cost a lot because they're very good quality.* ❖ ποιότητα

**2.149** **support** (v) /səˈpɔːt/
help sb by being kind to them when they have a problem • *My friends always support me when I feel sad.* ➤ support (n), supportive (adj) ❖ στηρίζω, υποστηρίζω

**2.150** **a bit** (adv) /ə bɪt/
a little; a small amount • *The surfers were a bit tired at the end of the competition.* ❖ λίγο, λιγάκι

**2.151** **reliable** (adj) /rɪˈlaɪəbl/
that can be trusted to do sth • *Cleo is never late. She's very reliable.* ➤ rely (v) ❖ αξιόπιστος
✎ Opp: unreliable

**2.152** **look forward to** (phr v) /lʊk ˈfɔːwəd tuː/
be happy waiting for sth good that is going to happen • *Are you looking forward to your holiday?* ❖ ανυπομονώ

**2.153** **arrive** (v) /əˈraɪv/
reach a place • *Bob was cooking dinner when his friends arrived.* ➤ arrival (n) ❖ φτάνω

**2.154** **positive** (adj) /ˈpɒzətɪv/
good or having a good effect • *Our teacher usually writes something positive on our homework.* ❖ θετικός

**2.155** **mention** (v) /ˈmenʃn/
to say or write something about sb/sth • *Max mentioned his visit to London in his email.* ❖ αναφέρω

**2.156** **negative** (adj) /ˈnegətɪv/
bad or having a bad effect • *Kay had a negative feeling that her classmates didn't like her.* ❖ αρνητικός

**2.157** **seem** (v) /siːm/
appear to be • *Hetty seems quite sociable because she's always chatting with people.* ❖ φαίνομαι

## Phrasal Verbs

| | |
|---|---|
| look after | take part in |
| look forward to | watch out |
| look like | |

# Video 2
# Happy Elephants Page 28

**2.158** **driver** (n) /ˈdraɪvə(r)/
sb who drives sth, e.g. a car, or rides an animal (often to lead a group of animals), e.g. an elephant or a camel • *The elephant driver was very kind and he helped Joe climb up onto the elephant's back.* ➤ drive (v) ❖ οδηγός

**2.159** **in captivity** (phr) /ɪn kæpˈtɪvəti/
in a place that you aren't free to get out of • *Some animals, like pandas, can live longer in captivity than in their natural home.* ❖ σε αιχμαλωσία

**2.160** **circus** (n) /ˈsɜːkəs/
a show that a group of people perform to entertain others sometimes in a big tent • *I feel sad to see wild animals in a circus.* ❖ τσίρκο

**2.161** **in the wild** (phr) /ɪn ðə waɪld/
in nature; in a natural place • *David enjoys going for long walks and taking photos of animals and flowers in the wild.* ❖ στην άγρια φύση

**2.162** **over** (prep) /ˈəʊvə(r)/
more than • *There are over 100 different kinds of birds in London Zoo.* ❖ πάνω από, περισσότερα από

**2.163** **sure** (adj) /ʃʊə(r)/
certain • *Are you sure these animals are happy in the zoo?* ❖ σίγουρος

**2.164** **worse** (adj) /wɜːs/
comparative form of bad • *In the past, life was worse for animals in captivity.* ❖ χειρότερα

**2.165** **gentle** (adj) /ˈdʒentl/
quiet and kind • *Be gentle with the kittens. They're very young.* ❖ ήρεμος, ευγενικός

**2.166** **believe** (v) /bɪˈliːv/
think that sth is true • *I don't believe it! I've got a new job.* ➤ belief (n) ❖ πιστεύω

**2.167** **keep** (v) /kiːp/
put sth/sb in a certain place and make them stay there • *Tony keeps his pet spider in a large box in his room.* ❖ κρατώ, φυλώ

**2.168** **transport** (n) /'trænspɔːt/
a way of carrying people from place to place • *Before people had cars, they used horses for transport.* ➣ transport (v) ❖ μεταφορά

**People**

| | |
|---|---|
| driver | policeman |
| girlfriend | trainer |
| neighbour | |
| police officer | |

# Vocabulary Exercises

**A  Circle the odd one out.**

| | | | |
|---|---|---|---|
| 1 | cheerful | horrible | sociable |
| 2 | beard | moustache | tan |
| 3 | bored | shocked | surprised |
| 4 | choice | culture | option |
| 5 | intelligent | mean | smart |
| 6 | blonde | tall | wavy |
| 7 | business | job | laziness |
| 8 | caring | kind | successful |

**B  Circle the correct words.**

1  Diane has lots of small **braces / freckles** on her face.
2  I was **looking like / looking forward to** my surfing lesson.
3  We had a **suncream / snack** at the beach because we were hungry.
4  What's the **similarity / quality** between these two photos?
5  I put on my swimming **costume / uniform** and went into the sea.
6  The bus arrived **early / nearly** this morning.
7  Joe was sleeping when **certainly / suddenly** the phone rang.
8  When you are surfing, **look after / watch out** for the sharks.

**C  Read the definitions and complete the words.**

1  somebody who lives in a house next to yours          n __ __ __ __ __ __ __ __
2  one of the two lines of hair above your eyes          e __ __ __ __ __ __ __
3  this covers your body          s __ __ __
4  how somebody or something looks          a __ __ __ __ __ __ __ __ __
5  talk about          d __ __ __ __ __ __
6  do something to make people have fun          e __ __ __ __ __ __ __ __
7  somebody who teaches animals to do things          t __ __ __ __ __ __
8  a man or woman who works in the police          p __ __ __ __ __ __   o __ __ __ __ __ __

26

**D** Complete the description with these words.

weird  curly  gentle  little  reliable  similar  traditional  worried

My ¹ _____ brother is quite ² _____ to me. We've both got short ³ _____ hair and brown eyes. Mum and Dad are ⁴ _____ because we don't want to do ⁵ _____ jobs like policemen or teachers. We want to try something really different and a bit ⁶ _____ like being street performers. We were trying to train our dog, Judy, to do tricks with us, but she's not very ⁷ _____ . She's a ⁸ _____ old Labrador and she prefers to sleep all day!

**E** Complete the sentences with words formed from the words in bold.

1  Don't be so _____ to your brother. You'll make him cry.          **KIND**
2  I gave the police a _____ of the man.                            **DESCRIBE**
3  These designs are very _____ . The colours are great.            **ATTRACT**
4  My friend doesn't often _____ with me because we like the same things.  **AGREE**
5  Did you get the _____ to the party?                              **INVITE**
6  What's the _____ between Olga and her sister?                    **DIFFERENT**
7  Angela smiled with _____ when she saw her dog.                   **HAPPY**
8  Can you describe your best friend's _____ ?                      **PERSON**

# 2 Grammar

## 2.1 Past Simple

| Κατάφαση |
|---|
| I/he/she/it/we/you/they play**ed** |

| Άρνηση |
|---|
| I/he/she/it/we/you/they **didn't** play |

| Ερώτηση |
|---|
| **Did** I/he/she/it/we/you/they play? |

| Σύντομες απαντήσεις | |
|---|---|
| **Yes**, I/he/she/it/we/you/they **did**. | **No**, I/he/she/it/we/you/they **didn't**. |

**Ορθογραφία:**
dance → dan**ced**   travel → trave**lled**   try → **tried**   stay → sta**yed**
**Σημείωση:** Κάποια ρήματα είναι ανώμαλα και δεν ακολουθούν αυτούς τους ορθογραφικούς κανόνες.
Δες τη λίστα ανωμάλων ρημάτων στις σελίδες 180-181. Είναι καλή ιδέα να μάθουμε τα ανώμαλα ρήματα που ακολουθούν το ίδιο πρότυπο στον Past Simple ταυτόχρονα, π.χ. *cut, hit, hurt, put* και *shut* όλοι παραμένουν το ίδιο στο Past Simple. Ενώ *blow, draw, fly, grow* και *throw* τελειώνουν όλοι με *'ew'* στον Past Simple (*blew, drew, flew, grew, threw*).
Χρησιμοποιούμε **Past Simple** για:
κάτι που ξεκίνησε και τελείωσε στο παρελθόν.
→ *She **finished** high school last year.*
ρουτίνα και συνήθειες που είχαμε στο παρελθόν (συχνά με επιρρήματα συχνότητας).
→ *My dad **often travelled** to other countries for his work.*
πράξεις που έγιναν η μία μετά την άλλη στο παρελθόν, για παράδειγμα όταν λέμε μια ιστορία.
→ *Sam's phone **rang** and he **answered** it.*
**Σημείωση:** Κάποιες συνηθισμένες χρονικές εκφράσεις που χρησιμοποιούνται συχνά με Past Simple είναι: *yesterday, last night/week/month/summer, a week/month/year ago, twice a week, once a month, at the weekend, in May, in the morning/afternoon/evening, at night, on Thursdays, on Monday mornings* κλπ.
→ *I **talked** to my cousins **yesterday**.*

## 2.2 Used To

| Κατάφαση |
|---|
| I/he/she/it/we/you/they **used to** play |

| Άρνηση |
|---|
| I/he/she/it/we/you/they **didn't use to** play |

| Ερώτηση |
|---|
| **Did** I/he/she/it/we/you/they **use to** play? |

| Σύντομες απαντήσεις | |
|---|---|
| **Yes**, I/he/she/it/we/you/they **did**. | **No**, I/he/she/it/we/you/they **didn't**. |

Χρησιμοποιούμε *used to* + **bare infinitive** (απαρέμφατο χωρίς *to*) για:
πράξεις που κάναμε συχνά στο παρελθόν, αλλά δεν κάνουμε τώρα πια.
→ *My mum **used to study** English at school.*
καταστάσεις που υπήρχαν στο παρελθόν αλλά δεν υπάρχουν τώρα.
→ *I **used to be** scared of big dogs, but now I like playing with them.*

## 2.3 Past Continuous

| Κατάφαση |
| --- |
| I/he/she/it **was** play**ing** <br> we/you/they **were** play**ing** |

| Άρνηση |
| --- |
| I/he/she/it **was not (wasn't)** play**ing** <br> we/you/they **were not (weren't)** play**ing** |

| Ερώτηση |
| --- |
| **Was** I/he/she/it play**ing**? <br> **Were** we/you/they play**ing**? |

| Σύντομες απαντήσεις | |
| --- | --- |
| **Yes**, I/he/she/it **was**. <br> **Yes**, we/you/they **were**. | **No**, I/he/she/it **wasn't**. <br> **No**, we/you/they **weren't**. |

**Ορθογραφία:**
rid**e** → rid**ing**   trave**l** → trave**lling**   fl**y** → fl**ying**
Χρησιμοποιούμε **Past Continuous** για:
πράξεις που ήταν σε εξέλιξη σε συγκεκριμένη χρονική στιγμή στο παρελθόν.
→ *Lynn **was talking** to her neighbour at seven o'clock yesterday evening.*
δύο ή περισσότερες πράξεις που ήταν σε εξέλιξη την ίδια χρονική στιγμή στο παρελθόν.
→ *Mum **was cutting** my hair and dad **was shaving** his beard.*
να δώσουμε το σκηνικό μιας ιστορίας.
→ *We **were standing** at the bus stop and the snow **was falling**.*
μια πράξη που ενώ ήταν σε εξέλιξη στο παρελθόν, διακόπηκε από μια άλλη.
→ *I **was walking** home when I **saw** the car crash.*
**Σημείωση:** Κάποιες συνηθισμένες χρονικές εκφράσεις που χρησιμοποιούνται συχνά με Past Continuous είναι: *while, as, all day/week/month/year, at eight o'clock last night, last Monday/week/month/year, this afternoon* κλπ.
→ *My cat **was sleeping** on the bed **all night**.*

## Grammar Exercises

**A** Circle the correct words.

1 Keith **works** / **worked** in a circus last summer.
2 Mike's grandad **made** / **making** musical instruments.
3 What did the girl **look** / **looked** like?
4 **Did** / **Were** you see the car crash?
5 I **went** / **go** to the park with my friends yesterday.
6 We **didn't** / **weren't** agree about the film.
7 Marjory **think** / **thought** the book was quite interesting.
8 What did you **ate** / **eat** for breakfast?

# 2 Grammar

**B** Choose the correct answer (A, B, or C).

1 Jim travelled to York two years ___ .
   A  ago          B  before        C  last

2 Did Mum ___ to work in a shop?
   A  used         B  use           C  using

3 We ___ our dogs to the animal doctor last week.
   A  bring        B  bringing      C  brought

4 The surfers were training ___ day.
   A  at           B  all           C  in

5 Lesley ___ to live in Edinburgh.
   A  used         B  use           C  using

6 There ___ use to be so many cars in our street.
   A  didn't       B  wasn't        C  weren't

7 The boys used to ___ their bikes to school.
   A  ride         B  rode          C  riding

8 ___ Carol use to train animals?
   A  Did          B  Was           C  Were


**C** Complete the sentences with the Past Continuous of the verbs in brackets.

1 The tourists _____ (travel) to Windsor Castle yesterday morning.

2 We _____ (look after) our neighbour's dog last week.

3 When Mum came home, I _____ (not do) my homework.

4 _____ you _____ (discuss) the problem when I called?

5 Corinna _____ (visit) her aunt in Brighton.

6 The children _____ (not laugh) at their dad's silly joke.

7 The elephant _____ (live) in captivity.

8 Ian _____ (annoy) his sister and she _____ (get) angry.

# 3 Let's Get Together

**3.1** **puffin** (n) /'pʌfɪn/
a bird with a large, brightly coloured beak that lives near the sea in northern parts of the world • *We saw some puffins on our trip to Iceland.* ❖ θαλασσοψιττακός, "παπαγάλος της θάλασσας"

**3.2** **Round Island** (n) /'raʊnd 'aɪlənd/
❖ Ράουντ Άιλαντ, νησί της Αλάσκα

**3.3** **Alaska** (n) /ə'læskə/
➢ Alaskan (adj, n) ❖ Αλάσκα

## Reading

**3.4** **fair** (n) /feə(r)/
an event where people can present and sell different things and entertain the public • *The school band is playing at the summer fair.*
❖ υπαίθρια γιορτή

**3.5** **sleepover** (n) /'sliːpəʊvə(r)/
a party where a group of friends all stay at one friend's home all night • *All the girls in my class are having a sleepover on Saturday at Mandy's house.* ❖ διανυκτέρευση ενός παιδιού στο σπίτι φίλου

**3.6** **fancy dress party** (n) /'fænsi dres 'paːti/
a party where people all wear funny clothes to look like sth/sb else • *I'm dressing up as a pirate for the fancy dress party.* ❖ μασκέ πάρτυ

**3.7** **costume** (n) /'kɒstjuːm/
special clothes you wear to look like sb/sth else • *Mum's helping us to make funny costumes to wear to the party.* ❖ στολή

**3.8** **Champions League** (n) /'tʃæmpiəns liːg/
❖ Τσάμπιονς Λιγκ

**3.9** **New Year's Eve** (n) /njuː jɪəz iːv/
the night of 31st December • *The friends and neighbours got together for a New Year's Eve party.* ❖ παραμονή πρωτοχρονιάς

**3.10** **event** (n) /ɪ'vent/
an occasion that is planned • *New Year's Eve is an important event in Scottish culture.* ❖ γεγονός

**3.11** **celebrate** (v) /'selɪbreɪt/
to do something enjoyable for a special reason • *We had a party to celebrate Grandad's birthday.* ➢ celebration (n) ❖ γιορτάζω

## Word Focus

**3.12** **settler** (n) /'setlə(r)/
sb who goes to live in a new place and starts a new community • *The first white settlers in South Africa were from the Netherlands.* ➢ settle (v) ❖ άποικος

**3.13** **harbour** (n) /'haːbə(r)/
an area on the coast where ships can stop for people to get on and off • *The children waved to the people on the boat as it sailed out of the harbour.* ❖ λιμάνι

**3.14** **spectacular** (adj) /spek'tækjʊlə(r)/
exciting to see • *The band gave a spectacular show on stage.* ❖ θεαματικός

**3.15** **Aussie** (n) /'ɒzi/
something or someone Australian • *Linda's family are all Aussies from Melbourne.*
❖ Αυστραλός

**3.16** **backyard** (n) /bæk'jaːd/
an open space at the back of a house • *My brothers were playing with a ball in the backyard.* ❖ αυλή (στο πίσω μέρος ενός σπιτιού)

**3.17** **invade** (v) /ɪn'veɪd/
to go into another country, town, etc. with an army to take control of it • *The Romans invaded France in 121BC.* ➢ invader (n), invasion (n) ❖ εισβάλλω

## Reading

**3.18** **British** (adj) /'brɪtɪʃ/
Britain (n) ❖ βρετανικός

**3.19** **public holiday** (n) /'pʌblɪk 'hɒlədeɪ/
a national holiday when businesses, schools, etc. are usually closed • *25th March is a public holiday in Greece.* ❖ αργία

**3.20** **bank** (n) /bæŋk/
a place where people go to save or take out money • *The banks are all closed in my country at weekends.* ❖ τράπεζα

**3.21** **post office** (n) /pəʊst 'ɒfɪs/
a place where people go to send letters, etc. • *Mum went to the post office to send some Christmas cards to our aunts in Australia.* ❖ ταχυδρομείο

**3.22** **relax** (v) /rɪ'læks/
rest and do something you enjoy • *Janet listened to some music to relax after her busy day.* ➢ relaxed (adj), relaxing (adj) ❖ χαλαρώνω

## Places

| | |
|---|---|
| backyard | harbour |
| bank | post office |

**3.23 fireworks** (n pl) /'faɪəwɜːks/
colourful explosions of light in the sky, usually used for celebrations • *We watched the fireworks over the harbour from our balcony on New Year's Eve.* ❖ πυροτεχνήματα

**3.24 important** (adj) /ɪm'pɔːtnt/
having a strong effect on sb/sth • *The First World War was an important event in European history.* ➢ importance (n) ❖ σημαντικός
✎ Opp: unimportant

**3.25 meat** (n) /miːt/
the soft part of an animal's body that other animals eat as food • *Heather doesn't eat meat, so she ate a cheese pie.* ❖ κρέας

**3.26 pie** (n) /paɪ/
a kind of food made from pastry filled with, e.g. meat, cheese, or fruit and baked in an oven • *To finish the meal, they had tasty apple pie and ice cream.* ❖ πίτα

**3.27 sandwich** (n) /'sænwɪtʃ/
a snack made from two pieces of bread put together with food in between them • *Would you like a cheese and tomato sandwich?* ❖ τοστ, σάντουιτς

**3.28 sprinkles** (n pl) /'sprɪŋklz/
small bits of coloured sugar to put on top of cakes • *Nick's birthday cake had sprinkles on top in his football team's colours.* ❖ χρωματιστή τρούφα

**3.29 square** (adj) /skweə(r)/
a shape that has four equal sides • *Jerry cut his birthday cake into small squares and gave everybody a piece to eat.* ➢ square (n) ❖ τετράγωνος

**3.30 coconut** (n) /'kəʊkənʌt/
a large nut that is hard outside and has a soft and white part inside with milky juice in the centre • *Tom made a hole in the coconut and drank the milk from inside.* ❖ καρύδα

**3.31 modern** (adj) /'mɒdn/
new and different from old styles • *My grandma doesn't like old furniture, so her home is very modern.* ❖ μοντέρνος,σύγχρονος

**3.32 freedom** (n) /'friːdəm/
the state of being free and not controlled by sb/sth else • *The ancient Greek cities fought together for their freedom when the Persians invaded their land.* ➢ free (v, adj) ❖ ελευθερία

**3.33 lifestyle** (n) /'laɪfstaɪl/
the way that you choose to live • *People in southern Europe have a different lifestyle from others in the north because the weather is warmer.* ❖ τρόπος ζωής

**3.34 conversation** (n) /ˌkɒnvə'seɪʃn/
a talk between two or more people • *We had a long conversation about Australian culture.* ❖ συζήτηση

**3.35 that's a pity** (phr) /ðæts ə 'pɪti/
you say this to show you feel sad or disappointed about sth • *That's a pity you can't come to the party.* ❖ είναι κρίμα

**3.36 luck** (n) /lʌk/
sth that makes sth good or bad happen by chance • *Good luck with your French exam.* ➢ lucky (adj) ❖ τύχη

**3.37 delicious** (adj) /dɪ'lɪʃəs/
having a very nice taste • *This cake is delicious. May I have another piece?* ❖ νόστιμος

**3.38 difficult** (adj) /'dɪfɪkəlt/
not easy • *It was difficult for Lee to learn to speak Arabic.* ➢ difficulty (n) ❖ δύσκολος

**3.39 fantastic** (adj) /fæn'tæstɪk/
very good; wonderful • *Greta had a fantastic holiday on Crete with her family, so they want to go back there next year.* ❖ φανταστικός, υπέροχος

**3.40 sausage** (n) /'sɒsɪdʒ/
a mixture of meat and other substances in a tube of skin • *A traditional English breakfast incudes sausages and eggs.* ❖ λουκάνικο

**3.41 barbecue** (n) /'baːbɪkjuː/
a meal or party outside where food is cooked on an open fire • *We invited the neighbours to our barbecue in our garden.* ❖ μπάρμπεκιου

# Vocabulary

Pages 34-35

**3.42 possible** (adj) /'pɒsəbl/
that can be done • *If Mum says it's possible, I'll invite all my classmates to my party.* ➢ possibility (n) ❖ δυνατός
✎ Opp: impossible

**3.43 candle** (n) /'kændl/
a small thin stick of coloured wax with a string inside that burns when you light it • *How many candles were on your birthday cake?* ❖ κεράκι

**3.44 confetti** (n) /kən'feti/
small pieces of coloured paper to throw over people at weddings, etc. • *Marjory and Bob got confetti all over their hair and clothes at their wedding.* ❖ κονφετί

**3.45** **sparkler** (n) /ˈspɑːklə(r)/
a small firework that you can hold or put on top of a cake to make a sparkly light • *The children's eyes shone in the light from the sparklers they were holding.* ➢ spark (v), sparkly (adj) ❖ αστράκι

**3.46** **streamer** (n) /ˈstriːmə(r)/
a long thin piece of coloured paper that you use to decorate a place for sth special • *We decorated the room with streamers and balloons for Annabelle's birthday party.* ❖ σερπαντίνα

| Party Decorations | Food |
|---|---|
| candle | coconut |
| confetti | meat |
| costume | pie |
| fireworks | sandwich |
| sparkler | sausage |
| streamer | sprinkles |

**3.47** **hang up** (phr v) /hæŋ ʌp/
end a phone call • *Julia said goodbye and hung up the phone.* ❖ κλείνω το τηλέφωνο

**3.48** **get on** (phr v) /get ɒn/
be friends with sb • *Do you get on well with your neighbours?* ❖ τα πάω κάλα με κάποιον

**3.49** **get together** (phr v) /get təˈgeðə(r)/
meet socially • *Let's get together for a chat tomorrow.* ➢ get-together (n) ❖ συναντιέμαι, συγκεντρώνομαι

**3.50** **go around** (phr v) /gəʊ əˈraʊnd/
visit someone at their home • *Gordon went around to his friend's house.* ❖ πηγαίνω επίσκεψη, επισκέπτομαι

**3.51** **go out** (phr v) /gəʊ aʊt/
leave your house to go and do a social activity • *Tracy usually goes out with her friends on Fridays.* ❖ βγαίνω

**3.52** **stay in** (phr v) /steɪ ɪn/
not go out • *I'm staying in to watch TV tonight.* ❖ μένω στο σπίτι

**3.53** **stay up** (phr v) /steɪ ʌp/
not go to bed • *We stayed up late on New Year's Eve.* ❖ μένω ξύπνιος

**3.54** **ask about** (phr v) /ɑːsk əˈbaʊt/
ask how sb is • *Jason called to ask about my sister when she was in hospital.* ❖ ρωτάω για
✎ Syn: ask after

**3.55** **take sb away** (phr v) /teɪk ˈsʌmbədi əˈweɪ/
go on holiday with sb • *My parents took us away to Bournemouth for the weekend.* ❖ παίρνω κάποιον κάπου για διακοπές

**3.56** **take sb out** (phr v) /teɪk ˈsʌmbədi aʊt/
go out with sb you have invited to come with you • *We're taking our grandparents out for a meal as a birthday surprise.* ❖ βγάζω κάποιον έξω (π.χ. για ραντεβού)

**3.57** **call back** (phr v) /kɔːl bæk/
phone sb that phoned you first • *I'm busy doing my homework now, so I'll call you back later.* ❖ ξανακαλώ

**3.58** **call off** (phr v) /kɔːl ɒf/
decide that sth will not happen at the planned time because it is too difficult or not possible • *They called off the football match because of the snow.* ❖ ακυρώνω

**3.59** **look up to** (phr v) /lʊk ʌp tuː/
admire or respect sb • *Rhona looks up to her older sister because she works really hard and has a successful business.* ❖ σέβομαι, θαυμάζω

**Phrasal verbs**

| | | |
|---|---|---|
| ask about | go around | stay up |
| call back | go out | take sb away |
| call off | hang up | take sb out |
| get on | look up to | |
| get together | stay in | |

**3.60** **respect** (v) /rɪˈspekt/
admire sb for their personality or the things they do • *I respect my English teacher because she's kind to us and teaches us well.* ➢ respect (n), respectful (adj) ❖ σέβομαι

**3.61** **folder** (n) /ˈfəʊldə(r)/
a way to store files on a computer • *Nancy puts her photos in different folders on her laptop.* ❖ φάκελος

**3.62** **inbox** (n) /ˈɪnbɒks/
the place where you see new emails on your computer • *There were two new emails in my inbox.* ❖ εισερχόμενα

**3.63** **delete** (v) /dɪˈliːt/
remove sth, e.g. words, emails or files on a computer • *Paul deleted all the emails that weren't important.* ❖ διαγράφω

**3.64** **junk** (n) /dʒʌŋk/
sth you don't need or want • *Most of the emails he gets are junk mail from people trying to sell things.* ❖ άχρηστος

**3.65** **save** (v) /seɪv/
keep sth; not delete sth on a computer • *Remember to save your text when you finish writing.* ❖ αποθηκεύω

**3.66** **reply** (v) /rɪˈplaɪ/
answer (an email, etc.) • *I was worried because Dave didn't reply to my email.* ➢ answer (n) ❖ απαντώ

**3.67**  **forward** (v) /ˈfɔːwəd/
send an email that you get from one person
to another person • *Jill forwarded the email
from her brother to her aunt in Edinburgh.*
❖ προωθώ

**3.68**  **receive** (v) /rɪˈsiːv/
get sth that sb sent to you • *Did you receive
an email from George about the fair?*
❖ παραλαμβάνω

**3.69**  **attachment** (n) /əˈtætʃmənt/
sth extra that you send with an email • *Jane
sent some photos of her home as attachments
to her email.* ➢ attach (v), attached (adj)
❖ επισύναψη

**3.70**  **device** (n) /dɪˈvaɪs/
sth like a small machine that you use for a
particular purpose • *You have to turn off
devices, like mobile phones, in the classroom.*
❖ συσκευή

**3.71**  **digital** (adj) /ˈdɪdʒɪtl/
showing information as electronic images
• *Can you show me how to take a good photo
with my new digital camera?* ❖ ψηφιακός

**3.72**  **mechanical** (adj) /məˈkænɪkl/
with parts that move with power from an
engine; related to a machine • *The car
stopped because of a mechanical problem.*
➢ mechanic (n), mechanically (adj)
❖ μηχανικός

**3.73**  **technology** (n) /tekˈnɒlədʒi/
the science used to discover and design
new things • *Modern technology helps us
to communicate with people around the
world very quickly.* ➢ technological (adj)
❖ τεχνολογία

**3.74**  **smartphone** (n) /ˈsmaːtfəʊn/
a mobile phone that can use internet and
apps • *Carol often sends emails from her
smartphone.* ❖ έξυπνο κινητό τηλέφωνο

**3.75**  **text** (n) /tekst/
a written message on a mobile phone • *Send
me a text when you get to the station and I'll
meet you there.* ➢ text (v) ❖ μήνυμα, SMS

**3.76**  **internet** (n) /ˈɪntənet/
the international computer network • *You can
look up the meanings of new words on the
internet.* ❖ διαδίκτυο, ίντερνετ

**3.77**  **letter** (n) /ˈletə(r)/
a message written on paper to send to sb
• *Sandra and Jack sent letters to their friends
and family to thank them for their wedding
presents.* ❖ γράμμα

**3.78**  **post** (n) /pəʊst/
a way of sending letters and parcels to other
people • *Daniel filled in a form for his new
passport and sent it by post.* ➢ post (v), postal
(adj) ❖ ταχυδρομείο

**3.79**  **fail** (n) /feɪl/
sth that isn't a success • *My exam result was
a fail, so I'll try to get a pass next time.* ➢ fail
(v), failure (n) ❖ αποτυχία, λάθος

**3.80**  **snail** (n) /sneɪl/
a small animal with a soft body that lives inside
a shell and moves very slowly • *The snails ate
the leaves of some plants in Fred's garden.*
❖ σαλιγκάρι

**3.81**  **recently** (adv) /ˈriːsntli/
not long before now • *Liz recently bought a
new smartphone and she's still learning how to
use it.* ➢ recent (adj) ❖ πρόσφατα

**3.82**  **desktop (computer)** (n) /ˌdesktɒp
(kəmˈpjuːtə(r))/
a computer that has a screen, keyboard and
tower that fits on a desk • *Thelma uses her
desktop at work and her smartphone when
she's travelling.* ❖ σταθερός υπολογιστής

**3.83**  **laptop (computer)** (n) /ˈlæptɒp
(kəmˈpjuːtə(r))/
a small computer that has a keyboard and
screen together, which you can carry easily
• *Tom watched a film on his laptop on the
plane.* ❖ λάπτοπ, φορητός υπολογιστής

**3.84**  **communicate** (v) /kəˈmjuːnɪkeɪt/
to share information with sb, e.g. by writing or
talking • *Wendy's friends in Ireland sometimes
communicate with her through Facebook.*
➢ communication (n) ❖ επικοινωνώ

**3.85**  **contact** (v) /ˈkɒntækt/
communicate with; get in touch with • *If you
need help with your homework, contact me
this evening.* ➢ contact (n) ❖ επικοινωνώ,
έρχομαι σε επαφή

**3.86**  **overseas** (adv) /ˌəʊvəˈsiːz/
in other countries, especially those across the
sea or ocean • *A lot of devices that we use
are made overseas in countries like China.*
❖ στο εξωτερικό

**3.87**  **click** (v) /klɪk/
press the computer mouse or touchpad to
choose sth on the screen • *Just click on the
screen to see the photos.* ➢ click (n) ❖ κάνω
κλικ

**3.88**  **net** (n) /net/
sth made from string or rope tied together with
spaces in between to catch sth, e.g. fish; short
form of the word *internet* • *The octopus was
caught in the fisherman's net.*
❖ δίχτυ, συντομογραφία της λέξης *διαδίκτυο*

**3.89**  **webcam** (n) /ˈwebkæm/
a camera on a computer • *My grandparents
use their webcam so that we can see them
when we talk on the laptop.* ❖ κάμερα
υπολογιστή, ουέμπκαμ

**3.90** **check** (v) /tʃek/
look at sth to see how it is • *Did you check your inbox this morning?* ➢ check (n)
❖ ελέγχω, τσεκάρω

**3.91** **ski** (v) /skiː/
move across snow on skis • *Ellen learnt to ski in Switzerland when she was ten years old.* ➢ skiing (n), skier (n) ❖ κάνω σκι

**3.92** **surf the net** (phr) /sɜːf ðə net/
use the internet, e.g. to find information • *Dad surfed the net to find a new job.* ❖ σερφάρω στο διαδίκτυο

**3.93** **waste time** (phr) /weɪst taɪm/
use time in a way that isn't useful when you should be doing sth else • *Your train leaves at six, so don't waste time chatting.* ❖ χάνω χρόνο

**3.94** **in touch** (phr) /ɪn tʌtʃ/
in contact • *I hope we can keep in touch when you go to study in Plymouth.* ❖ σε επαφή

**3.95** **company** (n) /ˈkʌmpəni/
being with other people; a group of people together • *Social events are better fun when you have company to go to them.* ❖ παρέα

**3.96** **social network** (n) /ˈsəʊʃl ˈnetwɜːk/
a website where people can communicate with lots of others; all the people you know socially • *She has thousands of friends on Facebook and other social networks.*
❖ κοινωνικό δίκτυο

---

**Look!**

Η λέξη **company** εκτός απο *παρέα*, σημαίνει και *εταιρία*. Προσέξτε πώς χρησιμοποιούμε το άρθρο στην δεύτερη περίπτωση.

*Jason is really good **company**.* (Ο Ιάσωνας είναι πολύ καλή παρέα.)

*Jason's is a good **company** to work for.* (Η Jason's είναι μια καλή εταιρία για να εργάζεσαι εκεί.)

---

## Technology & Communicating

| Nouns | | Verbs | save |
|---|---|---|---|
| attachment | net | check | update |
| desktop | post | click | |
| (computer) | smartphone | communicate | **Phrases** |
| device | social | contact | surf the net |
| folder | network | delete | in touch |
| inbox | text | download | |
| internet | webcam | forward | |
| junk | website | receive | |
| laptop | | repeat | |
| (computer) | **Adjectives** | reply | |
| letter | digital | respond | |
| | mechanical | | |

---

*Grammar* **Pages 36-37**

**3.97** **plan** (n) /plæn/
sth that you intend to do in the future • *Have you got any plans for the weekend?* ➢ plan (v), planned (adj), planning (n), planner (n)
❖ σχέδιο

**3.98** **arrangement** (n) /əˈreɪndʒmənt/
a plan or agreement to make sth happen • *We made arrangements to meet after school.*
➢ arrange (v) ❖ ρύθμιση, κάτι που κανονίζω

**3.99** **mall** (n) /mɔːl/
a building that has many shops, cafes, etc. in it • *James went shopping at the mall to get new shoes.* ❖ εμπορικό κέντρο

**3.100** **download** (v) /ˌdaʊnˈləʊd/
put a file from the internet onto your computer • *Sometimes Sheila downloads books to read on her tablet.* ❖ κατεβάζω

**3.101** **relative** (n) /ˈrelətɪv/
a family member • *Most of Eva's cousins and other relatives live in Newcastle.* ➢ relate (v), relation (n), relationship (n) ❖ συγγενής

**3.102** **match** (n) /mætʃ/
an event where two teams play against each other in a sport • *I enjoy watching football matches on TV with my friends.* ❖ αγώνας

---

**Look!**

Η λέξη **match** εκτός απο *αγώνας*, σημαίνει *ταίρι* και *σπίρτα*.

*Did you see the final goal in the **match**?* (αγώνας)

*Have you got a **match** to light the candles?* (σπίρτα)

*This T-shirt is a good **match** for your shorts.* (ταίρι)

---

**3.103** **passenger** (n) /ˈpæsɪndʒə(r)/
sb who is travelling on a type of transport, e.g. bus, car, boat, plane, train • *We waited for some passengers to get out of the bus before we got on it.* ❖ επιβάτης

**3.104** **business class** (n) /ˈbɪznəs klɑːs/
first class (travel) • *Tom's boss was paying for his trip to Brussels, so he travelled in business class on the train.* ❖ πρώτη θέση, επαγγελματική θέση (π.χ σε αεροπλάνο)

**3.105** **economy class** (n) /ɪˈkɒnəmi klɑːs/
second class (travel) • *They bought economy class tickets for the ferry because they weren't so expensive.* ❖ οικονομική θέση (π.χ. σε αεροπλάνο)

**3.106 row** (n) /rəʊ/
a group of people or things in a straight line next to each other • *We sat in the middle row at the cinema.* ❖ σειρά

**3.107 seat** (n) /siːt/
sth for sitting on • *I had a seat next to the window on the train.* ➤ seat (v), seating (n) ❖ θέση

**3.108 kick off** (n) /kɪk ɒf/
when a player kicks the ball to start a match in football or rugby • *What time is the kick off on Wednesday? I want to see the whole match.* ➤ kick off (phr v) ❖ έναρξη αγώνα ποδοσφαίρου ή ράγκμπι

**3.109 flight** (n) /flaɪt/
a journey by plane • *The flight to Aberdeen from London takes one hour and forty minutes.* ➤ fly (v) ❖ πτήση

**3.110 departure** (n) /dɪˈpɑːtʃə(r)/
leaving a place at a particular time • *All the flight departures from Zurich were late because of bad weather.* ➤ depart (v) ❖ αναχώρηση

**3.111 board** (v) /bɔːd/
get into a plane, boat, etc. to start travelling • *The passengers waited for three hours to board the plane that arrived late.* ➤ boarding (adj, n) ❖ επιβιβάζομαι

**3.112 boarding pass** (n) /ˈbɔːdɪŋ pɑːs/
a card that you show to board a plane • *Dad printed our boarding passes from the internet so that we didn't waste time at the airport.* ❖ κάρτα επιβίβασης

**3.113 midnight** (n) /ˈmɪdnaɪt/
twelve o'clock at night • *I finished my homework at midnight last night, so I'm very tired.* ❖ μεσάνυχτα

**3.114 movement** (n) /ˈmuːvmənt/
going from one place to another • *There was a loud noise and we saw a movement in the trees.* ➤ move (v, n), movable (adj) ❖ κίνηση

**3.115 in the middle** (phr) /ɪn ðə ˈmɪdl/
in the centre, between two or more other things • *The boat was in the middle of the river when it hit a rock.* ❖ στη μέση

**3.116 manager** (n) /ˈmænɪdʒə(r)/
sb who is responsible for a business, shop, club, etc. • *Margaret is the manager of a bookshop in the mall.* ➤ manage (v), manageable (adj) ❖ διευθυντής

**3.117 museum** (n) /mjuˈziːəm/
a building where very old objects are on display for people to see • *You'll have fun at the science museum in Paris.* ❖ μουσείο

**3.118 colleague** (n) /ˈkɒliːɡ/
sb who works in the same office as you • *Ian and his colleagues were having a chat in their lunch break.* ❖ συνάδελφος

**3.119 exhibition** (n) /ˌeksɪˈbɪʃn/
a show of things for people to see, e.g. in a museum • *There was an exhibition of Van Gogh paintings in the art gallery.* ➤ exhibit (v, n), exhibitor (n) ❖ έκθεση

**3.120 Egyptian** (adj) /iˈdʒɪpʃn/
➤ Egyptian (n), Egypt (n) ❖ αιγυπτιακός

**3.121 mummy** (n) /ˈmʌmi/
a dead body that is covered with bandages and oils, etc. to preserve it • *The mummies in the museum looked quite scary.* ➤ mummify (v) ❖ μούμια

**People**

| | | |
|---|---|---|
| settler | manager | visitor |
| actor | colleague | boyfriend |

**3.122 object** (n) /ˈɒbdʒɪkt/
any thing that is not a living thing • *The farmer found a strange stone object when he was digging in his field.* ❖ αντικείμενο, πράγμα

**3.123 tomb** (n) /tuːm/
a place where a dead body is put • *The pyramid was the tomb of an Egyptian queen.* ❖ τάφος, τύμβος

**3.124 glass case** (n) /ɡlɑːs keɪs/
a box made of glass used to keep sth in so it can be seen • *The oldest books in the exhibition were in glass cases to protect them.* ❖ γυάλινη θήκη

**3.125 include** (v) /ɪnˈkluːd/
have sth as part of sth else • *The party food included sandwiches, popcorn and small cheese pies.* ➤ inclusion (n), inclusive (adj) ❖ περιέχω

**3.126 furniture** (n) /ˈfɜːnɪtʃə(r)/
things like tables, chairs, cupboards, etc. • *We moved all the furniture out of the living room to paint the walls.* ❖ έπιπλα

**3.127 dead** (adj) /ded/
not living • *Our cat brought a dead bird into the house.* ➤ die (v), death (n) ❖ νεκρός

**Look!**

Η λέξη **furniture** (*έπιπλα*) είναι **uncountable** και έτσι την χρησιμοποιούμε χωρίς το άρθρο *a* και γράφουμε το ρήμα στον ενικό.
*Your new **furniture is** lovely.*

**3.128 afterlife** (n) /ˈɑːftəlaɪf/
a life that some people believe they will have after they die • *The paintings showed how ancient Egyptians imagined the afterlife to be.* ❖ μετά θάνατον ζωή

**3.129** **display** (n) /dɪˈspleɪ/
one or more things put in a place for people to look at • *I enjoy looking at the displays in the shop windows at the mall.* ➢ display (v) ❖ επίδειξη

**3.130** **ancient** (adj) /ˈeɪnʃənt/
very old • *Ancient Romans tried to take over the whole of Great Britain.* ❖ αρχαίος

**3.131** **X-ray** (n) /ˈeks reɪ/
a kind of photo that shows the bones inside your body • *The X-ray showed that Adam's arm was broken.* ➢ X-ray (v) ❖ ακτινογραφία

**3.132** **update** (v) /ˌʌpˈdeɪt/
add the newest information to sth • *You can update your details on the website if you change your email address.* ➢ update (n) ❖ ενημερώνω

**3.133** **website** (n) /ˈwebsaɪt/
a group of pages on the internet with information about a business, organisation or person • *The business sells holidays in Greece through its website.* ❖ ιστοσελίδα

# Listening    Page 38

**3.134** **wedding** (n) /ˈwedɪŋ/
an event where two people get married • *The band played and everybody danced at Sue and Frank's wedding.* ➢ wed (v) ❖ γάμος

**3.135** **concert** (n) /ˈkɒnsət/
a musical performance • *We're having a concert at the end of the school year and I'm singing with my class.* ❖ συναυλία

**3.136** **festival** (n) /ˈfestɪvl/
a public event where people perform music or theatre plays, dance, or show films • *David's rock band played at the street festival in Glasgow last year.* ➢ festive (adj) ❖ φεστιβάλ, γιορτή

# Speaking    Page 39

**3.137** **disco** (n) /ˈdɪskəʊ/
a place or party where pop music is played for people to dance to • *The music in the disco was so loud that I couldn't hear my friend, but we danced a lot.* ❖ ντίσκο

**3.138** **New Year** (n) /njuː jɪə(r)/
the first day of the year • *The Chinese celebrate New Year around the start of February.* ❖ πρωτοχρονιά

**3.139** **Christmas** (n) /ˈkrɪsməs/
25th December; the day that Christians celebrate as the birthday of Christ • *At Christmas, we usually have a big meal with a few friends and family members and give each other presents.* ❖ Χριστούγεννα

**3.140** **grammatically** (adv) /grəˈmætɪkli/
in a way that follows grammar rules • *The teacher will check your spelling and make sure your sentences are grammatically correct.* ❖ γραμματικά

**3.141** **respond** (v) /rɪˈspɒnd/
reply to sth that sb said or wrote • *Keith didn't respond to my emails, so I phoned to see if he was okay.* ➢ response (n), responsive (adj) ❖ ανταποκρίνομαι

**3.142** **boyfriend** (n) /ˈbɔɪfrend/
a man or boy who is a close friend • *My sister keeps talking about her new boyfriend, Steven.* ❖ φίλος

**3.143** **repeat** (v) /rɪˈpiːt/
do or say sth again in the same way • *Could you repeat your phone number to make sure I've got it right?* ➢ repetition (n), repetitive (adj) ❖ επαναλαμβάνω

# Writing    Pages 40-41

**3.144** **notice** (n) /ˈnəʊtɪs/
• *There was a big notice on the wall about the school fair.* ➢ notice (v), noticeable (adj) ❖ ανακοίνωση

**3.145** **break-dance** (v) /ˈbreɪkdɑːns/
a kind of modern dance, often done in the street • *Teresa is learning to break-dance at her dance school.* ➢ break-dancer (n) ❖ χορεύω μπρέικντανς

**3.146** **waltz** (v) /wɔːls/
dance with a partner in a traditional waltz • *The dancers waltzed around the room to classical music.* ➢ waltz (n) ❖ χορεύω βαλς

**3.147** **ballet** (n) /ˈbæleɪ/
a kind of dancing that tells a story with movements and music, but no words • *In my country, ballet classes are popular with young girls.* ❖ μπαλλέτο

# Video 3 Fat Tuesday    Page 42

**3.148** **Carnival** (n) /ˈkɑːnɪvl/
a celebration in spring before Lent • *In Greece we have lots of fancy dress parties and street parades at Carnival time.* ❖ καρναβάλι

**3.149** **Lent** (n) /lent/
the period of 40 days before Easter Sunday • *Irene never eats meat, so she enjoys the special foods that people cook without meat during Lent.* ➢ Lenten (adj) ❖ Σαρακοστή

**3.150** **parade** (n) /pəˈreɪd/
when people and vehicles move through the streets in a celebration • *We watched the people dancing in the Carnival parade from our hotel balcony.* ➤ parade (v) ❖ παρέλαση

**3.151** **float** (n) /fləʊt/
a car or truck that is decorated for a parade • *Everybody in our club helped to decorate our float for the festival with paper flowers.* ❖ άρμα

**3.152** **vehicle** (n) /ˈviːəkl/
sth that people can travel in from place to place, e.g. car, bus, truck • *It was difficult for vehicles to travel across the mountain road in the snow.* ❖ όχημα

**3.153** **decorate** (v) /ˈdekəreɪt/
add colours and other things to sth to make it look nice • *Everybody in our club helped to decorate our float for the festival with paper flowers.* ➤ decoration(s) (n), decorator (n) ❖ στολίζω

**3.154** **Easter** (n) /ˈiːstə(r)/
❖ Πάσχα

**3.155** **Roman** (n) /ˈrəʊmən/
❖ Ρωμαίος

**3.156** **feast** (n) /fiːst/
a very large meal • *The people in the village were enjoying their last big feast before Lent.* ➤ feast (v) ❖ μεγάλο γεύμα

**3.157** **Christian** (n) /ˈkrɪstʃən/
❖ Χριστιανός

**3.158** **rich food** (n) /rɪtʃ fuːd/
food that has a strong flavour • *If you eat rich food before you go to sleep at night, you might have bad dreams or a sore stomach.* ❖ φαγητό με πλούσια γεύση

### Special Events & Traditional Celebrations

| | | |
|---|---|---|
| barbecue | festival | Carnival |
| concert | parade | Christmas |
| disco | public holiday | Easter |
| exhibition | sleepover | Lent |
| fair | wedding | New Year |
| fancy dress | | New Year's Eve |
| party | | |
| feast | | |

# Vocabulary Exercises

**A** Circle the correct words.

1 The Romans built the **modern / ancient** walls around the old city.

2 Remember to **delete / save** his email address so that you can reply to him.

3 My grandfather thinks it's **delicious / difficult** to use the internet.

4 The neighbours are having a barbecue in their **harbour / backyard**.

5 The first **visitors / settlers** who lived in Australia didn't understand the Aboriginal people.

6 The boys were having a **conversation / letter** about the football match.

7 The ballet dancers looked so **common / spectacular** in their beautiful costumes.

8 I can't **communicate / contact** with my sister. She doesn't listen to me!

**B** Complete the sentences with the words you did not circle from Exercise A.

1 These sausages are really _____ . Can I have another one, please?

2 On a digital camera, you can _____ the photos that you don't want.

3 Cold weather is _____ in winter in Switzerland.

4 Were there many _____ at the art exhibition yesterday?

5 Did your dad receive the _____ from the bank?

6 You can _____ the manager by email.

7 Hillary uses her _____ smartphone to send photos to her friends.

8 The gulls flew behind the ship that was sailing out of the _____ .

**C** **Match to make sentences.**

1 New Year's day is a public ☐     **a** off is at seven o'clock.
2 The mummy is inside a glass ☐     **b** case at the museum.
3 I'm going to the post ☐     **c** pass from the website.
4 We always travel economy ☐     **d** holiday in Britain.
5 If you eat too much rich ☐     **e** office to send some Christmas cards.
6 In today's match, the kick ☐     **f** dress party.
7 Kate downloaded her boarding ☐     **g** class when we go on holiday.
8 Joe looked so funny at the fancy ☐     **h** food, you'll be sick.

**D** **Complete the sentences with these words.**

ask about    call off    get on    go out    hang up    look up to    stay up    take out

1 Do you often _____ to eat with your family?
2 Please don't _____ until I write down your number.
3 Sometimes I _____ late to watch films on TV.
4 My friends _____ Jerry because he can break-dance very well.
5 Dad likes to _____ Mum _____ for dinner on her birthday.
6 The band had to _____ the concert because the singer was ill.
7 My mum called to _____ tickets for the concert.
8 How do you _____ with your neighbours?

**E** **Do the crossword.**

**Across**

3 a website where people can communicate with lots of others
7 something like a small machine that you use for a particular purpose
8 special clothes you wear to look like somebody or something else
10 a public event where people perform music or theatre plays, dance, or show films
11 something extra that you send with an email

**Down**

1 a party where a group of friends all stay at one friend's home all night
2 the state of being free and not controlled by sb/sth else
3 a long thin piece of coloured paper that you use to decorate a place for sth special
4 a snack made from two pieces of bread put together with food in between them
5 colourful explosions of light in the sky, usually used for celebrations
6 when people and vehicles move through the streets in a celebration
9 an occasion that is planned

# 3 Grammar

## 3.1 Present Continuous for the future

Χρησιμοποιούμε **Present Continuous** για:
σχέδια και ό,τι έχουμε κανονίσει για το μέλλον.
→ *Is your class visiting the museum next week?*
**Σημείωση:** Χρονικές εκφράσεις που αφορούν το μέλλον (the future) χρησιμοποιούνται συχνά με Present Continuous όταν μιλάμε για το μέλλον. Για παράδειγμα: *tomorrow, next week/month/weekend, tonight, in a week/a few days.*

## 3.2 Prepositions of time

Χρησιμοποιούμε *at* με:
τις ώρες της ημέρας.
→ *The fair begins at ten o'clock.*
→ *We eat together at dinner time.*

τις παρακάτω εκφράσεις.
→ *at the weekend*
→ *at night*
→ *at the moment*
→ *at Easter*
→ *at Christmas*

Χρησιμοποιούμε *in* με:
μακρύτερες χρονικές περιόδους.
→ *in April*
→ *in summer*
→ *in the morning/afternoon/evening*
→ *in 1980*
→ *in the 1980s*

μια χρονική περίοδο για να δείξουμε πόση ώρα χρειάζεται για κάτι.
→ *She wrote the emails in ten minutes.*

μια χρονική περίοδο για να δείξουμε σε πόση ώρα κάτι θα συμβεί.
→ *We're having a party in three weeks from now.*

Χρησιμοποιούμε *on* με:
τις ημέρες και τις ημερομηνίες.
→ *on Tuesday*
→ *on Tuesday afternoon*
→ *on Saturday night*
→ *on 28th October*

## 3.3 Prepositions of place

Χρησιμοποιούμε *at* με:
σχετικές θέσεις.
→ *at the back/the front/the top/the bottom/the end*

γενικές ιδέες.
→ *at the table*
→ *at the door*
→ *at the cinema/theatre*
→ *at the airport/bank*
→ *at someone's house*
→ *at home*
→ *at school*
→ *at work*
→ *at a football match*

Χρησιμοποιούμε *in* με:
δοχεία.
- → *in his bag*
- → *in a box*
- → *in a bottle*

δωμάτια, κτίρια, χώρες, πόλεις, σημεία με όρια.
- → *in the living room*
- → *in the departure lounge*
- → *in hospital*
- → *in prison*
- → *in Ireland*
- → *in Dublin*
- → *in the backyard*
- → *in her car*

το νερό.
- → *in the river/sea/pond/lake/ocean*

άλλα πράγματα με περιεχόμενα.
- → *in the folder*
- → *in my inbox*
- → *in this book/picture*
- → *in your letter*
- → *in a row/line*

Χρησιμοποιούμε *on* με:
επιφάνειες.
- → *on the floor/wall/ceiling*
- → *on the blackboard/the page*
- → *on the road*
- → *Lunch is **on** the table. (**Σημείωση:** We sit **at** a table.)*
- → *Sit on this chair.*

τα μέσα μεταφοράς.
- → *on a bus/plane/boat/ship*

τους ορόφους.
- → *on the ground/first/second floor*
(**Σημείωση:** λέμε *in* the basement/attic (= στο υπόγειο/στην σοφίτα))

τα μέρη ενός αντικειμένου.
- → *on the front of the bus*
- → *on the back of her T-shirt*
- → *on the end of your finger*

τις λέξεις **right** (δεξιά) και **left** (αριστερά).
- → *on the right of the bank*
- → *on the left of the river*
- → *walk on the left*

## 3.4 Prepositions of direction

Χρησιμοποιούμε **from** για να δείξουμε πού άρχισε κάτι.
- → *When did you come home **from** school?*
- → *She sent me a letter **from** Canada.*
- → *Walk **from** here to the post office.*

Χρησιμοποιούμε **to** για να εκφράσουμε κίνηση από τη μια μεριά στην άλλη.
→ *go **to** school*
→ *come **to** Oxford*
→ *bring a friend **to** the party*
→ *give/lend something **to** someone*

Χρησιμοποιούμε **into** για να δείξουμε ότι κάτι μπήκε μέσα σε κάποιο μέρος.
→ *The cat came **into** the house.*
→ *The ball fell **into** the pool.*
→ *A bird flew **into** the forest.*

Χρησιμοποιούμε **onto** για να δείξουμε ότι κάτι μεταφέρθηκε σε μια θέση επάνω σε κάτι.
→ *The cat jumped **onto** the tree.*
→ *She dropped her books **onto** the floor.*
→ *The boy ran **onto** the road.*
(Συγκρίνετε: *The boy ran **on** the road.* = Το αγόρι ήταν πάνω στο δρόμο και άρχισε να τρέχει. Αυτό δείχνει την θέση και όχι την κατεύθυνση.)

Χρησιμοποιούμε **towards** για να δείξουμε ότι κάτι κινείται προς μια συγκεκριμένη κατεύθυνση.
→ *The children ran **towards** their mother.*

## 3.5 Prepositional Phrases

Χρησιμοποιούμε συνηθισμένες **prepositional phrases** (φράσεις με προθέσεις):
για να μιλήσουμε για χρόνο.
→ *I woke up **in the middle of** the night.*
→ *They're getting married **at the end of** the month.*

για να μιλήσουμε για τοποθεσία.
→ *The cat jumped **in front of** the tree.*
→ *She dropped her books **at the bottom of** the stairs.*
→ *The bird was sitting **on the top of** the tree.*

# Grammar Exercises

**A** Complete the conversation with the Present Continuous of the verbs in brackets.

**Mark:** We ¹ _____ (have) a barbecue on Saturday evening.

**Dina:** Great. So who ² _____ you _____ (invite)?

**Mark:** I ³ _____ (ask) some kids from my class to come, but I ⁴ _____ (not tell) all my classmates. It's a small backyard and my brother ⁵ _____ (send) some texts to ask his friends this afternoon.

**Dina:** ⁶ _____ Fiona _____ (come) to your barbecue?

**Mark:** No, she ⁷ _____ (stay) with her aunt in Paisley all weekend.

**Dina:** That's a pity. Who ⁸ _____ (cook) the food on Saturday? I'm sure you and your brother ⁹_____ (not do) it.

**Mark:** Why not? My parents ¹⁰ _____ (buy) the food, but they ¹¹ _____ (not cook) everything. Andrew and I ¹² _____ (make) sandwiches.

**Dina:** Okay. See you there.

# 3 Grammar

**B** Circle the correct words.

1 Do you walk **to** / **at** school every day?
2 Tony put the laptop **in** / **to** his bag.
3 I received the email **at** / **on** Friday morning.
4 Mum was **from** / **at** work when she called me.
5 We haven't got a school holiday **in** / **on** November.
6 There is somebody **at** / **to** the door. I'll see who it is.
7 The Carnival parade was coming down the road **on** / **towards** us.
8 How did you fall **into** / **onto** the pool?
9 My profile photo is **at** / **on** the left of the page.
10 I gave my mobile **on** / **to** my friend.

**C** Complete the sentences with prepositions.

1 Do you always go out with your friends _____ the weekend?
2 He wrote his first song _____ 2012.
3 Is your birthday _____ 5th April?
4 Write the answer _____ the board.
5 I'm writing a letter _____ the moment.
6 Why is Tom _____ hospital?
7 Peter has a photo _____ the back of his T-shirt.
8 Do your relatives live _____ South Africa?
9 She got home _____ school at four o'clock.
10 The man was standing _____ front of the window.

# 4 A Day in the Life

**Page 43**

**4.1** **Inuit** (n) /'ɪnjuɪt/
a Native American from a northern part
of Canada, Greenland or Alaska • *I can't
understand how Inuits can make homes in
the snow.* ❖ Εσκιμώος από τον Καναδά ή την
Αλάσκα

**4.2** **pick** (v) /pɪk/
cut or take small pieces of sth or small things
from sth else • *The farmer picked the stones
out of the horse's feet.* ➢ pick (n) ❖ κόβω,
μαζεύω

**4.3** **Greenland** (n) /'griːnˌlənd/
❖ Γροιλανδία

## Word Focus    Page 44

**4.4** **capital** (n) /'kæpɪtl/
the main city in a country • *Belfast is the
capital of Northern Ireland.* ❖ πρωτεύουσα

**4.5** **porridge** (n) /'pɒrɪdʒ/
a kind of breakfast food that is hot and
creamy, made from cooked oats • *A bowl
of hot porridge is the traditional breakfast in
Scotland.* ❖ κουάκερ, χυλός

**4.6** **physical education** (n) /'fɪzɪkl ˌedʒu'keɪʃn/
sports and exercise done as a class at school
• *Our class has physical education three times
a week in the school gym or the swimming
pool.* ❖ φυσική αγωγή, γυμναστική (στο
σχολείο)
✎ Syn: PE

**4.7** **steamed** (adj) /'stiːmd/
cooked with steam • *The Chinese often eat
steamed rice with other foods.* ➢ steam (v, n)
❖ μαγειρεμένος στον ατμό

**4.8** **gas** (n) /gæs/
sth that is not liquid and not solid, e.g. oxygen
• *Shona has a gas fire in her living room.*
❖ αέριο

**4.9** **boiling** (adj) /'bɔɪlɪŋ/
very hot • *He put the boiling water in the cup
to make tea.* ➢ boil (v) ❖ καυτός, βραστός

## Reading    Pages 44-45

**4.10** **typical** (adj) /'tɪpɪkl/
usual; common • *My typical day begins with
breakfast at seven.* ➢ typically (adj) ❖ τυπικός,
συνηθισμένος

**4.11** **congee** (n) /'kɒndʒi/
a kind of porridge made with rice • *When Tom
was feeling sick, his granny gave him congee
to eat.* ❖ λαπάς

**4.12** **international** (adj) /ˌɪntə'næʃnəl/
for people from many different countries
• *The restaurant sells a variety of delicious
international foods.* ➢ internationally (adv)
❖ διεθνής

**4.13** **foreign** (adj) /'fɒrən/
from another country • *Can you speak any
other foreign languages?* ➢ foreigner (n)
❖ ξένος

**4.14** **cafeteria** (n) /ˌkæfə'tɪəriə/
a self-service restaurant, often in a school or
other public building • *Do you have lunch in
the school cafeteria?* ❖ κυλικείο

**4.15** **during** (prep) /'djuərɪŋ/
all through a period of time • *Thousands of
tourists visit the Acropolis Museum during the
summer.* ❖ κατά τη διάρκεια

**4.16** **athlete** (n) /'æθliːt/
sb who takes part in sport, especially on a
track, e.g. running • *Frank loves running,
but he doesn't want to be a famous athlete.*
➢ athletic (adj), athletics (n) ❖ αθλητής

**4.17** **Olympic Games** (n) /ə,lɪmpɪk 'geɪmz/
an international sports event that happens
every four years • *The final swimming events
in the Olympic Games were on the news on
TV.* ❖ Ολυμπιακοί Αγώνες

**4.18** **on the way** (phr) /ɒn ðə weɪ/
going towards a place • *On the way to the
shops, Tanya found a little dog yesterday.*
❖ στο δρόμο

**4.19** **have a rest** (phr) /həv ə rest/
relax; take a break • *After five kilometres, the
group stopped walking to have a rest.* ❖ κάνω
διάλειμμα, ξεκουράζομαι

**4.20** **organise** (v) /'ɔːgənaɪz/
plan and prepare sth • *Helen needs a bigger
desk to organise her work.* ➢ organiser (n),
organisation (n) ❖ οργανώνω

**4.21** **language** (n) /'læŋgwɪdʒ/
the way of speaking and writing in a particular
country • *Can you speak any other foreign
languages?* ❖ γλώσσα

**4.22** **player** (n) /'pleɪə(r)/
sb who plays a sport or game • *Who is your
favourite football player?* ➢ play (v) ❖ παίχτης

## Vocabulary    Pages 46-47

**4.23** **dust** (v) /dʌst/
clean the dirt off furniture with a cloth •
*Amanda broke the jar when she was dusting
the table.* ➢ dust (n), duster (n), dusty (adj)
❖ ξεσκονίζω

**4.24**  **vacuum** (v) /ˈvækjuəm/
clean the floor with an electric cleaner
• *Who will vacuum the floor after the party?*
➢ vacuum (n) ❖ σκουπίζω (με ηλεκτρική σκούπα)

**4.25**  **carpet** (n) /ˈkɑːpɪt/
sth that you put on the floor to cover it
• *Please don't walk on the clean carpet with your wet football boots!* ❖ μοκέτα, χαλί

**4.26**  **do the washing up** (phr) /du ðə ˈwɒʃɪŋ ʌp/
wash plates, cups, etc. after using them
• *I made the dinner, so who wants to do the washing up? The kitchen is full of dirty dishes.* ❖ πλένω τα πιάτα

**4.27**  **sweep** (v) /swiːp/
clean a floor with a brush • *Ian swept up the leaves in the backyard.* ❖ σκουπίζω

**4.28**  **iron** (v) /ˈaɪən/
make clothes flat by pressing them with an iron
• *Could you iron my T-shirt for the basketball match?* ➢ ironing (n) ❖ σιδερώνω

**4.29**  **rise** (v) /raɪz/
move up • *The sun was rising when I got up this morning.* ❖ ανεβαίνω, σηκώνομαι

**4.30**  **dry** (v) /draɪ/
make sth dry • *Put the clothes out to dry in the sun.* ➢ dry (adj) ❖ στεγνώνω

**4.31**  **hairdryer** (n) /ˈheədraɪə(r)/
a device that you use to dry your hair with hot air • *You don't have to take a hairdryer on holiday because there's one in your hotel room.* ❖ σεσουάρ, πιστολάκι

**4.32**  **ready** (adj) /ˈredi/
prepared • *Are you ready to dance? Start the music!* ❖ έτοιμος

**4.33**  **hang (sth) out** (phr v) /hæŋ (ˈsʌmθɪŋ) aʊt/
attach sth to hang on a line outside your home, especially clothes • *I washed my trousers and hung them out to dry.* ❖ απλώνω

**4.34**  **tidy** (v) /ˈtaɪdi/
put things in order • *I always tidy my bedroom on Sunday afternoon.* ➢ tidy (adj) ❖ τακτοποιώ

**4.35**  **mess** (n) /mes/
an untidy and/or dirty state • *The kitchen was in a mess after the party.* ➢ mess (v), messy (adj) ❖ ακαταστασία, χάος

**4.36**  **housework** (n) /ˈhaʊswɜːk/
work that you need to do in your home, e.g. cooking and cleaning • *My parents are happy when I help them with the housework.* ❖ δουλειές του σπιτιού

---

### Housework

| | |
|---|---|
| do the washing up | iron |
| dry | sweep |
| dust | tidy |
| hang (sth) out | vacuum |

---

**4.37**  **pay** (v) /peɪ/
give money to buy sth; give sb money to do a job • *How much did you pay for your new school bag?* ➢ pay (n), payment (n), paid (adj), payable (adj) ❖ πληρώνω

**4.38**  **spend** (v) /spend/
use money to pay for sth • *Gina spends all her money on new clothes.* ❖ ξοδεύω

**4.39**  **rent** (v) /rent/
pay money to use sth (e.g. a house, flat or room) that belongs to sb else • *We rented a room with a view of Hyde Park in London.* ➢ rent (n), rental (n) ❖ ενοικιάζω

**4.40**  **flat** (n) /flæt/
a home on one floor of a building that has more than one floor • *George lives in a flat with his parents and his aunt lives in the flat downstairs.* ❖ διαμέρισμα

**4.41**  **lend** (v) /lend/
give sth of yours to sb to use for a short time
• *Could you lend me an umbrella because I forgot to bring mine?* ➢ lender (n) ❖ δανείζω

**4.42**  **borrow** (v) /ˈbɒrəʊ/
take sth that belongs to sb else to use for a short time and then give it back • *You can borrow books from the town library and take them back a week later.* ➢ borrower (n) ❖ δανείζομαι

**4.43**  **make money** (phr) /meɪk ˈmʌni/
get money from your job or by selling sth
• *Steve makes money by selling his old clothes and other things he doesn't need on the internet.* ❖ βγάζω λεφτά

**4.44**  **save money** (phr) /seɪv ˈmʌni/
keep money that you don't need to spend right now • *It's difficult to save money when you don't have a good job.* ➢ saving(s) (n) ❖ κάνω οικονομία, αποταμιεύω

**4.45**  **till** (n) /tɪl/
a machine that has a drawer where sb puts the money you pay for sth in a shop • *There are always alot of people waiting at the till in the supermarket at weekends.* ❖ ταμείο

**4.46**  **cashier** (n) /kæˈʃɪə(r)/
sb who works at the till in a shop, bank, etc.
• *The cashiers at this bank are not always very friendly when Mum goes to pay her bills.* ❖ ταμίας

**4.47** **customer** (n) /ˈkʌstəmə(r)/
sb who buys sth from a shop • *The customers were getting annoyed because there was only one cashier in the busy shop.* ❖ πελάτης

**4.48** **shelf** (n) /ʃelf/
a flat surface for storing things on a wall or in a cupboard • *I keep my school books on the shelves next to my bed.* ❖ ράφι

**4.49** **receipt** (n) /rɪˈsiːt/
a piece of paper that shows how much you paid for sth in a shop, etc. • *Keep your receipts because you might need to take something back to the shop.* ➢ receive (v) ❖ απόδειξη

**4.50** **trolley** (n) /ˈtrɒli/
a shopping cart for carrying things in a shop • *The children put some extra things they wanted into the shopping trolley, so their mum wasn't happy when she found out.* ❖ καρότσι (στο σουπερμάρκετ)

**4.51** **cash** (n) /kæʃ/
money in coins or notes • *Eric pays for everything in cash because he doesn't like using bank cards.* ❖ μετρητά

**4.52** **product** (n) /ˈprɒdʌkt/
sth that is grown or made for selling • *All the products in the village shop come from farms in the area.* ➢ produce (v), producer (n), production (n), productive (adj) ❖ προϊόν

---

**Shopping & Money**

| Verbs | Nouns |
|---|---|
| borrow | cash |
| lend | cashier |
| pay | customer |
| rent | dollar |
| spend | product |
| make money | receipt |
| save money | shelf |
| | till |
| | trolley |

---

**Containers & Quantity**

| bar | piece |
|---|---|
| can | slice |
| carton | tin |
| loaf | |

**4.53** **carton** (n) /ˈkɑːtn/
a small plastic or cardboard box that has food or drink inside • *I bought four cartons of ice cream and one carton of milk.* ❖ μικρό χάρτινο ή πλαστικό κουτί

**4.54** **loaf** (n) /ləʊf/
an amount of bread that is cooked in a shape • *We need a loaf of bread for the sandwiches.* ❖ φραντζόλα

**4.55** **tin** (n) /tɪn/
a metal container for food • *There are some tins of tomatoes in the kitchen cupboard.* ➢ tinned (adj) ❖ κονσέρβα

**4.56** **bar** (n) /bɑː(r)/
a long flat piece of sth with straight sides, e.g. chocolate, soap • *I ate a bar of chocolate and now I can't eat all of my dinner.* ❖ πλάκα, μπάρα

**4.57** **can** (n) /kən/
a metal container for food or drink • *We bought some cans of lemonade and cola for the barbecue.* ➢ canned (adj) ❖ μεταλλικό κουτί (κυρίως για αναψυκτικό)

**4.58** **olive** (n) /ˈɒlɪv/
a small green or black fruit that you can eat or use for its oil • *The pizza had tasty big black olives on top.* ❖ ελιά

# *Grammar*     Pages 48-49

**4.59** **Thailand** (n) /ˈtaɪlænd/
❖ Ταϊλάνδη

**4.60** **hotel** (n) /həʊˈtel/
a building where you pay for a room to stay in for a short time • *The hotel was very close to the sea, so we didn't need to swim in its pool.* ❖ ξενοδοχείο

**4.61** **tent** (n) /tent/
a shelter held up by poles and ropes that you use for camping • *Ben put up his tent and went inside it to sleep.* ❖ σκηνή

**4.62** **backpack** (n) /ˈbækpæk/
a large bag that you can carry on your back • *The campers were carrying large backpacks with their tents and clothes.* ❖ σακίδιο

**4.63** **pack** (v) /pæk/
put things into a bag or box • *I packed all my books in my school bag and went for the bus.* ❖ πακετάρω

**4.64** **prediction** (n) /prɪˈdɪkʃn/
what sb says will happen in the future • *Karen didn't believe Roger's prediction that the team would win the match.* ➢ predict (v), predictable (adj) ❖ πρόβλεψη

**4.65** **steak** (n) /steɪk/
a thick slice of meat • *The customer was unhappy because his steak wasn't cooked well.* ❖ μπριζόλα

**4.66** **tuna** (n) /ˈtjuːnə/
a large sea fish with light red meat • *Tony makes delicious pizza with tuna and other seafood.* ❖ τόνος

**4.67** **research** (n) /rɪˈsɜːtʃ/
a study to find out or prove facts about sth
• *In our science class, we did some research about healthy eating.* ❖ έρευνα, έρευνες

**4.68** **biscuit** (n) /ˈbɪskɪt/
a thin crispy cake • *Have a biscuit with your hot chocolate.* ❖ μπισκότο

**4.69** **dollar** (n) /ˈdɒlə(r)/
the kind of money used in some countries, e.g. the USA, Canada and Australia • *The taxi ride from the airport costs forty dollars.* ❖ δολάριο

**4.70** **traffic** (n) /ˈtræfɪk/
all the cars, buses, lorries, etc. on a street at the same time • *The bus was late because there was so much traffic.* ❖ κίνηση (στους δρόμους)

**4.71** **advice** (n) /ədˈvaɪs/
sth you tell sb to do to help them with a problem • *If you have any problem with grammar, ask your teacher for advice.*
➢ advise (v), advisable (adj) ❖ συμβουλή

**4.72** **luggage** (n) /ˈlʌgɪdʒ/
all the bags you're carrying when you're travelling • *Simon put his luggage in the back of the taxi and left for the airport.*
❖ αποσκευές, βαλίτσες

**4.73** **equipment** (n) /ɪˈkwɪpmənt/
the things you need to do a job or an activity
• *The students had a party to raise money to buy new equipment, like musical instruments, for the school.* ❖ εξοπλισμός

**4.74** **strawberry** (n) /ˈstrɔːbəri/
a small, juicy, red, summer fruit • *We're having ice cream with strawberries from the garden.*
❖ φράουλα

# Listening                                    Page 50

**4.75** **amount** (n) /əˈmaʊnt/
a quantity of sth • *My uncle won a large amount of money in a TV quiz.* ❖ ποσότητα

**4.76** **form** (n) /fɔːm/
type; kind • *What forms of music do you enjoy?* ❖ είδος, μορφή

**4.77** **espresso** (n) /eˈspresəʊ/
a very strong hot, black coffee in a small cup
• *Italians often drink a small cup of espresso for breakfast.* ❖ εσπρέσσο

**4.78** **cappuccino** (n) /ˌkæpuˈtʃiːnəʊ/
a hot coffee with lots of frothy milk on top
• *They make great cappuccino in this café.*
❖ καπουτσίνο

**4.79** **perhaps** (adv) /pəˈhæps/
maybe • *Perhaps we'll go to Thailand next year, but I'm not sure.* ❖ ίσως

**4.80** **comfortable** (adj) /ˈkʌmftəbl/
that has a relaxing feeling to wear or sit on, etc. • *This chair isn't comfortable to sit on for a long time.* ➢ comfort (v, n), comfortable (adv)
❖ άνετος
✎ Opp: uncomfortable

**4.81** **reach** (v) /riːtʃ/
get to a place/person • *When you reach the bank, turn left into Park Street.* ❖ φτάνω

# Speaking                                     Page 51

**4.82** **starter** (n) /ˈstɑːtə(r)/
a little food eaten before the main part of a meal • *In Britain, people often have soup for starters, especially in winter.* ➢ start (v)
❖ ορεκτικό

**4.83** **main course** (n) /meɪn kɔːs/
the main part of a meal • *Barbara had fish and salad for her main course.* ❖ κύριο πιάτο

**4.84** **dessert** (n) /dɪˈzɜːt/
a sweet eaten at the end of a meal • *We've got apple pie and ice cream for dessert.*
❖ επιδόρπιο

**4.85** **chocolate brownie** (n) /ˈtʃɒklət ˈbraʊni/
a kind of square, American chocolate cake • *How many eggs do I need to make chocolate brownies?* ❖ σοκολατένιο μπράουνι

**4.86** **prawn** (n) /prɔːn/
a shellfish with legs, a thin, hard back and a tail • *Prawns are funny looking little animals with ten legs.* ❖ γαρίδα

**4.87** **sparkling water** (n) /ˈspɑːklɪŋ ˈwɔːtə(r)/
a kind of fizzy drinking water • *Scientists did some research to see if sparkling water is bad for our bones.* ❖ ανθρακούχο νερό

**4.88** **garlic** (n) /ˈgɑːlɪk/
a small vegetable with a very strong taste and smell • *Greek people sometimes eat fish with garlic sauce on special days.* ❖ σκόρδο

**4.89** **still water** (n) /stɪl ˈwɔːtə(r)/
drinking water that is not fizzy • *I think still water is a more healthy drink than sparkling water.* ❖ πόσιμο νερό χωρίς ανθρακικό

**4.90** **tiramisu** (n) /ˌtɪrəmiˈsu/
a dessert made from slices of cake with chocolate and cream cheese • *Tiramisu is too sweet for me, so I had some fruit for dessert.*
❖ τιραμισού

**4.91** **tip** (n) /tɪp/
some extra money you give to sb who serves in a café, etc. • *How much should people pay taxi drivers as a tip?* ❖ φιλοδώρημα, πουρμπουάρ

**4.92** **book** (v) /bʊk/
ask sb to keep sth for you to use later • *We booked a holiday in the north of Scotland.* ➢ booking (n) ❖ κλείνω (τραπέζι, δωμάτιο, κλπ)

**4.93** **Americano** (n) /əˌmerɪˈkɑːnəʊ/
strong black American style coffee • *Mum never drinks Americano at night because then she can't sleep.* ❖ αμερικάνικος καφές

**4.94** **latte** (n) /ˈlɑteɪ/
a drink made with milk and a little coffee • *Latte is a more relaxing drink than most other coffees because it has so much milk.* ❖ λάτε

**4.95** **takeaway** (n) /ˈteɪkəweɪ/
a meal that you can collect at a restaurant to eat somewhere else • *We were too tired to cook, so we ordered a takeaway.* ❖ φαγητό σε πακέτο

### Drinks

| | |
|---|---|
| Americano | latte |
| cappuccino | sparkling water |
| espresso | still water |

# Writing
**Pages 52-53**

**4.96** **opinion** (n) /əˈpɪnjən/
what you think of sth • *What's your opinion of the new Italian restaurant? Do you like it?* ❖ γνώμη

**4.97** **exterior** (n) /ɪkˈstɪəriə(r)/
the outside part of a building • *Sam is painting the exterior walls of his house white.* ❖ εξωτερικό (κτιρίου)

**4.98** **sunbathe** (v) /ˈsʌnbeɪð/
stay outside in the sunshine to make your skin go brown • *Some people were swimming and others were sunbathing beside the pool.* ➢ sunbathing (n) ❖ κάνω ηλιοθεραπεία

**4.99** **awful** (adj) /ˈɔːfl/
not nice; very bad • *That meal was awful! I'm not eating there again.* ❖ απαίσιος

**4.100** **exciting** (adj) /ɪkˈsaɪtɪŋ/
interesting and making you feel excited • *I think travelling by plane is exciting.* ➢ excite (v), excited (adj), excitement (n) ❖ συναρπαστικός

**4.101** **exclamation mark** (n) /ˌekskləˈmeɪʃn mɑːk/
a mark you write after an exclamation; ! • *Don't use the exclamation mark '!' at the end of every sentence because that looks like you are shouting.* ❖ θαυμαστικό

### Look!

Προσέξτε την διάφορα μεταξύ των επιθέτων που τελειώνουν με **-ed** και **-ing**.
Όταν τελειώνουν με **-ed**, περιγράφουμε πώς αισθάνεται κάποιος.
*Jill's **excited** about getting a new bike.* (exci**ted** = ενθουσιασμένη)
*The children got bored quickly.* (be/get bor**ed** = βαρέθηκαν)
Ενώ, όταν τελειώνουν με **-ing**, περιγράφουμε πώς είναι κάτι ή κάποιος.
*Riding a bike is **exciting**.* (exci**ting** = συναρπαστικός)
*The children thought the game was **boring**.* (bor**ing** = βαρετός)

**4.102** **greeting** (n) /ˈɡriːtɪŋ/
sth you say when you meet sb or write when you start an email, letter, etc. • *'Hello' is a common English greeting.* ➢ greet (v) ❖ χαιρετισμός

**4.103** **informal** (adj) /ɪnˈfɔːml/
in a friendly and relaxed style • *Everybody wore informal clothes to the barbecue.* ❖ ανεπίσημος
✎ Opp: formal

**4.104** **sign off** (phr v) /saɪn ɒf/
end an email, letter, etc. • *Aunt Miranda signed off her email with 'Lots of love and kisses, Auntie M'.* ❖ υπογράφω

### Food

| | | |
|---|---|---|
| beef | olive | strawberry |
| biscuit | pasta | takeaway |
| boiling | pomegranate | tart |
| chocolate | pork | tiramisu |
| brownie | porridge | tuna |
| congee | prawn | venison |
| dessert | starter | |
| garlic | steak | |
| main course | steamed | |

# Video 4
# A Grizzly Encounter

**Page 54**

**4.105** **encounter** (n) /ɪnˈkaʊntə(r)/
an unplanned meeting • *Helen had a happy encounter with a dolphin when she went swimming in the sea.* ➢ encounter (v) ❖ (συνήθως απρόβλεπτη) συνάντηση

**4.106 grizzly bear** (n) /ˌɡrɪzli 'beə(r)/
a very big brown bear from North America or Russia • *When you see a grizzly bear hold your arms up and talk quietly or climb up a tree quickly.* ❖ αρκούδα Γκρίζλι

**4.107 staff** (n) /stɑːf/
all the people working in a place as a group • *The hotel staff were very friendly and helpful.* ❖ προσωπικό

**4.108 task** (n) /tɑːsk/
a piece of work • *Albert's job includes the task of feeding the animals at the zoo.* ❖ δουλειά, εργασία

**4.109 prepare** (v) /prɪ'peə(r)/
get ready to do sth • *Ken is preparing the invitations for his party.* ➤ preparation (n) ❖ προετοιμάζω

**4.110 powerful** (adj) /'paʊəfl/
strong; with a strong effect • *Grizzly bears are powerful big animals.* ➤ power (n) ❖ δυναμικός, ισχυρός

**4.111 hunt** (n) /hʌnt/
the action of trying to find sth/sb; the act of looking for sth/sb to catch or kill • *This year, our teacher planned an Easter egg hunt for the class and I found one egg.* ➤ hunt (v), hunter (n) ❖ κυνήγι

**4.112 treat** (n) /triːt/
sth extra given to a person or animal to eat for something special • *Patricia gives her dog little biscuits as a treat to help train him.* ➤ treat (v) ❖ λιχουδιά

**4.113 range (from)** (v) /reɪndʒ (frəm)/
have a variety of different types, sizes, etc. (from one thing to another) • *The animals in the zoo range from tiny insects to elephants.* ➤ range (n) ❖ κυμαίνομαι

**4.114 venison** (n) /'venɪsn/
meat from a deer • *Some butcher's shops in Scotland now sell venison as well as other meat because a lot of deer are kept on farms.* ❖ κρέας ελαφιού

**4.115 beef** (n) /biːf/
meat from a cow • *Angela is cooking beef and potatoes in the oven for Sunday dinner.* ➤ beefy (adj) ❖ βοδινό κρέας

**4.116 pork** (n) /pɔːk/
meat from a pig • *Because of their traditional ways of life, people from many countries don't like eating pork.* ❖ χοιρινό

**4.117 pomegranate** (n) /'pɒmɪɡrænɪt/
a large round red fruit with juicy seeds inside • *Heather puts juicy red pomegranate seeds on salads and they're so tasty.* ❖ ρόδι

**4.118 private** (adj) /'praɪvət/
that belongs to one person or group and not for everybody to use or know about • *Nobody likes people reading their private texts to friends.* ➤ privacy (n) ❖ ιδιωτικός, προσωπικός

**4.119 daily** (adj) /'deɪli/
of every day • *Can you describe your daily routine?* ❖ ημερήσιος

**4.120 mentally** (adv) /'mentəli/
related to the mind • *Are you mentally prepared for the maths exam?* ➤ mental (adj) ❖ διανοητικά

**4.121 healthy** (adj) /'helθi/
well and not getting ill easily • *Gordon keeps healthy by eating carefully and going for long walks.* ➤ health (n), healthily (adv) ❖ υγιής ✎ Opp: unhealthy

**4.122 hidden** (adj) /'hɪdn/
not able to be seen or found easily • *There was a hidden door behind the cupboard.* ➤ hide (v) ❖ κρυμμένος

# Vocabulary Exercises

**A Circle the odd one out.**

| | | | |
|---|---|---|---|
| 1 | olive | steak | strawberry |
| 2 | biscuit | tart | prawn |
| 3 | garlic | espresso | latte |
| 4 | cashier | customer | hairdryer |
| 5 | pay | save | spend |
| 6 | backpack | flat | hotel |
| 7 | cost | staff | tip |
| 8 | tuna | pork | venison |

**B** Circle the correct words.

1 Wait for me when you **reach** / **rise** the cafeteria.
2 Don't forget to **hang out** / **sign off** at the end of your email.
3 The cashier put the money into the **till** / **trolley** and gave me the receipt.
4 Tracy doesn't want to sleep in a **hunt** / **tent** because she's scared of snakes.
5 I'm learning to **dust** / **iron** my school clothes.
6 Eileen washed her hair and then had to **dry** / **sweep** it before she went out.
7 Would you please **borrow** / **lend** me some cash and I'll give it back tomorrow?
8 I took out the machine to **tidy** / **vacuum** the carpet.

**C** Complete the sentences with these words. Use each word only once.

amount   bar   can   carton   loaf   piece   slice   tin

1 Betty took out her _____ of chocolate and gave everyone a _____ of it.
2 I cut off a thick _____ from the _____ of bread to make a sandwich.
3 There was a small _____ of milk in the _____ .
4 I drank the _____ of cola and opened the _____ of tuna to eat it.

**D** Complete the sentences.

1 Will I order ice cream for d __ __ __ __ __ __ to finish the meal?
2 Jim paid a d __ __ __ __ __ for a cake in New York.
3 I can't reach the top s __ __ __ __ in the supermarket.
4 When you buy something, keep the r __ __ __ __ __ __ from the shop.
5 We'll have a break for lunch at m __ __ __ __ __ .
6 I'm not sure, but p __ __ __ __ __ __ I'll have pasta for my main course.
7 Our country won a lot of prizes d __ __ __ __ __ the Olympic Games.
8 You'll get ill if you s __ __ __ __ __ __ __ for too long in summer.

**E** Complete the sentences with words formed from the words in bold.

1 Derek wants to be a famous basketball _____ .          **PLAY**
2 We were _____ about watching the Olympic Games.          **EXCITE**
3 Timothy made a _____ to rent a flat in York.          **DECIDE**
4 Gorillas are very _____ animals.          **POWER**
5 I eat lots of fruit to stay _____ .          **HEALTH**
6 We found the _____ treasure under the tree.          **HIDE**
7 Rosie's cat likes sleeping in a _____ bed.          **COMFORT**
8 Let's have some soup for a _____ .          **START**

# 4 Grammar

## 4.1 *Will*

| Κατάφαση |
|---|
| I/he/she/it/we/you/they **will** help |
| **Άρνηση** |
| I/he/she/it/we/you/they **will not (won't)** help |
| **Ερώτηση** |
| **Will** I/he/she/it/we/you/they help? |

| Σύντομες απαντήσεις | |
|---|---|
| **Yes**, I/he/she/it/we/you/they **will**. | **No**, I/he/she/it/we/you/they **won't**. |

Χρησιμοποιούμε *will* για το μέλλον:
για αποφάσεις που παίρνουμε την ώρα που μιλάμε.
→ *I'll* ***vacuum*** *the carpet. It looks dirty.*
για υποσχέσεις.
→ *I promise, I'll* ***pay*** *for the meal.*
για να μιλήσουμε για μελλοντικά γεγονότα.
→ *The exam* ***will take*** *two hours.*
μετά από τα ρήματα *think, believe, expect, be sure* κλπ, καθώς και μετά από λέξεις όπως *probably, maybe,* κλπ.
→ *I think we'll* ***visit*** *Dubai in December.*
για να προσφέρουμε να κάνουμε κάτι για κάποιον.
→ *I'll* ***wash*** *your car.*
για να ζητήσουμε από κάποιον να κάνει κάτι.
→ ***Will*** *you* ***lend*** *me five euros, please?*

## 4.2 *Be Going To*

| Κατάφαση |
|---|
| I **am ('m) going to** help<br>he/she/it **is ('s) going to** help<br>we/you/they **are ('re) going to** help |
| **Άρνηση** |
| I **am ('m) not going to** help<br>he/she/it **is not (isn't) going to** help<br>we/you/they **are not (aren't) going to** help |
| **Ερώτηση** |
| **Am** I **going to** help?<br>**Is** he/she/it **going to** help?<br>**Are** we/you/they **going to** help? |

| Σύντομες απαντήσεις | |
|---|---|
| **Yes**, I **am**.<br>**Yes**, we/you/they **are**.<br>**Yes**, he/she/it **is**. | **No**, I'm not.<br>**No**, we/you/they **aren't**.<br>**No**, he/she/it **isn't**. |

Χρησιμοποιούμε *be going to* για:
μελλοντικά σχέδια και προθέσεις.
→ *Brian* ***is going to have*** *a barbecue on Saturday.*
προβλέψεις για το κοντινό μέλλον που στηρίζονται σε τωρινές καταστάσεις ή στοιχεία.
→ *They're playing tennis beside the swimming pool. I think the ball is* ***going to fall*** *into the water.*
**Σημείωση:** Κάποιες συνηθισμένες χρονικές εκφράσεις που χρησιμοποιούνται συχνά με *will* και *be going to* είναι: *this week/month/summer, tonight, this evening, tomorrow, tomorrow morning/afternoon/evening/night, next week/month/ year, at the weekend, in May, in a few minutes/ hours/days, on Tuesday, on Sunday morning,* κλπ.

## 4.3 Countable Nouns

Τα περισσότερα ουσιαστικά (nouns) είναι αριθμήσιμα (countable) και έχουν τον ενικό και τον πληθυντικό αριθμό.
→ banana → bananas
Συνήθως χρησιμοποιούμε *a* ή *an* με countable nouns.
→ *a* bag
→ *an* egg

Μπορούμε να χρησιμοποιήσουμε *some*, *any* ή έναν αριθμό (π.χ. *four*) με countable nouns στον πληθυντικό.
→ Have *some* biscuits.
→ We haven't got *any* apples.
→ I bought *two* tins of beans.

Χρησιμοποιούμε τα ρήματα στον ενικό ή στον πληθυντικό με countable nouns ανάλογα αν μιλάμε για ένα ή περισσότερα πράγματα.
→ The *cake is* delicious.
→ These *cakes are* amazing.

### Θυμηθείτε
Μερικά countable nouns δεν τελειώνουν με -s. Θυμηθείτε να χρησιμοποιήσετε το ρήμα στον πληθυντικό με αυτά.
→ The *children* are enjoying the game.

## 4.4 Uncountable Nouns

Μερικά ουσιαστικά είναι μη αριθμήσιμα (uncountable). Δεν έχουν πληθυντικό.

| | | | |
|---|---|---|---|
| advice | fun | knowledge | rubbish |
| biology | furniture | luggage | salt |
| cheese | hair | medicine | sugar |
| chocolate | health | milk | sugar |
| equipment | history | money | traffic |
| food | homework | music | water |
| fruit | information | research | weather |

Πάντα χρησιμοποιούμε τα ρήματα στον ενικό με uncountable nouns.
→ The equipment *is* new.
→ The water *wasn't* clean.

### Θυμηθείτε
Μερικά uncountable nouns τελειώνουν με -s. Θυμηθείτε να χρησιμοποιήσετε το ρήμα στον ενικό με αυτά.
→ The news *was* interesting.
→ Maths *is* difficult.

## 4.5 Quantifiers

Χρησιμοποιούμε *some* και με uncountable και με πληθυντικά uncountable nouns σε καταφατικές προτάσεις και σε αιτήματα ή προσφορές.
→ I borrowed *some* books from John.
→ Can you give me *some* help?
→ Would you like *some* bread?

Χρησιμοποιούμε *any* και με uncountable και με πληθυντικά uncountable nouns σε αρνητικές προτάσεις και σε ερωτήσεις.
→ There isn't *any* cheese on the pizza.
→ Did you see *any* birds in the park?

Χρησιμοποιούμε *a lot of/lots of* και με uncountable και με πληθυντικά uncountable nouns.
→ Harry has got *a lot of* money.
→ We ate *lots of* biscuits.

# 4 Grammar

Χρησιμοποιούμε *a little* με uncountable και *a few* με πληθυντικά uncountable nouns σε καταφατικές προτάσεις.
→ There was a **little** milk left in the fridge.
→ There were **a few** women in the post office.

Χρησιμοποιούμε *much* με uncountable και *many* με πληθυντικά uncountable nouns σε αρνητικές προτάσεις και σε ερωτήσεις.
→ We haven't got **much** money.
→ How **many** apples are on the tree?

## Grammar Exercises

**A** Match the sentences.

1  Vanessa is in front of the other athletes. ☐
2  I haven't got much money. ☐
3  What are you doing at the weekend? ☐
4  Mum came home from work and she's tired. ☐
5  When will you tidy your room? ☐
6  The kitchen is in a mess. ☐
7  When are you coming back? ☐
8  What are your holiday plans? ☐

a  I think I'll go to the beach.
b  I promise, I'll do it tomorrow.
c  We're going to travel to Spain in July.
d  She's going to win the race.
e  I'll probably be home at four o'clock.
f  I'll do the washing up.
g  Will you pay for the meal?
h  She's going to have a rest.

**B** Circle the correct words.

1  I think physics **isn't** / **aren't** a difficult subject.
2  Sam ate **a** / **an** apple tart.
3  The biscuits **was** / **were** really tasty.
4  Can you give me **an** / **some** information about the zoo?
5  Two **children** / **childrens** were playing in the garden.
6  These brownies **take** / **takes** twenty minutes to cook.
7  Put your **luggage** / **luggages** into the car.
8  Four women **work** / **works** in this supermarket.

**C** Complete the sentences with these words. Use each word only once.

any   few   little   lot   lots   many   much   some

1  I like a _____ salt on my food.
2  There weren't _____ men on the train.
3  Maria gave me _____ advice about how to cook prawns.
4  Did you hear _____ news about the crash?
5  I met a _____ friends at the café.
6  How _____ time do we have before the break?
7  I've got _____ of homework to do for tomorrow.
8  We got home late because there was a _____ of traffic on the road.

# 5 Home Sweet Home

**Page 57**

**5.1** **convert** (v) /kən'vɜːt/
change sth into sth else for a different use
• *Mum converted the extra bedroom into an office.* ➢ conversion (n), convertible (adj)
❖ μετατρέπω

**5.2** **former** (adj) /'fɔːmə(r)/
that used to be • *The museum is a former train station.* ❖ πρώην, τέως

**5.3** **water tower** (n) /'wɔːtə(r) 'taʊə(r)/
a large water tank on top of a high frame with water • *We could see the high water tower on the farm from miles away.* ❖ πύργος υδροδεξαμενής

**5.4** **air conditioner** (n) /eə(r) kən'dɪʃənə(r)/
a device that cools or heats and dries air
• *The sun doesn't shine on this side of the building, so we don't need an air conditioner in summer.* ➢ air conditioning (n) ❖ κλιματιστικό

**5.5** **toilet** (n) /'tɔɪlət/
a small room with a toilet; a bowl that you sit on to go to the toilet • *The house has two toilets; one is upstairs in the bathroom and the other is next to the hall downstairs.* ❖ τουαλέτα, λεκάνη τουαλέτας

## Word Focus
**Page 58**

**5.6** **running water** (n) /'rʌnɪŋ 'wɔːtə(r)/
water that comes straight from a tap • *Dad's grandparents in the village didn't have running water when they were young.* ❖ νερό βρύσης

**5.7** **tap** (n) /tæp/
a device from which water comes out
• *Remember to turn off the tap after you clean your teeth.* ❖ βρύση

**5.8** **animal skin** (n) /'ænɪml skɪn/
the skin of a dead animal • *Irene never buys shoes or bags made from animal skin because she loves animals.* ❖ δέρμα ζώου

**5.9** **nomad** (n) /'nəʊmæd/
sb who moves around and stays in different places • *A group of nomads was travelling across the Turkish desert with a herd of goats.* ➢ nomadic (adj) ❖ νομάς

**5.10** **permanent** (adj) /'pɜːmənənt/
that lasts forever • *Pauline's job in the café isn't permanent; it's only for the summer.* ➢ permanently (adv) ❖ μόνιμος

**5.11** **season** (n) /'siːzn/
one of the four parts of the year; spring, summer, autumn or winter • *My favourite season is autumn, when the leaves are brown.* ➢ seasonal (adj) ❖ εποχή

**5.12** **wood stove** (n) /wʊd stəʊv/
a device that burns wood for heating or cooking • *The air was filled with the smell of smoke from the wood stoves.* ❖ ξυλόφουρνος, σόμπα με ξύλο

**5.13** **chill out** (phr v) /tʃɪl aʊt/
relax • *Steven listens to music with his friends to chill out.* ❖ χαλαρώνω

## Reading
**Pages 58-59**

**5.14** **igloo** (n) /'ɪgluː/
an Eskimo house built of snow or ice • *Most Inuits live in towns and only a few live in traditional igloos.* ❖ ιγκλού

**5.15** **melt** (v) /melt/
heat sth, e.g. ice, to turn it into liquid • *The bar of chocolate melted in my pocket and it was a real mess.* ❖ λιώνω

**5.16** **instead** (adv) /ɪn'sted/
in place of sth/sb else • *They didn't want to stay at home, so they went for a walk instead.* ❖ αντί

**5.17** **blanket** (n) /'blæŋkɪt/
a large thick cover put onto a bed to keep you warm • *I needed an extra blanket on my bed because it was a cold night.* ❖ κουβέρτα

**5.18** **Mongolia** (n) /mɒŋ'gəʊliə/
➢ Mongolian (n, adj) ❖ Μογγολία

**5.19** **camel** (n) /'kæml/
a tall animal with one or two humps on its back
• *Camels can walk for a long time without drinking water.* ❖ καμήλα

**5.20** **ger** (n) /ger/
a tent used by nomads • *We rented a ger on a camping site for our summer holiday.* ❖ γκερ

**5.21** **outdoors** (adv) /ˌaʊt'dɔːz/
outside; not in a building • *It's too cold for us to play outdoors in winter.* ➢ outdoor (adj)
❖ έξω

**5.22** **cozy** (adj) /'kəʊzi/
warm and comfortable • *Our flat is small, but it's cozy in winter.* ❖ άνετος, βολικός

**5.23** **whole** (adj) /həʊl/
complete; all of sth • *The family spent the whole day at the beach.* ➢ whole (n), whole (adv) ❖ ολόκληρος

**5.24** **satellite dish** (n) /'sætəlaɪt dɪʃ/
a large device shaped like a dish that receives images and sounds from a satellite above the Earth • *Lots of homes have satellite dishes on their roofs so they can watch TV from other countries.* ❖ δορυφορικό πιάτο

**5.25** **solar panel** (n) /ˈsəʊlə(r) ˈpænl/
a piece of equipment with a flat side that collects heat from the sun to make electricity or heat water • *The solar panels on the roof of our home give us lots of hot water.* ❖ ηλιακό ταμπλό

**5.26** **electricity** (n) /ɪˌlekˈtrɪsəti/
energy that moves through wires to give power to machines, lights, etc. • *We couldn't watch TV because the electricity went off.* ➣ electric (adj) ❖ ηλεκτρική ενέργεια

**5.27** **houseboat** (n) /ˈhaʊsbəʊt/
a boat that is a kind of home (usually on a river or canal) • *On our visit to Holland, we saw colourful houseboats on the canals.* ❖ πλωτό σπίτι, σπίτι σε βάρκα

**5.28** **wardrobe** (n) /ˈwɔːdrəʊb/
a cupboard to hang clothes in • *Millie's room looked tidy because she quickly put everything into the wardrobe.* ❖ ντουλάπα για ρούχα

**5.29** **the rest** (n) /ðə rest/
everything else; all the other parts of sth • *Why don't you eat the rest of your dinner?* ❖ το υπόλοιπο

**5.30** **unexpected** (adj) /ˌʌnɪkˈspektɪd/
surprising; not expected or planned
• *Jean had an unexpected call from her Australian cousin in the middle of the night.* ➣ unexpectedly (adj) ❖ απρόβλεπτος
✎ Opp: expected

# Vocabulary
Pages 60-61

**5.31** **cottage** (n) /ˈkɒtɪdʒ/
a small house, especially in the countryside • *We stayed in a lovely little cottage near the sea for the weekend.* ❖ μικρό εξοχικό σπίτι

**5.32** **villa** (n) /ˈvɪlə/
a large house, usually with a garden • *It's my dream to live in a villa with a big garden.* ❖ βίλα

**5.33** **hallway** (n) /ˈhɔːlweɪ/
a small room or space where you go inside a house/building that has doors onto other rooms • *You can leave your coat and umbrella in the hallway.* ❖ χωλ

**5.34** **utility room** (n) /juːˈtɪləti rʊm/
a small room where you can use or keep household equipment, e.g. a washing machine • *Louise does her laundry in the utility room.* ❖ πλυσταριό

**5.35** **patio** (n) /ˈpætiəʊ/
a flat area outside a house where you can sit • *We often eat out on the patio on summer evenings.* ❖ αυλή

**5.36** **shed** (n) /ʃed/
a small building where you can keep things in • *Ian keeps his bicycle in the garden shed.* ❖ αποθήκη (έξω από σπίτι), καλύβι

## Homes & Buildings
| | |
|---|---|
| cottage | igloo |
| garage | shed |
| ger | villa |
| houseboat | |

**5.37** **tool** (n) /tuːl/
a device that you use to make or fix sth • *Roland took his tools out of the car to change the tyre.* ❖ εργαλείο

**5.38** **fix** (v) /fɪks/
correct sth that is broken; make sth work better • *Could you lend me some tools to fix my bicycle?* ❖ φτιάχνω, επιδιορθώνω

**5.39** **loads (of)** (n) /ləʊdz (əv)/
a large amount (of) • *We've got loads of time before the film starts. Let's go to the café.* ➣ load (v) ❖ μεγάλη ποσότητα, πολλά

**5.40** **shady** (adj) /ˈʃeɪdi/
without much sunlight • *They found a shady place for a picnic next to the tree.* ➣ shade (v, n)
❖ σκιερός, στη σκιά

**5.41** **smell** (v) /smel/
sense the smell/aroma of sth • *I can smell something nice. What's for dinner?* ➣ smell (n), smelly (adj) ❖ μυρίζω, οσφραίνομαι

## Look!
Χρησιμοποιούμε το ρήμα **smell** (*μυρίζω*) με δύο τρόπους, π.χ.:
*Your dog **smells** the food.* (Ο σκύλος σου μυρίζει το φαγητό.)
*Your dog **smells** terrible!* (Ο σκύλος σου βρωμάει!)

**5.42** **light** (v) /laɪt/
make sth begin to burn • *The nomads lit a fire to cook their food.* ➣ light (n) ❖ ανάβω

**5.43** **tumble dryer** (n) /ˈtʌmbl ˈdraɪə(r)/
a machine for drying clothes • *This tumble dryer is useful in winter when it's too wet to hang clothes out.* ❖ στεγνωτήριο ρούχων

**5.44** **lawnmower** (n) /ˈlɔːnməʊə(r)/
a machine for cutting grass • *The street gets noisy at the weekend when all the neighbours are using their lawnmowers.* ❖ χλοοκοπτική μηχανή, μηχανή γκαζόν

**5.45** **washing machine** (n) /ˈwɒʃɪŋ məʃiːn/
a machine for washing clothes, etc. • *There was water all over the floor when the washing machine broke down.* ❖ πλυντήριο ρούχων

**5.46** **dining table** (n) /ˈdaɪnɪŋ ˈteɪbl/
a table where you have meals • *Our dining table is at one end of our living room.* ❖ τραπεζαρία (έπιπλο)

**5.47** **fridge** (n) /frɪdʒ/
a machine for keeping food cool • *Katrina put the milk and cheese into the fridge.* ❖ ψυγείο

**5.48** **front door** (n) /frʌnt dɔː(r)/
the main door of a home • *There's somebody at the front door. I'll see who it is.* ❖ εξώπορτα
✎ Opp: back door

**5.49** **rug** (n) /rʌg/
a small carpet • *A traditional rug was on the bedroom floor.* ❖ χαλί

**5.50** **poster** (n) /ˈpəʊstə(r)/
a picture on a large piece of paper for decorating on a wall • *Suzanna has posters of her favourite singer in her room.* ❖ αφίσα

**5.51** **curtain** (n) /ˈkɜːtn/
a piece of cloth to cover a window • *She opened the curtains and saw the rain outside.* ❖ κουρτίνα

**5.52** **blinds** (n) /blaɪndz/
a cover for a window that you pull up or down • *A little light came into the room through the blinds.* ➣ blind (v, adj) ❖ στόρι

**5.53** **pillow** (n) /ˈpɪləʊ/
a cloth bag filled with sth soft that you use to rest your head on in bed • *Jake lay down resting his head on the pillow and went to sleep.* ❖ μαξιλάρι (κρεβατιού)

**5.54** **put away** (phr v) /pʊt əˈweɪ/
put (sth) in its correct place • *The children put away their books before they went to bed.* ❖ βάζω στην θέση, τακτοποιώ

**5.55** **pull up** (phr v) /pʊl ʌp/
make sth move up • *Lucy pulled up the blinds and opened the window.* ❖ τραβώ, ανοίγω (το στόρι)

**5.56** **switch on** (phr v) /swɪtʃ ɒn/
press sth (e.g. a switch or button) to make sth start working • *Jack switched on the TV to watch the news.* ❖ ανοίγω (π.χ. το φως)
✎ Opp: switch off

**5.57** **hang up** (phr v) /hæŋ ʌp/
put sth onto a hook or hanger to store it • *You can hang up your coat in the hallway.* ❖ κρεμάω

**5.58** **put up** (phr v) /pʊt ʌp/
hang sth on a wall • *The room looked nicer when we hung up some pictures.* ❖ εκθέτω, κρεμάω στον τοίχο

**5.59** **ideal** (adj) /aɪˈdiːəl/
perfect for a certain purpose • *The hotel was in an ideal place close to the sea.* ➣ ideally (adj) ❖ ιδανικός

---

### Phrasal Verbs

| | |
|---|---|
| chill out | pull up |
| grow up | switch on/off |
| put away | hang up |
| put up | |

---

# Grammar     Pages 62-63

**5.60** **since** (prep) /sɪns/
from a time in the past until the time of speaking • *I've known Terry since we were kids.* ❖ από κάποιο χρονικό σημείο

**5.61** **Peru** (n) /pəˈruː/
➣ Peruvian (adj, n) ❖ Περού

**5.62** **Chile** (n) /ˈtʃɪli/
➣ Chilean (adj, n) ❖ Χιλή

**5.63** **key** (n) /kiː/
a small metal object for opening or locking a door • *Have you got a key for the front door?* ➣ key (adj) ❖ κλειδί

**5.64** **company** (n) /ˈkʌmpəni/
a business • *Dad works for a company that makes clothes.* ❖ εταιρία

**5.65** **change** (v) /tʃeɪndʒ/
make sth different • *Matthew painted the living room to change the colour of the walls.* ➣ change (n), changeable (adj) ❖ αλλάζω

**5.66** **hour** (n) /ˈaʊə(r)/
a period of 60 minutes • *The school bus takes an hour to bring us home.* ➣ hourly (adj) ❖ ώρα

**5.67** **possession** (n) /pəˈzeʃn/
the state of having sth • *The bank took possession of the Smiths' house because they couldn't pay their bills.* ➣ possess (v) ❖ κυριότητα, ιδιοκτησία

**5.68** **car park** (n) /kaː(r) paːk/
a special area where you can leave cars (outside a building, etc.) • *There's a car park with space for fifty cars next to the sports centre.* ❖ πάρκινγκ

**5.69** **floor** (n) /flɔː(r)/
a level of a buiding • *Bob's flat is on the top floor.* ❖ όροφος

**5.70** **pay attention** (phr) /peɪ əˈtenʃn/
take care to do sth carefully; listen to or watch sb carefully • *Your writing will get better if you pay attention to spelling and grammar.* ❖ προσέχω, δίνω σημασία

**5.71** **adult** (n) /ˈædʌlt/
a grown-up person (usually sb over 18 years old) • *Young children need adults to look after them.* ➢ adult (adj) ❖ ενήλικας

**5.72** **feed** (v) /fiːd/
give food to • *Wendy fed her cat and gave it clean water to drink.* ➢ food (n) ❖ ταΐζω

**5.73** **survive** (v) /səˈvaɪv/
live through a difficult time • *People can't survive for a long time without drinking water.* ➢ survival (n), survivor (n) ❖ επιβιώνω

**5.74** **grow up** (phr v) /grəʊ ʌp/
become an adult • *James grew up on a farm, but now he's moved to the city.* ➢ grown-up (adj, n) ❖ μεγαλώνω (γίνομαι ενήλικας)

# Listening
Page 64

**5.75** **ketchup** (n) /ˈketʃəp/
a thick tomato sauce • *Would you like ketchup on your chips?* ❖ κέτσαπ

**5.76** **towel** (n) /ˈtaʊəl/
a cloth for drying your body or hair • *There were two big white towels in our hotel bathroom.* ❖ πετσέτα

**5.77** **printer** (n) /ˈprɪntə(r)/
a machine for printing words or pictures on paper • *The students used the school printer to make posters for the fair.* ➢ print (v), printed (adj), printing (n) ❖ εκτυπωτής

**5.78** **garage** (n) /ˈgærɑːʒ/
a small building or part of a building to put a car in • *Ann leaves her car in front of her house because she hasn't got a garage.* ❖ γκαράζ

**5.79** **drawer** (n) /drɔː(r)/
sth like a box that you can pull out and close for keeping things in that is a part of a desk, cupboard, etc. • *Len put his socks away in the drawer.* ❖ συρτάρι

## Furniture & Furnishings
| | |
|---|---|
| blanket | pillow |
| blinds | poster |
| bookshelf | rug |
| curtain | towel |
| dining table | wardrobe |
| drawer | |

# Speaking
Page 65

**5.80** **sailing** (n) /ˈseɪlɪŋ/
a sport in which you travel in a boat with sails • *On our holiday in Greece, we went sailing around the islands on a small boat.* ➢ sail (v, n), sailor (n) ❖ ιστιοπλοΐα

**5.81** **space** (n) /speɪs/
an area that is empty for people to use • *There is a lot of space where the children can play in the garden.* ➢ space (v), spacious (adj) ❖ χώρος

**5.82** **light** (adj) /laɪt/
not dark; full of light • *It gets light when the sun rises in the morning.* ➢ light (v, n) ❖ φωτεινός

**5.83** **bookshelf** (n) /ˈbʊkʃelf/
a shelf to keep books on • *My school books are on the bookshelf in my bedroom.* ❖ ράφι για βιβλία

**5.84** **untidy** (adj) /ʌnˈtaɪdi/
not tidy; in a mess • *Sophie's house is always untidy because she doesn't have time to tidy it.* ❖ ακατάστατος
✎ Opp: tidy

## Adjectives
| | |
|---|---|
| connected | permanent |
| cozy | shady |
| former | unexpected |
| ideal | untidy |
| light | whole |

# Writing
Pages 66-67

**5.85** **despite** (prep) /dɪˈspaɪt/
without being affected by • *We had a good time in London despite the bad weather.* ❖ παρά

**5.86** **heavy rain** (n) /ˈhevi reɪn/
more rain than usual • *Sandra didn't hang the washing out because of the heavy rain.* ❖ δυνατή βροχή

**5.87** **darling** (n) /ˈdɑːlɪŋ/
a name you call sb that you love • *Let's go out for dinner, darling.* ➢ darling (adj) ❖ αγάπη μου, χρυσό μου

**5.88** **cancel** (v) /ˈkænsl/
say that sth planned will not happen • *They cancelled the football match because of the snow.* ➢ cancellation (adj) ❖ ακυρώνω

**5.89** **cause** (n) /kɔːz/
sth/sb that makes sth happen • *The heavy rain was the cause of the traffic problems.* ➢ cause (v) ❖ αιτία

**5.90** **result** (n) /rɪˈzʌlt/
sth that happens because of sth else • *The traffic problems were the result of the heavy rain.* ➢ result (v) ❖ αποτέλεσμα

**5.91** **do the laundry** (phr) /du ðə ˈlɔːndri/
wash the clothes, etc. • *Neil has to do the laundry because all his shirts are dirty.* ❖ βάζω μπουγάδα/πλυντήριο

**5.92**  **excuse** (n) /ɪkˈskjuːs/
a reason that you give to explain why you do
or don't do sth ● *Alfie made an excuse not
to go to his cousin's wedding.* ➤ excuse (v)
❖ δικαιολογία

**5.93**  **I'm afraid** (phr) /aɪm əˈfreɪd/
a polite way to say you're sorry about sth ● *I'm
afraid I'll have to cancel my party because I'm
ill.* ❖ φοβάμαι (μεταφορικά), δυστυχώς

---

### Machines & Devices

| | |
|---|---|
| air conditioner | satellite dish |
| cart | solar panel |
| cooker | tap |
| freezer | tool |
| fridge | tumble dryer |
| key | washing machine |
| lawnmower | wood stove |
| printer | |

---

# Video 5
# The Horse Nomads of
# Mongolia                    Page 68

**5.94**  **ox** (n) /ɒks/
a bull used to pull farm equipment ● *The
farmer was using an ox to pull the equipment
to dig his field.* ❖ βόδι
✎ Plural: oxen

**5.95**  **cart** (n) /kɑːt/
a strong open vehicle with two or four wheels,
typically used for carrying loads and pulled
by a horse ● *The ancient Greek wall painting
showed the goddess, Athena, on a horse
pulling a cart.* ❖ κάρο

**5.96**  **camp** (n) /kæmp/
a place where people put tents to stay in
for a short time ● *We made our camp in the
middle of the forest for the night.* ➤ camp (v),
camper (n), campsite (n), camping (n) ❖ βάση,
κατασκήνωση

**5.97**  **centre** (n) /ˈsentə(r)/
the middle point or part ● *The school is in the
centre of the town.* ➤ central (adj) ❖ κέντρο

**5.98**  **gasoline** (n) /ˈgæsəliːn/
petrol; oil used to make an engine work ● *The
driver stopped to put some gasoline in his
truck.* ❖ βενζίνη
✎ Br Eng: petrol

**5.99**  **deeply** (adv) /ˈdiːpli/
very ● *A long hot bath is deeply relaxing at the
end of a busy day.* ➤ deepen (v), deep (adj),
depth (n) ❖ βαθειά

**5.100**  **connected** (adj) /kəˈnektɪd/
linked ● *Mark feels connected to nature
when he swims in the sea.* ➤ connection (n)
❖ συνδεδεμένος

**5.101**  **rope** (n) /rəʊp/
a strong thick string ● *The men tied the ropes
on the harbour to stop the boat moving.*
❖ σκοινί

**5.102**  **represent** (v) /ˌreprɪˈzent/
be a symbol that means sth ● *The sign above
the door represents Heracles and the lion that
he killed in Nemea.* ❖ συμβολίζω
✎ Syn: symbolise

**5.103**  **twists and turns** (phr) /twɪsts ənd tɜːns/
many bends, e.g. on a road, for a long way
● *The mountain road to Delphi is full of
twists and turns.* ❖ περίπλοκες περιστροφές,
ιδιαιτερότητες

---

## Vocabulary Exercises

**A**  **Circle the correct words.**

1  The room was nice and **light / shady** when I opened the curtains.

2  The boys have eaten the **rest / whole** cake.

3  Do you know how to **feed / fix** this broken tap?

4  We haven't got **space / possession** to play tennis in the garden.

5  I can **convert / smell** something good cooking.

6  This isn't Lynne's **ideal / permanent** home because she's just rented it for a month.

7  How did they **survive / change** in the desert for three weeks?

8  We've just heard some **untidy / unexpected** news.

**B** Put these words under the correct heading.

bookshelf  cottage  dining table  drawer  garage  hallway  houseboat  toilet  utility room  villa
wardrobe  ger

| Home | Room | Furniture |
|------|------|-----------|
| _____ | _____ | _____ |
| _____ | _____ | _____ |
| _____ | _____ | _____ |
| _____ | _____ | _____ |

**C** Circle two words in each group that can go with the phrasal verb.

1  hang up:    key / towel / igloo
2  switch on:  rug / printer / washing machine
3  put up:     curtain / pillow / poster
4  put away:   laundry / tool / patio
5  pull up:    blanket / blinds / light
6  grow up:    child / ketchup / ox

**D** Complete the sentences with these words.

air conditioner   car park   fridge   satellite dish   solar panel   tumble dryer   wood stove

1  Please put the cheese away into the _____ .
2  We have a _____ on top of our house, so we've got hot water every day.
3  My _____ has moved because of the wind and now there's no picture on my TV.
4  Grandma's cottage is warm when she lights the _____ .
5  Paul left his car in the street because the _____ was full.
6  When it's really hot in summer, we switch on the _____ .
7  In winter, Sam uses the _____ to dry his laundry.

**E** Do the crossword.

**Across**

2 a reason you give for something you did or didn't do

4 spring, summer, autumn or winter

8 a business

9 a machine to make food on

10 a sport you do in a boat with sails

11 a machine that keeps food very cold

**Down**

1 a large amount

3 something that gives power to machines

5 a person who travels a lot and doesn't have a permanent home

6 a machine for cutting the grass

7 sixty minutes

10 a small building to keep things in

# **5** Grammar

## 5.1 Present Perfect Simple

| Κατάφαση |
| --- |
| I/we/you/they **have ('ve)** walked<br>he/she/it **has ('s)** walked |

| Άρνηση |
| --- |
| I/we/you/they **have not (haven't) walked**<br>he/she/it **has not (hasn't) walked** |

| Ερώτηση |
| --- |
| **Have** I/we/you/they walk**ed**?<br>**Has** he/she/it walk**ed**? |

| Σύντομες απαντήσεις | |
| --- | --- |
| **Yes**, I/we/you/they **have**.<br>**Yes**, he/she/it **has**. | **No**, I/we/you/they **haven't**.<br>**No**, he/she/it **hasn't**. |

**Ορθογραφία**:
walk → walk**ed**    play → play**ed**    use → us**ed**    study → stud**ied**    travel → travel**led**
**Σημείωση:** Κάποια ρήματα είναι ανώμαλα και δεν ακολουθούν αυτούς τους ορθογραφικούς κανόνες.
Δες τη λίστα με τα ανώμαλα ρήματα στις σελ. 180 & 181.
Χρησιμοποιούμε **Present Perfect Simple** για:
κάτι που ξεκίνησε στο παρελθόν και ισχύει ακόμα.
→ *I **have studied** English for five years.*
κάτι που έγινε στο παρελθόν αλλά δεν αναφέρουμε πότε.
→ *We **have spent** a lot of money on our house.*
κάτι που έγινε στο πρόσφατο παρελθόν.
→ *Theo **has just bought** a new computer.*
εμπειρίες.
→ *I**'ve ridden** on a camel.*
**Σημείωση:** Χρονικές εκφράσεις που συνδέουν το παρελθόν με το παρόν χρησιμοποιούνται συχνά με Present Perfect Simple. Για παράδειγμα, *already, still, just, never, ever, yet, for, for ages/a long time, since.*
→ *I have had this mobile phone **for** two years.*

## 5.2 *Have been & Have gone*

Ο Present Perfect Simple για το ρήμα *be* είναι *have been.*
→ *We **have been** friends since our first day at school.*
Ο Present Perfect Simple για το ρήμα *go* είναι επίσης *have been* όταν σημαίνει 'πάω κάπου και επιστρέφω'.
→ *She **has been** to Madrid, but she**'s never been** to Barcelona.*
Ο Present Perfect Simple για το ρήμα *go* είναι και *have gone* όταν σημαίνει 'πάω κάπου και βρίσκομαι ακόμα εκεί, είμαι εκεί ακόμα'.
→ *He**'s gone** to the forest to get some wood and he'll be home soon.*

## 5.3 *For & Since*

Χρησιμοποιούμε συχνά *for* και *since* με Present Perfect Simple.
Το *for* αφορά κάποια χρονική περίοδο ενώ το *since* αφορά κάποια χρονική στιγμή.
→ *I have lived in Glasgow **for years**.*
→ *I have lived in Glasgow **since 2004**.*

## 5.4 Possessive *'s*

Χρησιμοποιούμε *'s* για δείξουμε ότι:
κάτι ανήκει σε κάποιον.
→ *Eva**'s** bike is blue and red.*
κάτι έχει κάποια συγκεκριμένη σχέση με κάποιον ή κάτι άλλο.
→ *Eva is Mark**'s** sister.*

Χρησιμοποιούμε **'s** μετά από ουσιαστικά στον ενικό αριθμό.
→ *The cat's food is in the bowl.*

Χρησιμοποιούμε **'s** μετά από ανώμαλα ουσιαστικά στον πληθυντικό αριθμό.
→ *The children's shoes are in the cupboard.*

Χρησιμοποιούμε **s'** μετά από ομαλά ουσιαστικά στον πληθυντικό αριθμό.
→ *The teachers' cars are in the car park.*

Χρησιμοποιούμε **s'** μετά από ονόματα που τελειώνουν με -s.
→ *It's James' house.*
→ *They're Ms Phillips' books.*

## 5.5 Possessive Adjectives & Possessive Pronouns

| Προσωπικές Αντωνυμίες | Κτητικά Επίθετα | Κτητικές Αντωνυμίες |
|---|---|---|
| I | my | mine |
| you | your | yours |
| he | his | his |
| she | her | hers |
| it | its | – |
| we | our | ours |
| you | your | yours |
| they | their | theirs |

Χρησιμοποιούμε **possessive adjectives** (κτητικά επίθετα) πριν από ουσιαστικά για να δείξουμε ότι κάτι ανήκει σε κάποιον ή έχει κάποια συγκεκριμένη σχέση με κάποιον.
→ *It's the **girl's** bike. It's **her** bike.*
→ *They're the **girls'** bikes. They're **their** bikes.*

Χρησιμοποιούμε **possessive pronouns** (κτητικές αντωνυμίες) για να δείξουμε ότι κάτι ανήκει σε κάποιον.
Possessive pronouns αντικαθιστούν ένα κτητικό επίθετο και ένα ουσιαστικό ή την κτητική μορφή και ένα ουσιαστικό.
→ *This is **your book**. It's **yours**.*
→ *It's **James' house**. It's **his**.*

# Grammar Exercises

**A** Put the words in the correct order to make sentences.

1 they / been / since / friends / year / have / last

_____

2 ? / has / lived / ever / he / flat / a / in

_____

3 just / the / fed / animals / has / the / woman

_____

4 not / we / far / walked / yet / have / very

_____

5 ? / you / finished / your / have / yet / homework

_____

**6** already / played / I / three / have / games / video

_____

**7** ? / where / have / they / up / put / posters / their

_____

**8** still / cleaned / they / haven't / windows / their

_____

**B** **Complete the sentences with the Present Perfect Simple of these verbs.**

do   go   go   not play   never see   stop   study   travel

**1** The nomads _____ to many parts of the country.

**2** _____ you _____ the laundry yet?

**3** Kate _____ an igloo.

**4** I _____ to the library and here are the books.

**5** _____ the camels _____ to drink some water?

**6** We _____ volleyball for a few weeks.

**7** The children _____ English since they were six years old.

**8** _____ Dad _____ to work already? His bag isn't here.

**C** **Choose the correct answers (A, B or C).**

**1** I haven't been to the cinema ___ ages.

A   for                      B   since                     C   from

**2** The ___ shirts are in the washing machine.

A   mens'                    B   mens                      C   men's

**3** That isn't my jacket. ___ is brown.

A   My                       B   Mine                      C   Mines

**4** Helen has three brothers. ___ names are Tom, Dave and Paul.

A   Their                    B   Theirs                    C   They're

**5** My ___ noses are black.

A   cat's                    B   cats                      C   cats'

**6** This isn't Mr Robertson's car. The red one is ___ .

A   he's                     B   hers                      C   his

**7** This photo belongs to you. It's ___ family photo.

A   your                     B   yours                     C   you're

**8** Where is ___ house?

A   Charles'                 B   Charle's                  C   Charles

# 6 The Place to Be

**6.1** **university** (n) /ˌjuːnɪˈvɜːsəti/
a place where you go to study a special subject after you've left school ● *My dad never went to university because he started working when he left school at sixteen.* ❖ πανεπιστήμιο

**6.2** **tower** (n) /ˈtaʊə(r)/
a very tall, narrow, building or structure ● *Rebecca went to see the Eiffel Tower in Paris.* ❖ πύργος

**6.3** **Georgia** (n) /ˈdʒɔːdʒə/
❖ Γεωργία (η χώρα)

## Reading                                    Page 70

**6.4** **building** (n) /ˈbɪldɪŋ/
a structure, e.g. a house, school, hospital, etc. ● *Our town is full of new buildings and it looks completely different from the past.* ➢ build (v), builder (n) ❖ κτίριο

**6.5** **return** (v) /rɪˈtɜːn/
give or bring back ● *I borrowed my friend's jacket and returned it today.* ➢ return (n) ❖ επιστρέφω

**6.6** **enter** (v) /ˈentə(r)/
go into ● *The door opened slowly, and a man in white entered the room.* ➢ entrance (n), entry (n) ❖ μπαίνω μέσα

**6.7** **in progress** (phr) /ɪn ˈprəʊgres/
happening now ● *Please don't enter the manager's office because there's a meeting in progress.* ❖ σε εξέλιξη

**6.8** **racket** (n) /ˈrækɪt/
a piece of equipment you use to hit a ball in a sport, e.g. tennis, badminton ● *Clive hit the ball too hard and broke his racket.* ❖ ρακέτα
✎ Syn: racquet

**6.9** **jewellery** (n) /ˈdʒuːəlri/
sth you wear for decoration ● *Cordelia always wears her gold jewellery when she goes out to special events.* ❖ κοσμήματα
✎ US Eng: jewelry

**6.10** **ring** (n) /rɪŋ/
a piece of jewellery that you wear on a finger ● *Jane's new ring fell off because it was too big for her finger.* ❖ δαχτυλίδι

**6.11** **necklace** (n) /ˈnekləs/
a piece of jewellery that you wear around your neck ● *Mum was wearing her new necklace with her black dress to go out for dinner.* ❖ κολιέ

**6.12** **tub** (n) /tʌb/
a bathtub ● *After his long run, Kevin filled the tub with hot water and had a relaxing hot bath.* ❖ μπανιέρα

## Word Focus                                 Page 70

**6.13** **tour guide** (n) /tʊə(r) gaɪd/
a person who takes tourists to interesting places and gives information about them ● *The tour guide told us some interesting facts about Ancient Sparta.* ❖ ξεναγός

**6.14** **somewhere** (adv) /ˈsʌmweə(r)/
some place in general ● *I've seen you somewhere before, but I can't remember where.* ❖ κάπου

**6.15** **banquet hall** (n) /ˈbæŋkwɪt hɔːl/
a large room where many people have a big meal together at long tables ● *In the castle at the top of Ancient Mystras, there was a banquet hall where the rich people had their feasts.* ❖ αίθουσα δεξιώσεων

**6.16** **locked** (adj) /lɒkt/
closed by using a key ● *The killer broke the window to get into the house because the doors were locked.* ➢ lock (v, n), locker (n) ❖ κλειδωμένος

**6.17** **bang** (v) /bæŋ/
hit sth very hard to make a noise ● *The toilet door wouldn't open, so Vincent banged on the door and shouted for help.* ➢ bang (n) ❖ χτυπώ δυνατά

**6.18** **once** (adv) /wʌns/
one time ● *Sally played golf once, but she didn't enjoy it much.* ❖ μια φορά

## Reading                                    Page 70

**6.19** **crazy** (adj) /ˈkreɪzi/
mad ● *Why is your hair green? You look crazy!* ➢ craziness (n) ❖ τρελός

**6.20** **notice** (v) /ˈnəʊtɪs/
see or hear sth ● *When did Jim go home? I didn't notice him leaving.* ➢ notice (n), noticeable (adj) ❖ παρατηρώ

**6.21** **far** (adj) /fɑː(r)/
not near ● *There were two small hotels at the far side of the village.* ➢ far (adv) ❖ μακρινός

**6.22** **report** (n) /rɪˈpɔːt/
a description of sth that happened ● *The police officer wrote a report on the crash.* ➢ report (v), reporter (n) ❖ αναφορά, ρεπορτάζ

**6.23**  **violent** (adj) /ˈvaɪələnt/
acting in a way that can hurt sb/sth • *The bear looks cute, but don't go close because it's a violent animal.* ➢ violence (n) ❖ βίαιος

**6.24**  **kill** (v) /kɪl/
to end the life of sb/sth • *The robbers killed a lot of people on their way out of the bank.* ➢ killer (n) ❖ σκοτώνω

**6.25**  **spooky** (adj) /ˈspuːki/
scary, very strange • *Everybody was afraid to walk along the spooky dark street at night.* ❖ ανατριχιαστικός

**6.26**  **someone** (pron) /ˈsʌmwʌn/
a person in general (when you don't know exactly who it is, or it isn't important) • *Someone sent me a text, but I don't know who it was because they didn't sign off with a name.* ❖ κάποιος
✎ Syn: somebody

**6.27**  **evil** (adj) /ˈiːvl/
very bad to others • *The evil prince killed his brother and became king.* ➢ evil (n) ❖ πολύ κακός, διαβολικός

**6.28**  **by herself** (phr) /baɪ hɜːˈself/
alone without help (for a girl or woman) • *Angela designed the new house by herself.* ❖ μόνη της

**6.29**  **allow** (v) /əˈlaʊ/
let sb do sth • *Young children aren't allowed to watch scary films in the cinema.* ❖ επιτρέπω

**6.30**  **flash** (n) /flæʃ/
a device that gives a quick bright light to take a photo • *Lizzie's photos weren't very good because she didn't use the flash on her camera.* ➢ flash (v) ❖ φλας (φωτογραφικής μηχανής)

**6.31**  **guided tour** (n) /ˈgaɪdɪd tʊə(r)/
a trip around a building, town, etc. with a tour guide • *Eric's travel company takes visitors on guided tours of the Peloponnese.* ❖ ξενάγηση, εκδρομή με ξενάγηση

**6.32**  **caution** (n) /ˈkɔːʃn/
great care so sth dangerous won't happen • *Caution! Don't swim here because of the sharks.* ➢ cautious (adj) ❖ προσοχή

**6.33**  **believe in** (phr v) /bɪˈliːv ɪn/
think that sth is true • *Do you believe in Santa Claus?* ❖ πιστεύω σε

**6.34**  **haunted** (adj) /ˈhɔːntɪd/
that people say has ghosts inside • *At the top of the hill is a haunted castle where the prince killed his sons.* ➢ haunt (v) ❖ στοιχειωμένος

# Vocabulary
Pages 72-73

**6.35**  **corner shop** (n) /ˈkɔːnə(r) ʃɒp/
a small shop that sells food and other things near your home • *Our corner shop is useful because it's always open late at night.* ❖ μικρό μπακάλικο της γειτονιάς

**6.36**  **factory** (n) /ˈfæktri/
a building where people make things • *Many people in my town have had no jobs since the car factory closed.* ❖ εργοστάσιο

**6.37**  **petrol station** (n) /ˈpetrəl steɪʃn/
a place where you stop to put petrol, etc. in a car • *They were lucky to find a petrol station open in a village after driving so many miles.* ❖ βενζινάδικο

**6.38**  **pharmacy** (n) /ˈfɑːməsi/
a shop where you can buy medicines • *Judy bought some suncream from the pharmacy.* ➢ pharmacist (n) ❖ φαρμακείο
✎ Syn: chemist's

**6.39**  **shopping centre** (n) /ˈʃɒpɪŋ sentə(r)/
a group of shops with a common area for cars to park • *The shopping centre is always really busy at weekends.* ❖ εμπορικό κέντρο
✎ Syn: mall

**6.40**  **stadium** (n) /ˈsteɪdiəm/
a place where sports are played with rows of seats around for people to watch • *Everyone stood up excitedly when the teams entered the stadium.* ❖ στάδιο

**6.41**  **theatre** (n) /ˈθɪətə(r)/
a place where people go to watch live performances • *I'm going to see a Shakespeare play at the theatre next week.* theatrical (adj) ❖ θέατρο

**6.42**  **tank** (n) /tæŋk/
a container for water or other liquid • *Olivia stopped at the petrol station because her petrol tank was nearly empty.* ❖ δεξαμενή, ενυδρείο

**6.43**  **fill up** (phr v) /fɪl ʌp/
make sth full • *The walking group stopped to fill up their water bottles at the tap by the road.* ❖ γεμίζω

**6.44**  **take up** (phr v) /teɪk ʌp/
start doing sth new, e.g. a hobby or sport • *Grace is never at home at weekends because she's taken up horse-riding.* ❖ ξεκινάω κάτι καινούργιο (π.χ. χόμπι ή σπορ)

**6.45**  **run out of** (phr v) /rʌn aʊt əv/
use all that you have of sth • *We've run out of spaghetti, so can you go and buy a packet?* ❖ ξεμένω

**6.46**  **sell out** (phr v) /sel aʊt/
have sold everything of one kind • *I couldn't get tickets for the concert because they were already sold out.* ❖ ξεπουλάω

**6.47** **play** (n) /pleɪ/
a performance of a story that is acted in a theatre ● *We're going to see a famous play by Shakespeare next week.* ❖ θεατρικό έργο

**6.48** **put on** (phr v) /pʊt ɒn/
organise a performance ● *Our class put on a play about helping wildlife.* ❖ ανεβάζω (θεατρική παράσταση)

**6.49** **look for** (phr v) /lʊk fə(r)/
try to find ● *Tom looked for his glasses everywhere, but he couldn't find them.* ❖ ψάχνω

**6.50** **worker** (n) /'wɜːkə(r)/
sb who works ● *The workers in the shoe factory work for eight hours a day.* ❖ εργάτης

**6.51** **break down** (phr v) /breɪk daʊn/
stop working because of a mechanical problem ● *Ron can't do the laundry because the washing machine has broken down.* ➢ breakdown (n) ❖ χαλάω, έχω μηχανική βλάβη

**6.52** **work out** (phr v) /wɜːk aʊt/
exercise your body ● *Veronica works out three times a week at the gym.* ➢ workout (n) ❖ κάνω γυμναστική, γυμνάζομαι

**6.53** **come down with** (phr v) /kʌm daʊn wɪθ/
become ill because of ● *I feel awful because I've come down with a cold.* ❖ αρρωσταίνω

**6.54** **flu** (n) /fluː/
an illness like a bad cold with headaches, fever and pains, etc. ● *All the students in my class had the flu last month.* ❖ γρίπη

**6.55** **medicine** (n) /'medsn/
sth you drink or eat to make you well when you're ill ● *The doctor told Tim to take his medicine every eight hours.* ❖ φάρμακο

**6.56** **air** (n) /eə(r)/
the gases that are all around us ● *Irene opened a window to let some air in.* ➢ air (v) ❖ αέρας, ατμόσφαιρα

**6.57** **polluted** (adj) /pə'luːˌtɪd/
dirty and not safe to use ● *You can't drink the water from the river because it is polluted.* ➢ pollute (v), pollution (n) ❖ μολυσμένος

**6.58** **everywhere** (adv) /'evriweə(r)/
in all places ● *Maria doesn't have a car and she cycles everywhere.* ➢ everywhere (pron) ❖ παντού

**6.59** **peaceful** (adj) /'piːsfl/
quiet with nothing to worry about ● *My family moved to the island to have a peaceful life.* ➢ peace (n), peacefully (adv) ❖ ήρεμος

**6.60** **service** (n) /'sɜːvɪs/
sth helpful for sb to use ● *The services at the sports centre include showers, toilets and a cafeteria.* ➢ serve (v), servant (n) ❖ υπηρεσία

**6.61** **fire station** (n) /'faɪə(r) 'steɪʃn/
a building where firefighters are with their equipment and vehicles ● *Our class visited a fire station and we learnt about how to put out fires.* ❖ πυροσβεστικός σταθμός

**6.62** **police station** (n) /pə'liːs 'steɪʃn/
a building where police officers work ● *Pat went to the police station to give a report about his lost laptop bag.* ❖ αστυνομικό τμήμα

**6.63** **dangerous** (adj) /'deɪndʒərəs/
that can hurt sb or damage sth ● *It's dangerous to cross the busy street here.* ➢ danger (n) ❖ επικίνδυνος

**6.64** **gain** (v) /geɪn/
get sth that you didn't have ● *We gained a few new friends at the summer camp.* ➢ gain (n) ❖ αποκτώ

**6.65** **knowledge** (n) /'nɒlɪdʒ/
all the facts you know about everything ● *Dimitris couldn't understand the tourists because he has no knowledge of foreign languages.* ➢ know (v), knowledgeable (adj) ❖ γνώση

**6.66** **item** (n) /'aɪtəm/
an object ● *I made a list of items that I needed before I went shopping.* ❖ αντικείμενο

**6.67** **stamp** (n) /stæmp/
a small piece of paper to stick on sth before you post it ● *The postman returned the letter to me because I forgot to put a stamp on it.* ❖ γραμματόσημο

**6.68** **bill** (n) /bɪl/
sth that shows an amount you have to pay for things or a service ● *Has Sandra paid her electricity bill yet?* ❖ λογαριασμός

**6.69** **past** (adv) /pɑːst/
to a position that is further than a particular point ● *The bus went past the park on the way to the museum.* ❖ (περνάω) από ένα συγκεκριμένο σημείο

## Look!

Χρησιμοποιούμε τη λέξη **past** ως επίρρημα σε διάφορες περιπτώσεις, π.χ.:
*He walked **past** my house.* (Πέρασε μπροστά από το σπίτι μου.)
*It's half **past** five.* (Είναι πέντε και μισή.)
και ως ουσιαστικό.
*She lived in the castle in the **past**.* (Έμενε στο κάστρο στο παρελθόν.)
Προσέξτε την διαφορά με τη λέξη **passed** (*πέρασα*) που ακούγεται το ίδιο.
*I **passed** the park on my way home.* (Πέρασα μπροστά από το πάρκο καθώς πήγαινα στο σπίτι μου.)

**6.70**  **breathe** (v) /briːð/
take air into your body and let it out through your mouth or nose • *People can't breathe under the sea.* ➢ breath (n) ❖ αναπνέω

**6.71**  **fresh** (adj) /freʃ/
clean and new; grown not long ago • *There aren't many fresh strawberries in the shops in winter.* ➢ freshness (n) ❖ καθαρός, φρέσκος

**6.72**  **row** (v) /rəʊ/
make a boat move across water by pulling on oars • *There was no wind for the sails, so I rowed the boat to the island.* ➢ rowing (n) ❖ κωπηλατώ

**6.73**  **continue** (v) /kənˈtɪnjuː/
keep doing sth • *Kate told her sister to be quiet, but she continued playing loud music.* ❖ συνεχίζω

**6.74**  **run away** (phr v) /rʌn əˈweɪ/
get out of a place suddenly; escape from somewhere • *Oliver ran away from the evil man who made children work for him.* ❖ δραπετεύω

**6.75**  **directions** (n pl) /dəˈrekʃnz/
instructions about how to go somewhere • *Tanya asked someone for directions to get to the underground station.* ➢ direct (v, adj), directly (adv) ❖ οδηγίες

**6.76**  **follow** (v) /ˈfɒləʊ/
keep going along a road • *Follow the street to the corner and you'll see the bus stop.* ❖ ακολουθώ

**6.77**  **get off** (phr v) /get ɒf/
go out of a bus, train, plane or ship • *We got off the bus outside the school.* ❖ κατεβαίνω

**6.78**  **get on** (phr v) /get ɒn/
to go into a bus, train, plane or ship • *Sue got on the plane at Heathrow airport.* ❖ ανεβαίνω

**6.79**  **get to** (phr v) /get tuː/
arrive at • *The train got to the station at six o'clock.* ❖ φτάνω σε

---

### Phrasal Verbs

| | |
|---|---|
| get off | break down |
| get on | work out |
| get to | come down with |
| run away | sell out |
| run out of | fill up |
| put on | take up |
| look for | |

---

**6.80**  **turn** (v) /tɜːn/
move in a different direction • *I didn't know which way to turn at the end of the road.* ➢ turn (n) ❖ στρίβω

**6.81**  **right** (adv) /raɪt/
on the right side • *We turn right at the traffic lights.* ➢ right (adj) ❖ δεξιά

**6.82**  **left** (adv) /left/
on the left side • *Turn left at the corner of King's Road.* ➢ left (adj) ❖ αριστερά

**6.83**  **straight on** (adv) /streɪt ɒn/
in a direct line • *Walk straight on and turn right at the bank.* ❖ ευθεία

# Grammar      Pages 74-75

**6.84**  **contrast** (n) /ˈkɒntraːst/
a clear difference between two things • *There is a big contrast between our quiet village and the centre of London.* ➢ contrast (v) ❖ αντίθεση

**6.85**  **Russia** (n) /ˈrʌʃə/
➢ Russian (adj, n) ❖ Ρωσία

**6.86**  **lift** (n) /lɪft/
a machine that moves people and things to a higher level in a building • *You can take the lift to the sixth floor.* ➢ lift (v) ❖ ασανσέρ, ανελκυστήρας

**6.87**  **roundabout** (n) /ˈraʊndəbaʊt/
a crossroads where you drive round a circle to enter another street • *Take the first right at the roundabout to get to the port.* ❖ κυκλική διασταύρωση

**6.88**  **app** (n) /æp/
a piece of software on a smartphone • *This app is useful to see what the weather will be like.* ❖ εφαρμογή σε κινητό τηλέφωνο

**6.89**  **temple** (n) /ˈtempl/
a building where people pray to their god(s) • *Every year, many tourists visit the temple of Apollo Epicurius in Messinia.* ❖ ναός

**6.90**  **column** (n) /ˈkɒləm/
a tall stone pole that holds up the roof of a building or a statue • *The temple once had fifty columns holding up its roof.* ❖ κολόνα

**6.91**  **sightseeing** (n) /ˈsaɪtsiːɪŋ/
the tourist activity of visiting interesting places to look at them • *Andy is planning to go on a sightseeing tour of Rome.* ➢ sightseer (n) ❖ περιήγηση σε αξιοθέατα

**6.92**  **vowel** (n) /ˈvaʊəl/
one of the letters: a, e, i, o, u • *The five English vowels are a, e, i, o and u.* ❖ φωνήεν

**6.93**  **exist** (v) /ɪgˈzɪst/
live; be • *Televisions didn't exist before the twentieth century.* ➢ existence (n) ❖ υπάρχω

**6.94**  **in general** (phr) /ɪn ˈdʒenrəl/
usually; generally • *I don't watch football matches in general, but I enjoyed the World Cup Final.* ➢ generally (adv) ❖ γενικά

**6.95** **the Alps** (n pl) /ðə ælps/
➢ alpine (adj) ❖ οι Άλπεις

**6.96** **yacht** (n) /jɒt/
a sailing boat • *The yachts sailed quickly into the nearest harbour when the storm got closer.*
❖ ιστιοφόρο

**6.97** **yachtsman** (n) /'jɒtsmən/
a man who sails a yacht • *The restaurant at the harbour attracts a lot of yachtsmen when they tie up their boats for the night.*
❖ ιστιοπλόος
✎ Also: yachtswoman (female form)

**6.98** **signal** (n) /'sɪgnəl/
a movement or sound sb makes to send information to sb • *We lit a fire as a signal for any passing ships or planes to find us.*
➢ signal (v) ❖ σήμα

**6.99** **voyage** (n) /'vɔɪɪdʒ/
a journey by ship (or spaceship) • *The voyage to the island of Santorini took eight hours.*
❖ ταξίδι στη θάλασσα (ή στο διάστημα)

**6.100** **collect** (v) /kə'lekt/
find things of a particular kind to use them
• *Our class collected clothes and toys to give to poor children.* ➢ collection (n) ❖ μαζεύω

**6.101** **bucket** (n) /'bʌkɪt/
a container for carrying liquid or other things
• *In the past, farmers carried cow's milk in buckets.* ❖ κουβάς

**6.102** **Kenya** (n) /'kenˌjə/
➢ Kenyan (adj, n) ❖ Κένυα

**6.103** **Nepal** (n) /nə'pɔːl/
➢ Nepalese (adj, n) ❖ Νεπάλ

**6.104** **the Mediterranean** (n) /ðə ˌmedɪtə'reɪniən/
➢ Mediterranean (adj) ❖ η Μεσόγειος

**6.105** **the Himalayas** (n pl) /ðə ˌhɪmə'laɪəs/
➢ Himalayan (adj) ❖ τα Ιμαλάια

**6.106** **Sicily** (n) /'sɪˌsəli/
➢ Sicilian (adj, n) ❖ Σικελία

**6.107** **wildlife** (n) /'waɪldlaɪf/
animals and plants that live naturally in an area • *Water pollution in the lake is very bad for the wildlife and the plants and animals are dying.* ❖ πανίδα και χλωρίδα, άγρια φύση

**6.108** **the United States** (n) /ðə ju'naɪtɪd steɪts/
❖ οι Ηνωμένες Πολιτείες (Αμερικής)

### Countries, Mountains & Sea

| | |
|---|---|
| Denmark | Sicily |
| Georgia | the Alps |
| Kenya | the Himalayas |
| Nepal | the Mediterranean |
| Russia | the United States |

# Listening Page 76

**6.109** **half** (n) /hɑːf/
one of two equal parts of sth • *Why were you half an hour late for the lesson?* ❖ μισός

**6.110** **half past** (phr) /hɑːf pɑːst/
thirty minutes after • *The film started at half past eight.* ❖ και μισή

**6.111** **weekly** (adj) /'wiːkli/
once a week • *We do our weekly shopping on Friday afternoon when the supermarket isn't so busy.* ➢ week (n) ❖ εβδομαδαίος

**6.112** **marbles** (n pl) /'mɑːblz/
small round glass balls used to play a game
• *The children were sitting on the carpet playing marbles.* ❖ μπίλιες

**6.113** **tricycle** (n) /'traɪsɪkl/
a vehicle like a bike with three wheels • *My little sister has a small tricycle that she rides in the backyard.* ❖ τρίκυκλο

**6.114** **teddy** (n) /'tedi/
a toy bear • *Mum still has a very old teddy that she had when she was a baby.* ❖ (λούτρινο) αρκουδάκι

**6.115** **childhood** (n) /'tʃaɪldhʊd/
the years when sb is a child • *Amal spent her childhood in South Africa, and then moved to Germany when she grew up.* ❖ παιδική ηλικία

**6.116** **explore** (v) /ɪk'splɔː(r)/
go around a place to learn things about it
• *We put up our tents and began to explore the island.* ➢ explorer (n), exploration (n) ❖ εξερευνώ

### Shops & Buildings

| | |
|---|---|
| banquet hall | skyscraper |
| corner shop | stadium |
| factory | temple |
| fire station | theatre |
| petrol station | underground station |
| pharmacy | university |
| police station | youth hostel |
| shopping centre | |

# Speaking Page 77

**6.117** **underground station** (n) /ˌʌndə'graʊnd 'steɪʃn/
a place where people get off and on an underground train • *Liverpool Street and Charing Cross are two of the underground stations in London.* ❖ σταθμός του μετρό

**6.118** **exactly** (adv) /ɪg'zæktli/
used to ask for more details • *Where exactly will I wait for you?* ➢ exact (adj) ❖ ακριβώς

**6.119**   **crossroads** (n pl) /ˈkrɒsrəʊdz/
a place where two or more streets meet • *Turn right at the crossroads into Tower Street.*
❖ διασταύρωση

**6.120**   **traffic lights** (n pl) /ˈtræfɪk laɪts/
a set of three lights, coloured red, orange and green, to control the movement of vehicles on the streets • *There was a bad crash at the traffic lights because one driver didn't stop when they were red.* ❖ φανάρια

## On the Road

| Nouns | Verbs | Adverbs |
|---|---|---|
| crossroads | continue | left |
| guided tour | explore | past |
| roundabout | follow | right |
| route | pass | straight on |
| traffic lights | turn | |

# Writing                    Pages 78-79

**6.121**   **sequence** (n) /ˈsiːkwəns/
a logical order of things one after the other
• *This radio station plays the songs in the same sequence every day, so it's a bit boring.*
❖ σειρά

**6.122**   **structure** (n) /ˈstrʌktʃə(r)/
the way sth is put together • *We are learning to use new grammatical structures in our English class.* ❖ δομή

**6.123**   **eventually** (adv) /ɪˈventʃuəli/
in the end, after a lot of things happened
• *Dad failed his driving test three times and eventually passed it the fourth time he tried.*
❖ τελικά

**6.124**   **finally** (adv) /ˈfaɪnəli/
in the end • *Finally, we got home after walking for hours.* ➤ final (adj) ❖ τελικά

**6.125**   **regards** (n) /rɪˈgɑːdz/
best wishes • *Dorothy always signs off her emails with 'Best regards'.* ❖ χαιρετισμούς

**6.126**   **administrator** (n) /ədˈmɪnɪstreɪtə(r)/
sb who organises things in a company
• *Susan is an administrator in the university office and she organises the bills that students pay.* ❖ διαχειριστής

**6.127**   **route** (n) /ruːt/
the way from one place to another • *I take the same route to school every day.* ❖ διαδρομή

**6.128**   **youth hostel** (n) /juːθ ˈhɒstl/
a building where young people can stay cheaply for a holiday • *When the rain got too heavy, the boys packed up their tents and went to stay in a youth hostel for the rest of the week.* ❖ ξενώνας νεότητας

**6.129**   **headteacher** (n) /ˌhed ˈtiːtʃə(r)/
the person in charge of a school • *Our headteacher is planning a special event for the whole school at the end of the school year.*
❖ διευθυντής σχολείου
✎ Syn: principal

# Video 6
# One of a Kind          Page 80

**6.130**   **skyscraper** (n) /ˈskaɪskreɪpə(r)/
a very tall building with many floors • *I couldn't believe the size of the skyscrapers in Dubai. All the modern buildings were huge.*
❖ ουρανοξύστης

**6.131**   **architect** (n) /ˈɑːkɪtekt/
sb who designs buildings, bridges, etc.
• *The new bridge was designed by a famous Spanish architect.* ❖ αρχιτέκτονας

## People & Jobs

| | |
|---|---|
| administrator | sailor |
| architect | tour guide |
| engineer | worker |
| headteacher | yachtsman |

**6.132**   **inspire** (v) /ɪnˈspaɪə(r)/
to give somebody an idea to do something
• *Agatha's strange dream inspired her to write her first book.* ➤ inspiration (n), inspiring (adj)
❖ εμπνέω

**6.133**   **unique** (adj) /juˈniːk/
the only one of a kind • *The old bridge across the River Forth is unique because there's no other exactly like it.* ❖ μοναδικός

**6.134**   **edge** (n) /edʒ/
the top of the outside part of sth • *Don't sit on the edge of the yacht when we're sailing.*
❖ άκρη

**6.135**   **pass** (v) /pɑːs/
move • *Trains pass through the Channel Tunnel every day.* ❖ περνώ

**6.136**   **turbine** (n) /ˈtɜːbaɪn/
a machine that liquid or wind goes through to give power • *There are three wind turbines on the hill above our village to make electricity.*
❖ τουρμπίνα

**6.137**   **engineer** (n) /ˌendʒɪˈnɪə(r)/
sb who designs or makes engines • *Rosemary studied hard at university to become an engineer for a company that makes cars.*
➤ engineering (n) ❖ μηχανικός

**6.138**   **Denmark** (n) /ˈdenmɑːk/
➤ Danish (adj, n) ❖ Δανία

# Vocabulary Exercises

## A Match.

1 corner ☐     a tour
2 guided ☐     b centre
3 petrol ☐     c shop
4 youth ☐      d guide
5 banquet ☐    e hall
6 tour ☐       f hostel
7 traffic ☐    g lights
8 shopping ☐   h station

## B Complete the sentences with words from Exercise A.

1 I hope we find a _____ before we run out of petrol.
2 Paul and his friends are staying at a _____ in the countryside for the weekend.
3 Mum sometimes meets her friends at the café in the _____ .
4 Tom buys his weekly magazine at the small _____ on his street.
5 The _____ told us to wear good boots for the long walk up the steps to the temple.
6 The _____ of London included a boat ride on the River Thames.
7 Cinderella dropped her shoe as she ran out of the _____ at midnight.
8 Drive slowly because you'll have to stop at the _____ .

## C Circle the correct words.

1 Julie needs to buy some **flu / medicine / jewellery** from the pharmacy because she feels ill.
2 Everyone is different in some way because we're all **spooky / violent / unique**.
3 Is the exam still in **progress / general / service** or can I go into the class now?
4 Can you give me **regards / marbles / directions** to get to the park?
5 Steven bought a **bill / stamp / display** to post his letter.
6 You can take the **roundabout / turbine / lift** to go up to the tenth floor.
7 We sailed across the Mediterranean on a beautiful **yacht / tricycle / tub**.
8 The building was **designed / explored / polluted** by a famous architect.
9 We walked for hours and **exactly / eventually / weekly** we reached the stadium.
10 You need a **racket / ring / necklace** to play tennis.

## D Complete the phrasal verbs in these sentences.

1 I got _____ the bus and I was looking out of the window when it finally got _____ the bus station.
2 Mark has taken _____ acting and he's in the Shakespeare play they're putting _____ at the town theatre.
3 The truck didn't break _____ , but the driver forgot to fill it _____ with petrol.
4 The police are looking _____ the man that ran _____ with the jewellery.
5 Charlie always runs _____ money because he doesn't believe _____ saving it up.
6 Tina can't work _____ at the gym today because she's come _____ the flu.

**E** **Complete the sentences with words formed from the words in bold.**

1 We heard the sound of _____ inside the theatre.                            **LAUGH**
2 Many tall new _____ are in the centre of the city.                         **BUILD**
3 The cottage is in a _____ village in the countryside.                      **PEACE**
4 A _____ at the olive oil factory gave us a guided tour.                    **WORK**
5 _____, the car broke down and he had to call for help.                     **SUDDEN**
6 Mum's going for her _____ visit to the hairdresser.                        **WEEK**
7 Do you have any _____ about sailing a yacht?                               **KNOW**
8 We can't swim here because of the _____ in the sea.                        **POLLUTE**
9 Adele spent her _____ growing up happily in Paris.                         **CHILD**
10 Lock your doors and windows because there's a _____ in town.             **KILL**

# 6 Grammar

## 6.1 Demonstratives

Χρησιμοποιούμε *this* + **singular noun** ή **uncountable noun** (ουσιαστικό ενικού αριθμού ή μη αριθμήσιμο ουσιαστικό) για να δείξουμε ότι κάτι βρίσκεται κοντά μας στο χώρο ή στο χρόνο.
→ **This** house is mine.
→ **This** tour is interesting.

Χρησιμοποιούμε *these* + **plural noun** (ουσιαστικό πληθυντικού αριθμού) για να δείξουμε ότι κάτι βρίσκεται κοντά μας στο χώρο ή στο χρόνο.
→ Do you like **these buildings**?

Χρησιμοποιούμε *that* + **singular noun** ή **uncountable noun** (ουσιαστικό ενικού αριθμού ή μη αριθμήσιμο ουσιαστικό) για να δείξουμε ότι κάτι βρίσκεται πιο μακριά από μας στο χώρο ή στο χρόνο.
→ **That** castle on the hill is called Palamidi.
→ **That** film we saw last night was great.

Χρησιμοποιούμε *those* + **plural noun** (ουσιαστικό πληθυντικού αριθμού) για να δείξουμε ότι κάτι βρίσκεται πιο μακριά από μας στο χώρο ή στο χρόνο.
→ **Those** tourists took a lot of selfies at that castle.

## 6.2 The Indefinite Article: *A/An*

Χρησιμοποιούμε *a* πριν από μια λέξη που αρχίζει με ήχο συμφώνου.
→ **a** building
→ **a** unique tour

Χρησιμοποιούμε *an* πριν από μια λέξη που αρχίζει με ήχο φωνήεντος.
→ **an** underground station
→ **an** hour
→ **an** ATM

Χρησιμοποιούμε *a/an*:
με countable nouns (αριθμήσιμα ουσιαστικά) ενικού αριθμού.
→ We live in **a** flat.
για να αναφέρουμε κάτι για πρώτη φορά. (Όταν το αναφέρουμε ξανά, χρησιμοποιούμε *the*).
→ I read **a** book. **The** book was about **a** haunted house.
για να δείξουμε επάγγελμα, ιδιότητα, κλπ.
→ She is **an** architect.

## 6.3 The Definite Article: *The*

Χρησιμοποιούμε *the* με countable nouns (αριθμήσιμα ουσιαστικά) ενικού και πληθυντικού αριθμού, και με uncountable nouns (μη αριθμήσιμα ουσιαστικά), για να μιλήσουμε για κάτι συγκεκριμένο όταν το ουσιαστικό αναφέρεται για δεύτερη φορά.
→ They were sailing **a** boat. **The** boat was a large yacht.
Επίσης χρησιμοποιούμε *the* πριν από:
ουσιαστικά που τα θεωρούμε μοναδικά.
→ **The** sun is rising.
ονόματα κινηματογράφων, θεάτρων, ξενοδοχείων, πλοίων, κλπ.
→ I saw a film at **the** Odeon cinema.
→ Where is **the** Tower Hotel?
ονόματα ποταμών, ερήμων, οροσειρών, και ονομασίες ή ουσιαστικά που περιέχουν τη λέξη *of*.
→ I went skiing in **the** Alps.
→ Is **the** River Severn polluted?
χώρες ή ομάδες χωρών με όνομα πληθυντικού αριθμού.
→ I'm visiting **the** Netherlands soon.
→ She's moved to **the** United States.

μουσικά όργανα.
→ He plays **the** guitar and **the** drums.
εθνικότητες.
→ **The** British drink a lot of tea.
επίθετα που τα χρησιμοποιούμε σαν ουσιαστικά.
→ A lot of people are helping **the** homeless.
λέξεις όπως beach, countryside, station, jungle, κλπ.
→ Many different animals live in **the** jungle.
τις λέξεις morning, afternoon, evening.
→ We often go swimming in **the** afternoon.

Δεν χρησιμοποιούμε **the** πριν από:
κύρια ονόματα.
→ **Alice** is **Rachel's** cousin.
ονόματα αθλημάτων και παιχνιδιών, χρώματα, μέρες, μήνες, ποτά, αργίες και γιορτές, γεύματα και γλώσσες (που δεν ακολουθούνται από τη λέξη language).
→ **Blue** is my favourite colour.
→ We had **dinner** with **Aunt Jane** on **Saturday**.
**Σημείωση:** Όταν αναφερόμαστε συγκεκριμένα σε κάποιο γεύμα, χρώμα, πότο, κλπ. χρησιμοποιούμε **the**.
→ The **dinner** we had with you was delicious.
→ The **meal** was expensive.
πεδία μελέτης, μαθήματα.
→ Do you like **history**?
ονόματα χωρών, πόλεων, οδών (ΑΛΛΑ: the High Street, the United Kingdom), πλατείες, γέφυρες (ΑΛΛΑ: the Golden Gate Bridge), πάρκα, σταθμούς, μεμονωμένα βουνά, νησιά, λίμνες, ηπείρους.
→ **Canberra** is the capital of **Australia**.
→ They live in **White Street** near **West Station**.
τις λέξεις bed, church, school, hospital, prison, college, university, court, κλπ, όταν μιλάμε για κάτι σχετικό με τον κύριο σκοπό του χώρου αυτού. (Η λέξη work δεν παίρνει ποτέ the.)
→ Tracy is studying at **university**. (βρίσκεται εκεί γιατί είναι φοιτήτρια).
→ Tracy's dad is going to **the university** to drive her home. (Ο πατέρας δεν σπουδάζει στο πανεπιστήμιο, απλώς πήγε εκεί για να πάρει την Tracy και να την πάει στο σπίτι.)
μεταφορικά μέσα σε εκφράσεις όπως by car, κλπ. (ΑΛΛΑ in the car).

## Grammar Exercises

→ I go to work **by train**.

**A** Complete the sentences with **this, that, these** or **those**. Use each word twice.

1 _____ cakes are still hot and they smell delicious. Can I have one?
2 Look at _____ wind turbines up there on top of the hill.
3 Here! _____ necklace is for you. I hope you like it.
4 Who lives in _____ house on the other side of the street?
5 _____ flowers smell nice. I'll put them in water now.
6 Who took _____ photo that's hanging on the wall?
7 _____ boats look very far away. Where are they sailing to?
8 Is _____ ring yours? I found it in the bathroom.

**B** Circle the correct answers.

1 They stayed at **a** / **an** hotel in **–** / **the** Brisbane.
2 This is **a** / **the** nice cup of **–** / **a** tea.
3 Not many plants grow in **a** / **the** deserts in **–** / **the** Africa.
4 Do **–** / **the** French really eat **–** / **the** snails?
5 We saw **a** / **the** moon above in **–** / **the** sky.
6 Can I take **a** / **an** underground train to **–** / **the** Victoria Station?
7 **–** / **A** dinner will be ready in **a** / **an** hour.
8 I usually go to **–** / **a** school by **–** / **the** bus.

**C** Complete the sentences with *a*, *an*, *the* or *–* .

1 Geoffrey studied ___ technology at ___ university in ___ Wales.
2 ___ Sardinia is ___ island in ___ Mediterranean.
3 ___ blankets on ___ bed in my room are ___ yellow.
4 ___ capital of ___ Netherlands is ___ Amsterdam.
5 ___ Aunt Joan is ___ architect and she loves designing ___ skyscrapers.
6 Can you tell me ___ way to ___ Ingram Street in ___ Glasgow?
7 ___ Lambros and his wife are ___ tour guides in ___ Alps.
8 I like having ___ meal at ___ restaurant, but I hated what I had to eat in ___ hospital.

# 7 Time Out!

**7.1** **time out** (phr) /taɪm aʊt/
free time; a break from work or studying • *Now my exams are finished, I really need some time out.* ❖ διάλειμμα

**7.2** **participant** (n) /pɑːˈtɪsɪpənt/
sb who takes part in an activity or event
• *Anyone over 10 years old can be a participant in this race.* ➢ participate (v), participation (n) ❖ συμμετέχων

**7.3** **attempt** (v) /əˈtempt/
try • *Barbara is attempting to run faster than ever, and I think she's going to do it.* ➢ attempt (n) ❖ επιχειρώ

**7.4** **course** (n) /kɔːs/
a race track • *One of the racing cars broke down in the middle of the course.* ❖ πίστα

**7.5** **Taiwan** (n) /taɪˈwɑːn/
❖ Ταϊβάν

## Reading
**Page 84**

**7.6** **skill** (n) /skɪl/
sth you are good at • *Molly is learning new painting skills in her art class.* ➢ skilful (adj) ❖ δεξιότητα

**7.7** **baking** (n) /ˈbeɪkɪŋ/
preparing food and then cooking it in an oven
• *The smell of fresh home baking filled the air when we reached grandma's cottage.* ➢ bake (v), baker (n), baked (adj) ❖ ψήσιμο

**7.8** **robotics** (n) /rəʊˈbɒtɪks/
the activity of creating and operating a robot
• *Marios love science, so he goes to a robotics club every weekend.* ❖ ρομποτική

**7.9** **gardening** (n) /ˈgɑːdnɪŋ/
the activity of creating and looking after a garden • *Alistair enjoys gardening and he grows his own vegetables.* ➢ garden (n), gardener (n) ❖ κηπουρική

**7.10** **origami** (n) /ˌɒrɪˈgɑːmi/
the activity of folding paper to make artistic shapes • *Claire is good at origami and she can make paper animals very quickly.* ❖ οριγκάμι

**7.11** **advert** (n) /ˈædvɜːt/
an advertisement; sth printed or shown to attract you to buy or do sth • *I looked at loads of hotel adverts on the internet to find the perfect place for a holiday.* ➢ advertise (v), advertising (n) ❖ διαφήμιση

**7.12** **be into** (phr v) /bi ˈɪntə/
enjoy (sth) • *My dad's really into rock music from the 1970s.* ❖ ασχολούμαι με

**7.13** **juggle** (v) /ˈdʒʌgl/
throw things (e.g. balls) in the air and catch them • *The circus clowns were juggling with real fruit and they didn't drop anything.* ➢ juggler (n), juggling (n) ❖ δίνω παράσταση σαν ζογκλέρ

**7.14** **unicycle** (n) /ˈjuːnɪsaɪkl/
a one-wheeled thing like a bike • *How can you ride a unicycle without falling?* ❖ ποδήλατο με μία ρόδα

**7.15** **wheel** (n) /wiːl/
a round object that helps a vehicle move along the road • *Ellie crashed her bicycle and one of the wheels came off.* ➢ wheel (v) ❖ τροχός, ρόδα

**7.16** **practise** (v) /ˈpræktɪs/
do sth often to get better at it • *Pavlina had a chance to practise speaking German when she went to Austria.* ➢ practice (n) ❖ εξασκώ

**7.17** **ability** (n) /əˈbɪləti/
being able to do sth • *Simon has the ability to sing and play the piano.* ➢ able (adj) ❖ ικανότητα
✎ Opp: inability

**7.18** **confidence** (n) /ˈkɒnfɪdəns/
the feeling of being sure of what you or sb else can do • *Sadie never sings in front of others because she doesn't have enough confidence.* ➢ confident (adj) ❖ αυτοπεποίθηση

**7.19** **perform** (v) /pəˈfɔːm/
do an act in front of people • *The ballet dancers performed beautifully.* ➢ performance (n), performer (n) ❖ δίνω παράσταση, εκτελώ

## Reading
**Pages 84-85**

**7.20** **session** (n) /ˈseʃn/
a period of time set for an activity • *I've just had a two-hour swimming session and I'm so tired.* ❖ συνεδρία

**7.21** **program** (v) /ˈprəʊgræm/
design sth with a set of instructions that it has to follow to do sth • *This car is programmed to drive by itself.* ➢ program (n), programmer (n) ❖ προγραμματίζω

**7.22** **workshop** (n) /ˈwɜːkʃɒp/
a group meeting where you can learn to
do sth practical; a session where you can
discuss a subject in a small group ● *There
was a photography workshop at the fair where
people could learn to use their cameras better.*
❖ σεμινάριο, εργαστήριο

---

**Look!**

Χρησιμοποιούμε τη λέξη **workshop** σε δυο
περιπτώσεις με διαφορετικές σημασίες:
*You can learn about our projects in the
**workshops** during the exhibition.* (= μια ομαδική
συζήτηση θέματος σε σεμινάριο)
*Sandra makes jewellery in her **workshop**.*
(= εργαστήριο όπου φτιάχνουμε κάτι)

---

**7.23** **pop** (adj) /pɒp/
a type of music that has simple words and
beats to sing and dance to ● *Georgina has
posters of her favourite pop singer on her wall.*
➣ pop (n) ❖ μουσική ποπ

**7.24** **classical** (adj) /ˈklæsɪkl/
in a style of music that most people know
from many years ago, usually with lots of
instruments playing ● *Yiannis plays relaxing
classical music on his piano.* ❖ κλασσική

**7.25** **musical** (n) /ˈmjuːzɪkl/
a performance with singing and dancing
● *We're performing the musical of the Harry
Potter story in our school theatre.* ➣ music (n),
musician (n), musical (adj) ❖ μιούζικαλ

**7.26** **join** (v) /dʒɔɪn/
become a member of sth ● *A new boy has
joined our basketball team and he's a great
player.* ❖ γίνομαι μέλος

**7.27** **pronoun** (n) /ˈprəʊnaʊn/
a word used in place of a noun ● *The pronoun
'she' refers to a girl or woman.* ❖ αντωνυμία

**7.28** **that's a shame** (phr) /ðæts ə ʃeɪm/
used to say sth makes you sad or
disappointed ● *That's a shame about the
concert being cancelled. I was looking forward
to it.* ❖ είναι κρίμα

**7.29** **solve** (v) /sɒlv/
find a way to do sth ● *It took me ages to solve
the crossword puzzle.* ➣ solution (n) ❖ επιλύω

# Vocabulary     Pages 86-87

**7.30** **brush** (n) /brʌʃ/
a small tool with hard hairs at the end used
for putting paint onto paper, etc. for painting
pictures ● *Don't forget to clean your brushes
when you've finished painting.* ➣ brush (v)
❖ πινέλο
✎ Syn: paintbrush

---

**Look!**

Το ουσιαστικό **brush**, εκτός απο *πινέλο*,
σημαίνει επίσης *βούρτσα* και *σκούπα*.
*Use a thin **brush** to paint the small details.*
(= πινέλο)
*Your hair is a mess. Haven't you got a **brush**?*
(= βούρτσα)
*Where's the **brush** to clean the balcony?*
(= σκούπα)

---

**7.31** **controller** (n) /kənˈtrəʊlə(r)/
a small device for controlling moves in
a computer/video game ● *This robot will
do whatever you like when you move the
controller.* ➣ control (v, n) ❖ ελεγκτής

**7.32** **selfie stick** (n) /ˈselfiː stɪk/
a long stick that can hold a camera to take
photos of yourself ● *Rita and Alex took some
good photos of themselves with different views
by using their selfie stick.* ❖ μπαστούνι σέλφι

**7.33** **sleeping bag** (n) /ˈsliːpɪŋ bæg/
a bag that you use to sleep in, e.g. for
camping ● *We got into our sleeping bags in
the tent and told stories until we went to sleep.*
❖ υπνόσακος

**7.34** **gaming** (n) /ˈgeɪmɪŋ/
playing games on a computer ● *Alvy bought
a really fast computer because he enjoys
gaming on the internet with his friends.*
➣ game (v, n), gamer (n) ❖ gaming, παιχνίδια
στον υπολογιστή

**7.35** **Scotland** (n) /ˈskɒtlənd/
➣ Scot (n), Scottish (adj) ❖ Σκωτία

**7.36** **hiking** (n) /ˈhaɪkɪŋ/
the activity of going for long walks in the
countryside ● *Chris goes hiking in the hills
around Athens once a month.* ➣ hike (v, n),
hiker (n) ❖ πεζοπορία

**7.37** **the Highlands** (n pl) /ðə ˈhaɪləndz/
the high mountains in the north of Scotland
● *On our bus tour of the Highlands, we saw
some amazing views of Scottish mountains
and rivers.* ❖ τα Χάιλαντς της βόρειας Σκωτίας

**7.38**  **yoga** (n) /'jəʊgə/
a type of exercise that keeps you fit and helps
you relax • *Yoga is a great form of exercise
for all ages and it helps you to breathe better.*
❖ γιόγκα

**7.39**  **chess** (n) /tʃes/
a game for two people played by moving
specially shaped pieces on a board with black
and white squares • *Alice plays chess as a
hobby with her friends.* ❖ σκάκι

**7.40**  **running** (n) /'rʌnɪŋ/
the sport of running on a track • *A lot of people
go running in the park for exercise.* ➢ run (v),
runner (n) ❖ τρέξιμο στίβου

**7.41**  **table tennis** (n) /'teɪbl tenɪs/
a sport played with small rackets and a ball on
a table with a net across the middle • *On our
camping holiday, my friends and I played table
tennis every day after swimming.* ❖ πινγκ-πονγκ
✎ Syn: ping pong

**7.42**  **crazy (about sth)** (adj) /'kreɪzi (ə'baʊt
'sʌmθɪŋ)/
enthusiastic or excited (about sth) • *I'm not
crazy about gaming because I can't sleep well
if I play at night.* ❖ ξετρελαμένος με

**7.43**  **involved (in sth)** (adj) /ɪn'vɒlvd (ɪn 'sʌmθɪŋ)/
(be) doing (sth); take part (in sth) • *Our
teacher is involved in planning the school
athletics competition.* ➢ involve (v),
involvement (n) ❖ μπλεγμένος (με κάτι),
ενασχολούμενος (με κάτι)

**7.44**  **keen (on sth)** (adj) /kiːn (ɒn 'sʌmθɪŋ)/
interested (in sth) • *Jim is very keen on
football and he goes to watch matches every
Saturday.* ❖ το να μου αρέσει πολύ κάτι;
ενθουσιασμένος (με κάτι)

---

### Expressing Likes

| | |
|---|---|
| crazy (about sth) | be into |
| involved (in sth) | keen (on sth) |

---

**7.45**  **preposition** (n) /ˌprepə'zɪʃn/
a word used before a noun or pronoun to show
where, when or how sth is done • *Maria is
studying the different words to use with the
prepositions 'on', 'at' and 'in'.* ❖ πρόθεση

**7.46**  **alive** (adj) /ə'laɪv/
living • *The yachtsman was lucky to be
alive after his boat sailed onto the rocks.*
❖ ζωντανός

**7.47**  **lost** (adj) /lɒst/
not able to find your way; not knowing where
you are • *The hiking group got lost in the
forest because they followed the wrong path.*
➢ lose (v) ❖ χαμένος

**7.48**  **realise** (v) /'riːəlaɪz/
start to understand (that sth is happening
or true) • *They realised they were going
the wrong way when they came to the river.*
➢ realisation (n) ❖ συνειδητοποιώ

**7.49**  **search** (v) /sɜːtʃ/
look for • *I searched for my keys everywhere,
and then found them in the door.* ➢ search (n)
❖ ψάχνω

# Grammar                                    Pages 88-89

**7.50**  **dictionary** (n) /'dɪkʃənri/
a book that gives the meanings of words
• *Tom uses his French dictionary to
understand the meaning of words he doesn't
know.* ❖ λεξικό

**7.51**  **stressed** (adj) /strest/
worried; not relaxed • *I always get so stressed
about taking exams.* ➢ stress (v, n), stressful
(adj) ❖ πιεσμένος, στρεσαρισμένος

**7.52**  **correctly** (adv) /kə'rektli/
in the right way • *Dennis spelt all the words
correctly in his word test and got full marks.*
➢ correct (v, adj), correction (n) ❖ σωστά,
ορθά

**7.53**  **skateboarding** (n) /'skeɪtbɔːdɪŋ/
the activity of riding a skateboard
• *Skateboarding is exciting, but it's dangerous
to do on a busy street.* ➢ skateboard (v, n),
skateboarder (n) ❖ σκέιτ-μπορντ (άθλημα,
δραστηριότητα)

**7.54**  **snowboarding** (n) /'snəʊbɔːdɪŋ/
the sport/activity of riding a board on snow
down a hill • *Did you know that snowboarding
is a sport in the Winter Olympics?*
➢ snowboard (v, n), snowboarder (n)
❖ σνόου-μπορντ (άθλημα, δραστηριότητα)

**7.55**  **win** (v) /wɪn/
be the first in a competition, match or race, etc.
• *Which team won the Champions League last
year?* ➢ winner (n) ❖ νικώ

**7.56**  **horror film** (n) /'hɒrə(r) fɪlm/
a film that is made to be scary • *I get scared
if I watch horror films alone at night.* ❖ ταινία
τρόμου

**7.57**  **be worth** (phr) /bi wɜːθ/
be useful enough to do; have a value • *Is it
worth paying to see a film at the cinema or
better to watch it on TV?* ❖ αξίζει τον κόπο

**7.58**  **gymnastics** (n) /dʒɪm'næstɪks/
exercises that make you strong and able
to bend easily • *The sports club offers
gymnastics for children from 6-12 years old.* ➢
gymnast (n), gymnastic (adj), gym (n)
❖ ενόργανη γυμναστική

**7.59** **fitter** (adj) /ˈfɪtə(r)/
comparative form of *fit*; healthier and stronger
• *Ron feels much fitter since he started running as a hobby.* ➤ fitness (n), fit (adj) ❖ σε καλύτερη φυσική κατάσταση

**7.60** **woodwork** (n) /ˈwʊdwɜːk/
the activity of making things from wood
• *Mum made a chair at her woodwork class.*
❖ ξυλουργική

**7.61** **talent** (n) /ˈtælənt/
a natural ability • *Leonardo had great talent as an artist and produced amazing paintings.*
➤ talented (adj) ❖ ταλέντο

# Listening
Page 90

**7.62** **board game** (n) /bɔːd ɡeɪm/
any game played with pieces that you move on a board (on a table, etc.) • *Sometimes I play chess or other board games with my family.*
❖ επιτραπέζιο παιχνίδι

**7.63** **quiz** (n) /kwɪz/
a game or competition where you answer questions to win points • *Our team came first in the school history quiz.* ❖ σπαζοκεφαλιά, κουίζ

**7.64** **drums** (n pl) /drʌms/
a musical instrument that is round and is empty inside, which you play by hitting with sticks or your hands • *I couldn't hear the TV because my brother was making so much noise on his drums in his room.* ➤ drummer (n)
❖ ντραμς

**7.65** **competitive** (adj) /kəmˈpetətɪv/
wanting very much to win or be more successful than other people • *If you want to be a professional athlete, you must be very competitive.* ➤ compete (v), competition (n), competitor (n) ❖ ανταγωνιστικός

**7.66** **absolutely** (adv) /ˈæbsəluːtli/
very much; completely • *The film was absolutely fantastic.* ➤ absolute (adj)
❖ τελείως, απολύτως, εντελώς

**7.67** **actually** (adv) /ˈæktʃuəli/
in fact • *I didn't know that Marie was actually from France.* ➤ actual (adj) ❖ στην πραγματικότητα

**7.68** **in actual fact** (phr) /ɪn ˈæktʃuəl fækt/
in fact • *Paul sounds Spanish, but in actual fact, he's from Portugal.* ❖ στην πραγματικότητα

### Adverbs
| | |
|---|---|
| absolutely | before |
| actually | correctly |
| anywhere | |

### Useful Phrases
| | |
|---|---|
| be worth | in common |
| for sale | that's a shame |
| in actual fact | time out |

# Speaking
Page 91

**7.69** **stage** (n) /steɪdʒ/
a part of a theatre where people perform
• *Natalie was nervous about going on stage to sing.* ❖ θεατρική σκηνή

**7.70** **audience** (n) /ˈɔːdiəns/
the people who watch a performance in a cinema or theatre • *The audience were thrilled when the lead singer came down off the stage to sing among them.* ❖ ακροατήριο

**7.71** **violin** (n) /ˌvaɪəˈlɪn/
a musical stringed instrument that you hold on your shoulder to play • *Marinos placed his violin under his chin and began to play a beautiful tune.* ❖ βιολί

**7.72** **in common** (phr) /ɪn ˈkɒmən/
with the same ideas/interests; being similar
• *My best friend and I have got lots of things in common, so we do a lot of activities together.*
❖ κοινά στοχεία (με)

**7.73** **scan** (v) /skæn/
look at all the parts of sth • *Len scanned the online adverts to find a new job.* ➤ scan (n), scanner (n) ❖ ρίχνω γρήγορη ματιά

### Activities
| | |
|---|---|
| athletics | origami |
| baking | quiz |
| board game | robotics |
| chess | running |
| competition | skateboarding |
| drama club | snowboarding |
| gaming | stamp collecting |
| gardening | table tennis |
| gymnastics | woodwork |
| hiking | yoga |

### Equipment
| | |
|---|---|
| brush | selfie stick |
| controller | sleeping bag |
| drums | unicycle |
| machine | violin |
| model | wheel |

# Writing

Pages 92-93

**7.74** **suggestion** (n) /sə'dʒestʃən/
an idea that sb gives sb else to do sth
• *I agreed with Mary's suggestion to go dancing.* ➤ suggest (v) ❖ πρόταση

**7.75** **imperative** (n) /ɪm'perətɪv/
the form of a verb that you use to give an order, warning, etc. • *The phrase 'Be careful!' is an imperative.* ❖ προστακτική

**7.76** **persuade** (v) /pə'sweɪd/
talk sb into doing sth or believing sth is true
• *Have you persuaded your parents to buy tickets for the concert?* ➤ persuasion (n), persuasive (adj) ❖ πείθω

**7.77** **DJ** (abbr) /'diː dʒeɪ/
short form of 'disc jockey'; sb who plays recorded music in a public place • *We asked the DJ to play our favourite One Direction song.* ❖ DJ

**7.78** **mix** (v) /mɪks/
put things together to form sth different • *The DJ mixed the songs to create a non-stop dance session with music from the eighties and nineties.* ➤ mixture (n) ❖ αναμιγνύω

**7.79** **offer** (v) /'ɒfə(r)/
say you will do sth; say you can give sth to sb
• *Clive has offered to help carrying the band's equipment.* ➤ offer (n) ❖ προσφέρω

**7.80** **stamp collecting** (n) /stæmp kə'lektɪŋ/
collect different stamps as a hobby • *Grandad enjoys stamp collecting and some of his old stamps are worth a lot of money.* ❖ κάνω συλλογή γραμματοσήμων, φιλοτελισμός

**7.81** **drama club** (n) /'drɑːmə klʌb/
a club for people interested in acting and producing plays • *Our school drama club is putting on an ancient Greek play and I'm playing the part of Theseus.* ❖ δραματικός όμιλος

**7.82** **per** (prep) /pə(r)/
for each • *The tickets for the show cost five pounds per person.* ❖ ανά

**7.83** **brave** (adj) /breɪv/
not afraid to do sth • *You have to be brave to try snowboarding.* ❖ θαρραλέος

**7.84** **for sale** (phr) /fə(r) seɪl/
ready for you to buy • *There were some snacks and drinks for sale at the exhibition.* ❖ προς πώληση, πωλείται

## People

| | |
|---|---|
| audience | performer |
| DJ | skateboarder |
| participant | |

## Places

| | |
|---|---|
| circus | stage |
| course | Scotland |
| desert | Taiwan |
| hill | the Highlands |

# Video 7
# Mechanical Lizard Car

Page 94

**7.85** **desert** (n) /'dezət/
a large area of land that is very dry and hot
• *The nomads travelled for hours across the sand in the desert.* ❖ έρημος

**7.86** **rat** (n) /ræt/
a small animal like a big mouse with a long thin tail • *There was so much rubbish in the streets and we could see rats eating food from the bins.* ❖ αρουραίος

**7.87** **off-road** (adj) /ɒf rəʊd/
that can drive on difficult ground • *This truck is specially designed for off-road driving across the countryside.* ❖ εκτός δρόμου

**7.88** **lizard** (n) /'lɪzəd/
a small reptile with four short legs and a long tail • *When we opened the window, a tiny green lizard ran up the wall of the cottage.* ❖ σαύρα

**7.89** **machine** (n) /mə'ʃiːn/
a device that works with electricity or with an engine • *Imagine how life was before people had flying machines to travel anywhere in the world.* ❖ μηχάνημα

**7.90** **model** (n) /'mɒdl/
a small copy of sth • *George wanted to buy a model robot after he watched Star Wars.* ❖ μοντέλο, μακέτα

**7.91** **before** (adv) /bɪ'fɔː(r)/
at a time in the past • *The Smiths have never been to Denmark before.* ❖ πριν από

**7.92** **anywhere** (adv) /'eniweə(r)/
in any place • *I can't find the tickets anywhere. Where can they be?* ❖ οπουδήποτε

**7.93** **hill** (n) /hɪl/
an area of land like a small mountain
• *It wasn't easy to ride our bikes up the hill.* ➤ hilly (adj) ❖ λόφος

**7.94** **hold** (v) /həʊld/
have sth in your hand (or arms) • *The gorilla picked up her baby and held it gently in her arms.* ❖ κρατώ

**7.95** **operate** (v) /ˈɒpəreɪt/
use or make sth (e.g. a machine) work • *Do you know how to operate this tumble dryer?* ➢ operation (n), operator (n) ❖ λειτουργώ

**7.96** **steep** (adj) /stiːp/
this describes a slope that goes up or down very quickly • *I had to get off my bicycle and push it up the steep hill.* ❖ απότομο, με μεγάλη κλίση, πολύ επικλινές

**7.97** **accident** (n) /ˈæksɪdənt/
sth (usually bad) that happens without you expecting it • *Drive carefully or you might cause an accident.* ➢ accidental (adj), accidentally (adv) ❖ ατύχημα

### Adjectives

| | |
|---|---|
| active | off-road |
| alive | pop |
| brave | shy |
| classical | steep |
| fit | stressed |
| lost | |

### Verbs

| | |
|---|---|
| attempt | practise |
| hold | realise |
| join | scan |
| juggle | search |
| mix | solve |
| operate | suggest |
| perform | win |
| persuade | |

# Vocabulary Exercises

**A Circle the correct words.**

1 Michael **suggested / persuaded / offered** us to go hiking in the Highlands.
2 Betty is taking art classes to learn a new **talent / skill / unicycle**.
3 You'll meet more people if you **join / hold / mix** our youth club.
4 Have they **searched / scanned / solved** the mystery of the haunted house yet?
5 They were hot and thirsty after walking for an hour in the **desert / stage / machine**.
6 Every **controller / performer / DJ** in the dancing competition received a small prize.
7 Some African performers danced while others were banging their traditional **drums / violin / wheel** loudly.
8 That's a **shame / fact / course** you can't go to the party. I hope you feel better soon.
9 A few sessions of yoga will stop you feeling **fit / stressed / brave** and help you relax.
10 If you **practise / attempt / program** running for an hour every day, you might win the race.

**B Match the words with the meanings.**

| | | | | | |
|---|---|---|---|---|---|
| 1 | anywhere | ☐ | a | completely |
| 2 | before | ☐ | b | in fact |
| 3 | correctly | ☐ | c | ready for you to buy |
| 4 | actually | ☐ | d | at an earlier time |
| 5 | absolutely | ☐ | e | in any place |
| 6 | for sale | ☐ | f | in the right way |

**C** Complete the sentences with these words.

actual   alive   common   crazy   involved   keen   lost   steep

1   I'll never be able to run to the top of this _____ hill.
2   How long have you been _____ in acting?
3   Richard is absolutely _____ about robotics. He never misses a session.
4   The sailors were lucky to be _____ when their boat hit the rocks.
5   We phoned our tour guide for help when we got _____ in the mountains.
6   I thought Sarah liked skateboarding, but in _____ fact she hates it.
7   Tom and Harry have some things in _____ . They both like sports and gaming.
8   David is very _____ on baking and he makes great cheese pies.

**D** Read the meanings and complete the words.

1   somebody who takes part in an activity or event          p __ __ __ __ __ __ __ __ __
2   a small reptile with four short legs and a long tail      l __ __ __ __ __
3   a bag that you use to sleep in                            s __ __ __ __ __ __ __  b __ __
4   a long stick that holds a camera to take photos          s __ __ __ __ __  s __ __ __ __
5   a book that gives the meanings of words                  d __ __ __ __ __ __ __ __ __
6   a club for people interested in acting, etc.             d __ __ __ __  c __ __ __ __
7   a game played on a board with black and white squares    c __ __ __ __
8   any game played with pieces you move on a board          b __ __ __ __  g __ __ __

**E** Find ten words from Unit 7. Then complete the sentences with these words.

| | | | | | | | | | | | |
|---|---|---|---|---|---|---|---|---|---|---|---|
| I | C | I | R | C | A | N | A | V | E | M | G |
| S | E | S | S | O | V | E | B | T | A | O | E |
| E | L | F | I | M | U | C | I | R | C | U | S |
| S | E | D | E | P | G | N | L | I | O | D | T |
| S | U | G | G | E | S | T | I | O | N | P | A |
| I | R | Y | R | T | I | O | T | C | F | R | C |
| O | S | P | U | I | L | I | Y | O | I | E | C |
| N | E | R | A | T | T | A | S | F | D | S | I |
| S | U | G | R | I | F | U | S | I | E | E | D |
| L | P | I | M | O | D | E | L | D | N | D | E |
| R | O | N | F | N | C | E | R | T | C | O | N |
| E | N | T | I | O | N | A | D | V | E | R | T |

1 There was a terrible _____ at the traffic lights.
2 You need a lot of _____ to perform on stage.
3 I agree with your _____ to go surfing.
4 Have you read this _____ for snowboarding lessons?
5 You're so good at juggling! You should be in a _____ .
6 Who do you think will win the singing _____ ?
7 I think our team has the _____ to win this match.
8 The neighbour's cat chased the hungry _____ out of the garden.
9 This is a small _____ of an off-road vehicle.
10 A one-hour _____ at the tennis court costs £3.50.

# 7 Grammar

## 7.1 Zero Conditional

| *If* clause | Main clause |
|---|---|
| present simple | present simple |

Χρησιμοποιούμε **zero conditional** για να μιλήσουμε για τα αποτελέσματα μιας πράξης ή μιας κατάστασης που ισχύουν πάντα. Μπορούμε να χρησιμοποιήσουμε το **when** στη θέση του **if**.
→ *If I **sleep** well, I **feel** better in the morning.*
→ *When I **sleep** well, I **feel** better in the morning.*

## 7.2 First Conditional

| *If* clause | Main clause |
|---|---|
| present tense | *will* + bare infinitive |

Χρησιμοποιούμε **first conditional** για να μιλήσουμε για τα αποτελέσματα μιας πράξης ή μιας κατάστασης που είναι πιθανό να συμβεί τώρα ή στο μέλλον.
→ *If you **are** hungry, I**'ll make** sandwiches.*
→ *If you **study** hard, you**'ll learn** quickly.*
Μπορούμε να χρησιμοποιήσουμε **can**, **could**, **may** ή **might** στην κύρια πρόταση στη θέση του **will**. Μπορούμε επίσης να χρησιμοποιήσουμε προστακτική (imperative).
→ *If you enjoy walking, you **could** go hiking with us.*
→ *If you want to join the club, **call** this number.*

## 7.3 Gerunds

Σχηματίζουμε τα **gerunds** (γερούνδια) με τα ρήματα και την κατάληξη *-ing*. Μπορούμε να χρησιμοποιούμε το gerund:
σαν ουσιαστικό.
→ *Stamp **collecting** is her favourite hobby.*
μετά από προθέσεις.
→ *Nicky is interested **in joining** the chess club.*
μετά από το ρήμα *go* όταν μιλάμε για δραστηριότητες.
→ *We **go swimming** in the sea in summer.*
Χρησιμοποιούμε επίσης gerund (γερούνδιο) μετά από κάποια ρήματα και φράσεις.

| | |
|---|---|
| enjoy | keep |
| finish | like |
| hate | love |
| it's no good | miss |
| it's no use | practise |
| it's (not) worth | prefer |

→ *She **likes taking** photos.*
→ ***It's no good getting** a dog if you haven't got time to look after it.*

## 7.4 Infinitives: Full Infinitives

Σχηματίζουμε full infinitives με *to* και το ρήμα. Μπορούμε να χρησιμοποιούμε **full infinitives**:
για να εξηγήσουμε το σκοπό μιας πράξης.
→ *I joined a class **to learn** woodwork.*
μετά από επίθετα π.χ. *afraid, scared, happy, glad, sad*
→ *She was **sad to leave** the team.*
μετά από τις λέξεις *too* και *enough*.
→ *He's **too** young **to join** the men's team.*
→ *Our team weren't good **enough to win** the match.*

Χρησιμοποιούμε επίσης **full infinitives** μετά από κάποια ρήματα και φράσεις.

| | |
|---|---|
| ask | learn |
| begin | need |
| choose | offer |
| decide | plan |
| fail | prepare |
| forget | start |
| hope | want |
| invite | would like |

→ He **forgot to bring** his tennis racket.
→ We **chose to stay** at a youth hostel.

## 7.5 Bare Infinitives

Χρησιμοποιούμε **bare infinitives** (απαρέμφατα χωρίς *to*) μετά από:
modal verbs.
→ You **can use** my sister's bicycle if you want to go cycling with me.
*had better* για να δώσουμε συμβουλή.
→ You **had better wear** your helmet.
*would rather* για να μιλήσουμε για προτίμηση. Συχνά χρησιμοποιούμε τη λέξη *than*.
→ I **would rather play** tennis than watch it on TV.

# Grammar Exercises

**A** Complete the sentences with the correct form of the verbs in brackets.

1 If you exercise more, you _____ (feel) fitter.
2 When ice _____ (get) warmer, it becomes water.
3 I _____ (text) you when I arrive at the hotel.
4 If you see an accident, _____ (phone) the police.
5 If you _____ (be) thirsty, you can have some lemonade.
6 When I get up early on Sundays, I always _____ (make) breakfast for my family.
7 If you see Emma, _____ (tell) her to call me.
8 Ask your friend to send me a text if she _____ (want) to come hiking with us.

**B** Circle the correct words.

1 If you spend too much time gaming, **hurt** / **you might hurt** your eyes.
2 You can **borrow** / **to borrow** my skateboard if you like.
3 It's not worth **to spend** / **spending** a lot of money on clothes.
4 He's taking lessons **to learn** / **learning** to drive.
5 I would rather **go** / **to go** for a walk in the rain than stay at home.
6 Katy enjoys **to bake** / **baking** her own bread.
7 I'll be happy **to feed** / **feeding** your cats when you're on holiday. It's no problem.
8 Are you interested in **travelling** / **to travel** to Scotland?

# 7 Grammar

**C** **Complete the sentences with the correct form of these verbs.**

attempt   bring   eat   learn   pay   take   wear   go

1 If you go skateboarding, you should _____ a helmet.
2 Frances offered _____ for the tickets to the theatre.
3 The weather wasn't warm enough _____ swimming.
4 Are you prepared _____ to drive in the snow?
5 The cake is too hot _____ right now. I've just taken it out of the oven.
6 William is keen on _____ to sail a boat.
7 You had better _____ enough water with you when you cross the desert.
8 Dad forgot _____ his glasses and he can't read the menu.

# 8 Personal Best

**8.1** **whitewater rafting** (n) /waɪt 'wɔːtə(r) 'raːftɪŋ/
The sport of travelling down a very fast river in a raft • We tried whitewater rafting on the Alfeios River in Greece and it was so exciting. ❖ ράφτινγκ

**8.2** **creek** (n) /kriːk/
a small river; an area like a very narrow bay where the sea flows into the land • The river wasn't very deep so we were able to walk across the stones to the other side of the creek. ❖ ποταμάκι

# Reading

**8.3** **ice hockey** (n) /aɪs 'hɒki/
a sport played on ice by two teams of six players who use hockey sticks to hit a rubber puck into a net to score goals • Ice hockey is popular in cold countries like Canada. ❖ χόκεϋ επί πάγου

**8.4** **general public** (n) /'dʒenrəl 'pʌblɪk/
the ordinary people who are not members of a special group, club, etc. • We're doing a special performance for a small audience tonight, and then the show opens to the general public next week. ❖ ευρύτερο κοινό

**8.5** **admission** (n) /əd'mɪʃən/
the entry to or cost of entering an event or building • How much is the ticket for admission to the Acropolis Museum? ➢ admit (v) ❖ είσοδος

**8.6** **VIP** (abbr) /ˌviː aɪ 'piː/
a very important person with a high position; a celebrity • We felt like VIPs when we got the best seats in the theatre. ❖ VIP

**8.7** **drill** (n) /drɪl/
a way to learn sth by doing it many times • Once a year, we do an earthquake drill at school to practise what we would do if it really happened. ➢ drill (v) ❖ άσκηση

**8.8** **preview** (n) /'priːvjuː/
a performance for a few people before a film, play or show opens for the general public • The reporters who attended the theatre preview said the actors gave a brilliant performance. ➢ preview (v) ❖ μια παράσταση πριν την πρεμιέρα, αβάν πρεμιέρ

**8.9** **stand** (n) /stænd/
an area of a stadium with seats where people sit to watch a match, race, etc. • George and his friends watched the final from the best seats in the centre of the stand. ➢ stand (v) ❖ κερκίδα, διάζωμα

**8.10** **impaired view** (v) /ɪm'peəd vjuː/
the view from an area of a stadium where you can't see the full playing field • I didn't exactly see the winning goal because I was in the impaired view area at the opposite end of the stadium. ➢ impair (v), impairment (n) ❖ εμποδιζόμενη/μειωμένη ορατότητα

**8.11** **long jump** (n) /'lɒŋ dʒʌmp/
a sport where people run up to a line and then jump as far as they can • How far did Teresa jump in the long jump at the school sports day? ❖ άλμα εις μήκος

**8.12** **hurdle** (n) /'hɜːdl/
sth that you have to jump over in a race; sth that gets in your way • Tony fell over the second hurdle and broke his leg. ➢ hurdler (n) ❖ εμπόδιο (στίβος)

**8.13** **helmet** (n) /'helmɪt/
a hard hat that you wear on your head to protect it • Put on your helmet before you start skateboarding. ❖ κράνος

**8.14** **skates** (n pl) /skeɪts/
a kind of shoe with wheels, rollers or a blade on the bottom • Remember to bring your skates to play ice hockey. ➢ skate (v), skater (n) ❖ πατίνια

**8.15** **glove** (n) /glʌv/
sth that covers your hand and each finger • It's freezing outside, so wear your hat and gloves. ❖ γάντι

**8.16** **shoulder pad** (n) /'ʃəʊldə(r) pæd/
a piece of hard material (e.g. plastic or rubber) that you wear on your shoulders inside a shirt so you won't get hurt • American football players always seem huge because they're wearing shoulder pads. ❖ επωμίδα, προστατευτικό ώμου

**8.17** **shin guard** (n) /ʃɪn gaːd/
a piece of hard material (e.g. plastic or rubber) that you wear on the lower front part of your leg so you won't get hurt • Cricket players have to wear shin guards because their legs might get hit by a ball. ❖ επικαλαμίδα

**8.18** **elbow pad** (n) /'elbəʊ pæd/
a piece of hard material (e.g. plastic or rubber)
that you wear on the middle bone of your arm
so your elbow won't get hurt • *The skater
broke her arm when she fell because she
wasn't wearing elbow pads.* ❖ προστατευτικό
αγκώνα

**8.19** **brochure** (n) /'brəʊʃə(r)/
a small magazine with pictures and information
about sth • *Jill brought home some holiday
brochures to choose where to go this year.*
❖ φυλλάδιο, μπροσούρα

**8.20** **Jamaica** (n) /dʒə'meɪkə/
➢ Jamaican (adj, n) ❖ Τζαμάικα

**8.21** **baseball** (n) /'beɪsbɔːl/
a game with two teams of nine players in
which a player uses a bat to hit a ball and
others run to catch it • *My American cousins
are all crazy about baseball, but I prefer
football.* ❖ μπέιζμπωλ

**8.22** **originally** (adv) /ə'rɪdʒənəli/
at the beginning before sth changed in some
way • *This theatre was originally a factory
building.* ➢ original (adj), origin (n) ❖ αρχικά

## Word Focus                                    Page 96

**8.23** **colony** (n) /'kɒləni/
an area of the world where people have
travelled to from a powerful country and taken
control of the people and land • *Australia was
once a British colony.* ➢ colonise (v), colonial
(adj), colonisation (n) ❖ αποικία

**8.24** **independent** (adj) /ˌɪndɪ'pendənt/
free to do things without being controlled
or helped by sb else • *Scotland was an
independent country before it became part of
the United Kingdom in 1707.* ➢ independence
(n) ❖ ανεξάρτητος

**8.25** **rule** (v) /ruːl/
control and have power over a country • *The
Romans ruled part of Britain in ancient times,
but they couldn't control Scotland.* ➢ ruling
(adj), ruler (n), rule (n) ❖ κυβερνώ, διέπω

**8.26** **govern** (v) /'gʌvn/
control and make laws to rule a country
• *The British governed India from 1858 to
1947 when India became independent again.*
➢ government (n), governor (n) ❖ κυβερνώ

**8.27** **authorities** (n pl) /ɔː'θɒrətiz/
the organisations with the power to make
decisions to control a country or area • *If
you're planning an outdoor concert, you'll have
to get permission from the authorities first.*
➢ authorise (v), authority (n) ❖ Αρχές

**8.28** **bullfighting** (n) /'bʊlfaɪtɪŋ/
the activity of killing bulls in front of an
audience • *Bullfighting was popular in ancient
times, but many people believe it's wrong now.*
➢ bullfighter (n), bullfight (n) ❖ ταυρομαχία

**8.29** **entertainment** (n) /ˌentə'teɪnmənt/
activities for people to enjoy themselves • *TV
is not such a popular form of entertainment as
it was in the past.* ➢ entertain (v), entertaining
(adj), entertainer (n) ❖ ψυχαγωγία

**8.30** **bull** (n) /bʊl/
a male cow • *Be careful when you're passing
the farm because the bulls might chase you.*
❖ ταύρος

# Reading                                    Pages 96-97

**8.31** **unwind** (v) /ˌʌn'waɪnd/
relax • *I love listening to music to unwind after
I've finished my homework.* ❖ χαλαρώνω

**8.32** **the West Indies** (n) /ðə ˌwest 'ɪndɪz/
➢ West Indian (adj, n) ❖ οι Δυτικές Ινδίες

**8.33** **fascinating** (adj) /'fæsɪneɪtɪŋ/
very interesting • *We heard a fascinating story
about how people used to travel in the past.*
➢ fascinate (v), fascinated (adj), fascination
(n) ❖ γοητευτικός

**8.34** **war** (n) /wɔː(r)/
a long period of fighting between countries
or groups • *Millions of lives were lost during
the First World War between 1914 and 1918.*
➢ warring (adj), warrior (n) ❖ πόλεμος

**8.35** **run (for)** (v) /rʌn (fə(r))/
continue to happen (for a period of time)
• *The film ran for four weeks at the Odeon.*
❖ διαρκώ, κρατάω

**8.36** **the Caribbean** (n) /ðə ˌkærɪ'biːən/
❖ η Καραϊβική

> ### Countries, Nationalities & Seas
>
> | | |
> |---|---|
> | Alaska | Jamaican |
> | Cuba | the West Indies |
> | Cuban | the Aegean |
> | Hawaii | the Caribbean |
> | Jamaica | |

**8.37** **marathon** (n) /'mærəθən/
a race that is about 26 miles or 42 kilometres
long • *Thousands of runners took part in
the London marathon.* ➢ marathon (adj)
❖ Μαραθώνιος

**8.38** **synonym** (n) /'sɪnənɪm/
a word with the same meaning as another
word • *The adjectives 'big' and 'large' are
synonyms.* ❖ συνώνυμο

**8.39** **sauna** (n) /ˈsɔːnə/
a small room that is very hot, sometimes with steam, which you sit in or lie down in to clean yourself • *Sometimes Tracy has a sauna at the gym after her workout.* ❖ σάουνα

**8.40** **due to** (prep) /djuː tuː/
because of • *The bus couldn't get to the village due to the snow on the road.* ❖ εξ αιτίας, λόγω

**8.41** **repair** (n) /rɪˈpeə(r)/
an action to fix sth that is broken or not working correctly • *My bicycle needs some small repairs before I can use it again.* ➢ repair (v), repaired (adj) ❖ επισκευή

**8.42** **secure** (adj) /sɪˈkjʊə(r)/
safe; not easy to move out of place • *We felt secure when we sailed our yacht safely into the harbour.* ➢ secure (v), security (n) ❖ ασφαλής
✎ Opp: insecure

**8.43** **thief** (n) /θiːf/
sb who steals sth • *A thief got into the house and stole the computer and some cash when the Smiths were at work.* ➢ theft (n) ❖ κλέφτης
✎ Plural: thieves

**8.44** **provide** (n) /prəˈvaɪd/
give sth for sb to use • *The sports centre provides rackets, balls and any other equipment you need when you pay for a session.* ➢ provider (n), provision (n) ❖ προμηθεύω

**8.45** **aerobics** (n) /eəˈrəʊbɪks/
physical exercises to help you breathe better and become stronger • *Mum goes to her aerobics class at the sports centre three times a week to keep fit.* ➢ aerobic (adj) ❖ αεροβική

**8.46** **timetable** (n) /ˈtaɪmteɪbl/
schedule • *On the door of the gym, there's a timetable that shows when each class is on.* ➢ timetabled (adj) ❖ πρόγραμμα

**8.47** **goggles** (n pl) /ˈɡɒɡlz/
special glasses to cover your eyes for sports in the snow or swimming • *I don't like swimming underwater without my goggles because the water hurts my eyes.* ❖ γυαλιά

**8.48** **changing room** (n) /ˈtʃeɪndʒɪŋ rʊm/
an area where people can change clothes before and after taking part in sports • *When I got to the swimming pool, I put on my swimsuit in the changing room.* ➢ change (v, n) ❖ αποδυτήρια

**8.49** **push** (v) /pʊʃ/
press on sth with your hand or finger • *Push the handle on the side of this machine to make it work.* ➢ push (n) ❖ πιέζω, σπρώχνω

**8.50** **button** (n) /ˈbʌtn/
a small round or square part of sth that you press to make sth work • *When you push this button, the door will open.* ❖ κουμπί

**8.51** **assistance** (n) /əˈsɪstəns/
help (to do sth) • *Could you give me some assistance to put up the tennis net, please?* ➢ assist (v), assistant (n) ❖ βοήθεια

**8.52** **fan** (n) /fæn/
sb who likes a particular sport or team • *The fans went wild when their team scored the winning goal.* ❖ οπαδός

# Vocabulary Pages 98-99

**8.53** **net** (n) /net/
a piece of sports equipment in a playing area which players hit with a ball to score points (e.g. football, basketball) or hit a ball over (e.g. tennis, volleyball) • *Andy hit the ball over the net to win the final game.* ➢ net (v) ❖ δίχτυ

**8.54** **court** (n) /kɔːt/
the area where a game is played in tennis, badminton, basketball or volleyball • *The basketball fans ran onto the court to meet the players at the end of the game.* ❖ γήπεδο

**8.55** **goal** (n) /ɡəʊl/
a point scored in a sport by hitting a ball into a net, e.g. football, hockey • *When Henderson scored his third goal, Liverpool won the match.* ❖ γκολ

**8.56** **pitch** (n) /pɪtʃ/
the area where a game of football, rugby or hockey, etc., is played • *David ran with the ball and kicked it to the other side of the pitch.* ❖ γήπεδο

**8.57** **bat** (n) /bæt/
a piece of sports equipment for hitting a ball • *Kelly hit the ball hard with the baseball bat.* ➢ bat (v) ❖ ρόπαλο, ρακέτα

**8.58** **stand on your hands** (phr) /stænd ɒn jɔː(r) hændz/
do a handstand • *Be careful when you stand on your hands because you might fall over and hurt your back.* ➢ handstand (n) ❖ το να κάνω κατακόρυφο

**8.59** **the Aegean** (n) /ðə iːˈdʒiːən/
❖ το Αιγαίο

**8.60** **opponent** (n) /əˈpəʊnənt/
a person or team that you are playing against • *Our opponents were too good for our team to beat and we lost the match 3–1.* ❖ αντίπαλος

**8.61** **referee** (n) /ˌrefəˈriː/
sb who controls a game in a sport (e.g football, basketball) • *The referee gave Miguel a yellow card for being rude to him during the match.* ➢ referee (v) ❖ διαιτητής

**8.62 goalkeeper** (n) /ˈgəʊlkiːpə(r)/
a player who stops the ball from going into the goal when the other team tries to score • *Steve kicked the ball towards the net, but the goalkeeper caught it.* ❖ τερματοφύλακας

**8.63 whistle** (n) /ˈwɪsl/
a small piece of equipment that makes a high noise when you blow into it • *We were glad when the referee blew the final whistle and the game was over.* ➢ whistle (v) ❖ σφυρίχτρα

**8.64 tournament** (n) /ˈtʊənəmənt/
a sports competition that includes different levels of games until only two teams/players are left in the final • *Gary was so happy to win the chess tournament.* ❖ τουρνουά

**8.65 forever** (adv) /fərˈevə(r)/
for always; for a long time • *I want my team to stay at the top of the League forever.* ❖ για πάντα

**8.66 bounce** (v) /baʊns/
move sth up and down; move up and down or hit against sth and come back • *You can bounce the basketball, but you're not allowed to kick it.* ❖ αναπηδώ, κάνω κάτι να αναπηδήσει

**8.67 score** (v) /skɔː(r)/
win a point in a game, test, etc. • *The Liverpool fans went wild when the team scored the winning goal.* ❖ σκοράρω

**8.68 coach** (n) /kəʊtʃ/
a sports trainer • *Leo's tennis coach taught him how to serve the ball over the net.* ➢ coach (v), coaching (n) ❖ προπονητής

### People

| | |
|---|---|
| authorities | lover |
| coach | motorcyclist |
| colony | opponent |
| diver | referee |
| fan | runner |
| general public | thief |
| goalkeeper | VIP |
| gymnast | |

**8.69 beat** (v) /biːt/
win more points or do better than another team or opponent so that you win • *When Charlotte saw the other girl running past her, she knew she couldn't beat her in the race.* ❖ νικάω

**8.70 point** (n) /pɔɪnt/
a mark that counts on the score of a game or competition • *At the end of the word game, we counted our points to see who had the best score.* ❖ πόντος

**8.71 pass out** (phr v) /pɑːs aʊt/
lose your senses; fall down and become unconscious • *Nick passed out when the football hit him on the head.* ❖ λιποθυμώ

**8.72 warm up** (phr v) /wɔːm ʌp/
prepare for an exercise session by doing light exercises to stretch the muscles • *The players ran round the pitch to warm up before the game began.* ➢ warm-up (n) ❖ κάνω προθέρμανση

**8.73 drop out** (phr v) /drɒp aʊt/
stop taking part in sth • *Hilda dropped out of her Spanish lessons because she wanted to go to zumba instead.* ➢ dropout (n) ❖ παρατάω

**8.74 catch up** (phr v) /kætʃ ʌp/
reach others who are in front of you or at a higher level • *Sam is doing extra homework to catch up with the lessons that he missed when he was ill.* ❖ προφταίνω

**8.75 equal** (adj) /ˈiːkwəl/
that is the same as sth/sb else • *The score was equal at the end of the first game, so we played again to decide the winner.* ➢ equally (adv), equal (n) ❖ ίσος, ισοδύναμος

**8.76 unconscious** (adj) /ʌnˈkɒnʃəs/
having lost your senses, as if you're sleeping because of sth that happened to you • *When we got to the car, the driver and passenger were both unconscious, so we called an ambulance.* ➢ unconsciously (adv) ❖ αναίσθητος

### Phrasal Verbs & Phrases

| | |
|---|---|
| catch up | dream come true |
| drop out | stand on your hands |
| pass out | |
| warm up | |

# Grammar  Pages 100-101

**8.77 motocross** (n) /ˈməʊtəʊkrɒs/
the sport of motorbike racing off-road on rough country tracks • *The motocross riders and their bikes were covered in mud after the race.* ❖ μότοκρος

**8.78 refuse** (v) /rɪˈfjuːz/
say you don't want sth from sb; say you won't do sth that sb asks you to • *My parents refused to let me stay out very late.* ➢ refusal (n) ❖ απορρίπτω, αρνούμαι

**8.79 permission** (n) /pəˈmɪʃn/
the act of saying that sb is allowed to do sth • *Our teacher gave us permission to leave the room when we finished our test.* ➢ permit (v) ❖ άδεια

**8.80** **motorcyclist** (n) /ˈməʊtəsaɪklɪst/
sb who rides a motorbike ● *The police
motorcyclists rode after the thieves and
stopped them at the crossroads.* ➢ motorcycle
(n) ❖ μοτοσυκλετιστής

**8.81** **swimsuit** (n) /ˈswɪmsuːt/
sth you wear to go swimming ● *Don't forget to
pack your swimsuits for the holiday.* ❖ μαγιό

**8.82** **abseil** (v) /ˈæbseɪl/
move down a rope on a straight rock face or
wall using your feet and hands ● *You have
to be very brave or completely mad to abseil
down the outside of Europe's highest building.*
➢ abseiling (n) ❖ κατεβαίνω (από βράχο,
τοίχο, κτλ.) χρησιμοποιώντας σχοινί

**8.83** **lifejacket** (n) /ˈlaɪfdʒækɪt/
a small plastic jacket that you fill with air to
keep you up in the sea ● *The island beach
was covered with lifejackets from the people
who arrived on the boats.* ❖ σωσίβιο

**8.84** **forbid** (v) /fəˈbɪd/
say that sth is not allowed ● *The law forbids
the sale of cigarettes to people under the age
of 16.* ➢ forbidden (adj) ❖ απαγορεύω

**8.85** **obligation** (n) /ˌɒblɪˈgeɪʃn/
sth that you must do ● *There's no obligation to
go climbing if you don't want to.* ➢ oblige (v)
❖ υποχρέωση

**8.86** **necessity** (n) /nəˈsesəti/
sth that is needed ● *Helmets are a basic
necessity for riders on motorbikes and people
doing dangerous sports like snowboarding.*
➢ necessary (adj) ❖ ανάγκη

**8.87** **scooter** (n) /ˈskuːtə(r)/
a children's vehicle which has a board that
moves on small wheels with a long handle for
the rider to hold ● *Some children were riding
their scooters in the playground.* ❖ σκούτερ

**8.88** **drink station** (n) /drɪŋk ˈsteɪʃn/
an area where participants can stop for a drink
during a race ● *During the marathon, there
are many drink stations where the runners can
have a drink and some fruit or chocolate to
keep them going.* ❖ αναψυκτήριο

**8.89** **riding** (n) /ˈraɪdɪŋ/
the activity of riding a horse ● *Luckily, Owen
was wearing his helmet when he went riding
because he fell off his horse.* ➢ ride (v), rider
(n) ❖ ιππασία

## Places

| | |
|---|---|
| changing room | gym |
| court | pitch |
| creek | ski slope |
| drink station | stand |

# Listening

**8.90** **thirtieth** (num) /ˈθɜːtiəθ/
the number 30th ❖ τριακοστός

**8.91** **fortieth** (num) /ˈfɔːtiəθ/
the number 40th ❖ τεσσαρακοστός

**8.92** **fiftieth** (num) /ˈfɪftiəθ/
the number 50th ❖ πεντηκοστός

**8.93** **sixtieth** (num) /ˈsɪkstiəθ/
the number 60th ❖ εξηκοστός

**8.94** **seventieth** (num) /ˈsevntiəθ/
the number 70th ❖ εβδομηκοστός

**8.95** **eightieth** (num) /ˈeɪtiəθ/
the number 80th ❖ ογδοηκοστός

**8.96** **ninetieth** (num) /ˈnaɪntiəθ/
the number 90th ❖ ενενηκοστός

**8.97** **thirty-second** (num) /ˈθɜːti ˈsekənd/
the number 32nd ❖ τριακοστός δεύτερος

**8.98** **thirty-third** (num) /ˈθɜːti θɜːd/
the number 33rd ❖ τριακοστός τρίτος

## Ordinal Numbers

| | |
|---|---|
| thirtieth | eightieth |
| fortieth | ninetieth |
| fiftieth | thirty-second |
| sixtieth | thirty-third |
| seventieth | |

**8.99** **watersport** (n) /ˈwɔːtə(r) spɔːt/
a sport that takes place on water ● *You have
to be a good swimmer to do water sports like
rafting because you might fall into the river.*
❖ θαλάσσιο σπορ

**8.100** **discount** (n) /ˈdɪskaʊnt/
a lower price than usual; an amount cut off a
price ● *Students are allowed a 50% discount
on train tickets.* ❖ έκπτωση

# Speaking

**8.101** **zumba** (n) /ˈzʊmbə/
a type of aerobics mixed with Latin dancing
steps ● *Dancing to the music makes zumba
classes more fun than basic aerobics.*
❖ ζούμπα

## Sports & Activities

| | |
|---|---|
| aerobics | motocross |
| baseball | riding |
| bullfighting | watersport |
| ice hockey | whitewater rafting |
| long jump | zumba |
| marathon | |

## Equipment

| | |
|---|---|
| bat | net |
| button | pedal |
| elbow pad | sauna |
| glove | shin guard |
| goggles | shoulder pad |
| helmet | skates |
| hurdle | swimsuit |
| lifejacket | tyre |
| locker | whistle |

# Writing
**Pages 104-105**

**8.102** **blog** (n) /blɒg/
a piece of writing on a website that sb writes about events, opinions, etc. • *Have you read our new travel blog following the adventures of Heracles?* ➤ blog (v), blogger (n) ❖ μπλογκ

**8.103** **electric** (adj) /ɪˈlektrɪk/
that produces a sense of thrilling excitement; that works with electricity • *The actor gave an electric performance of Hamlet.* ➤ electrical (adj), electricity (n) ❖ ηλεκτρικός

**8.104** **truly** (adv) /ˈtruːli/
really; absolutely • *Seeing the River Amazon must be a truly wonderful experience.* ➤ true (adj), truth (n) ❖ αληθινά, πραγματικά

**8.105** **easily** (adv) /ˈiːzəli/
with no difficulty • *You can easily get to the top of the mountain if you follow the path.* ➤ easy (adj), ease (n) ❖ εύκολα

**8.106** **unbelievable** (adj) /ˌʌnbɪˈliːvəbl/
that you can't believe is true or possible • *An unbelievable number of fans came to see the game and many of them couldn't get into the stadium.* ➤ unbelievably (adv) ❖ απίστευτα
✎ Opp: believable

**8.107** **touch** (v) /tʌtʃ/
be right beside sth with no space in between; put your hand or part of your body on sth • *The ball touched the net before the goalkeeper could stop it.* ➤ touching (adj), touch (n) ❖ αγγίζω

**8.108** **emotion** (n) /ɪˈməʊʃn/
a feeling • *When she received her trophy, she showed her emotions and suddenly started crying.* ➤ emotional (adj) ❖ συναίσθημα

**8.109** **thrilled** (adj) /θrɪld/
very excited • *I was thrilled to hear the result of the match.* ➤ thrill (v, n), thrilling (adj) ❖ ενθουσιασμένος

**8.110** **dream come true** (phr) /driːm kʌm truː/
sth you always wanted very much that actually happens • *Vanessa's win at Wimbledon was a dream come true.* ❖ όνειρο που έγινε πραγματικότητα

**8.111** **disaster** (n) /dɪˈzɑːstə(r)/
a very bad event, especially one where sth is damaged and/or people are hurt • *When our team lost 6–0, it was a complete disaster for us.* ➤ disastrous (adj) ❖ καταστροφή

**8.112** **upset** (adj) /ʌpˈset/
unhappy and worried • *Ken was feeling ill and he was really upset about not being able to run in the marathon.* ➤ upset (v), upsetting (adj) ❖ ταραγμένος, στενοχωρημένος

**8.113** **disappointed** (adj) /ˌdɪsəˈpɔɪntɪd/
unhappy when sth doesn't go as well as you wanted it to • *We felt disappointed that we had to cancel our holiday.* ➤ disappoint (v), disappointing (adj), disappointment (n) ❖ απογοητευμένος

**8.114** **ceremony** (n) /ˈserəməni/
a traditional event where people do things in a special way • *They had their wedding ceremony in a small village by the sea.* ➤ ceremonial (adj) ❖ τελετή

## Adjectives & Adverbs

| | |
|---|---|
| amazed | secure |
| confident | thrilled |
| disappointed | unbelievable |
| electric | upset |
| equal | brilliantly |
| fascinating | easily |
| gentle | forever |
| independent | originally |
| rubber | truly |

# Video 8
# A Muni Adventure
**Page 106**

**8.115** **adventure** (n) /ədˈventʃə(r)/
a journey or experience that is exciting and may be dangerous • *The first time I travelled by plane was a big adventure for me.* ➤ adventurous (adj) ❖ περιπέτεια

**8.116** **pedal** (n) /ˈpedl/
a small part of a bicycle that you push with your foot to make the wheels move; a control operated by foot inside a vehicle • *Which pedal should I press to stop the car?* ➤ pedal (v) ❖ πεντάλι

**8.117** **tyre** (n) /ˈtaɪə(r)/
a rubber cover around the edge of a wheel • *I had to walk home because my bicycle had a flat tyre.* ❖ λάστιχο

**8.118 strength** (n) /streŋθ/
how strong sth is • *After her accident, Liz got back the strength in her arm again with a few minutes exercise every day.* ➣ strengthen (v), strong (adj) ❖ δύναμη

**8.119 ski slope** (n) /skiː sləʊp/
the area on the side of a mountain that you ski down • *Daniel went snowboarding on the ski slope at Aviemore in the Highlands.* ❖ πίστα σκι

**8.120 rubber** (adj) /ˈrʌbə(r)/
made of a strong material that can bend easily without breaking • *You need a small rubber ball to play tennis.* ➣ rubber (n) ❖ λαστιχένιος

**8.121 knob** (n) /nɒb/
a round handle or switch on sth • *I tried to turn the knob, but the door was locked.* ❖ στρογγυλό πόμολο, διακόπτης

**8.122 grip** (n) /grɪp/
ability to move without losing hold on sth • *These new tyres have a good grip on the wet road.* ➣ grip (v) ❖ κράτημα

**8.123 endurance** (n) /ɪnˈdjʊərəns/
being able to do sth difficult for a long time without getting too tired • *Mountain climbing needs skills and endurance because you can't stop when you're half way up or down.* ➣ endure (v) ❖ αντοχή

**8.124 exercise** (v) /ˈeksəsaɪz/
do activities to make your body fitter • *You can exercise your whole body at our zumba classes.* ➣ exercise (n) ❖ γυμνάζομαι, ασκούμαι

**8.125 concentration** (n) /ˌkɒnsnˈtreɪʃn/
the act of focussing all your thoughts and attention on one thing • *You need total concentration on the game to win at chess.* ➣ concentrate (v) ❖ συγκέντρωση

**Verbs**

| | |
|---|---|
| abseil | push |
| beat | refuse |
| bounce | rule |
| cheer | run (for) |
| dive | score |
| exercise | surf |
| forbid | touch |
| govern | unwind |
| provide | |

**Qualities**

| | |
|---|---|
| concentration | strength |
| endurance | |

# Vocabulary Exercises

**A** Circle the odd one out.

| | | | |
|---|---|---|---|
| 1 | button | tournament | knob |
| 2 | unwind | forbid | refuse |
| 3 | upset | amazed | disappointed |
| 4 | net | tyre | pedal |
| 5 | bounce | cheer | touch |
| 6 | blog | brochure | hurdle |
| 7 | court | goal | point |
| 8 | diver | locker | runner |

**B** Match.

| | | | | |
|---|---|---|---|---|
| 1 | shin | ☐ | a | room |
| 2 | long | ☐ | b | station |
| 3 | changing | ☐ | c | guard |
| 4 | shoulder | ☐ | d | hockey |
| 5 | life | ☐ | e | public |
| 6 | drink | ☐ | f | jump |
| 7 | ice | ☐ | g | pad |
| 8 | general | ☐ | h | jacket |

**C** Circle the correct words.

1 Sarah had to **drop out / pass out / warm up** of the tennis tournament when she hurt her arm.
2 The play **caught / scored / ran** for three years at the National Theatre.
3 Do you feel **confident / secure / gentle** enough to perform in front of an audience?
4 I need a new pair of **goggles / gloves / skates** because these are too small for my feet.
5 I held on to the paddle on the side of the rubber boat when we went whitewater **diving / rafting / riding** down the river.
6 It would be a fascinating **creek / drill / adventure** to travel on a cruise to Alaska.
7 Does the club **provide / rule / govern** safety equipment for the general public or only for members?
8 You can **exercise / beat / abseil** as often as you like at our gym.
9 The crowd cheered when the first runners in the **marathon / war / stand** reached the finishing line.
10 Suddenly, the frightened **bat / bull / goalkeeper** jumped over the gate and ran out of the stadium to find his freedom.

**D** Complete the blog with these words.

ceremony  disaster  discount  dream  opponent  referee  stand  pitch  VIP  whistle

At last, it was a ¹ _____ come true! I was sitting with my best friend watching the opening ² _____ of the Cup Final at Wembley. I felt like a real ³ _____ because we had the best seats in the ⁴ _____ . In actual fact, we bought our tickets at ⁵ _____ prices for students, so it didn't cost us too much. The ⁶ _____ dropped the ball and Liverpool's captain kicked it down the ⁷ _____ . Our team was playing against their biggest ⁸ _____ , Manchester United, but they played so badly that we lost the match 4–1. It was an absolute ⁹ _____ for Liverpool fans like us! We heard the final ¹⁰ _____ and we were so disappointed when the game was over.

**E** Complete the sentences with words formed from the words in bold.

1 The team played _____ , but they didn't win the match.                          BRILLIANT
2 The fans were _____ to meet the World Cup winners at the airport when they returned home.  THRILL
3 Driving a car needs a lot of _____ on the road.                                  CONCENTRATE
4 You don't need much _____ to do zumba and it is great fun.                        STRONG
5 I'm sure the ball wasn't out. The referee's decision was _____ !                 BELIEVE
6 Samaras scored his _____ goal for Celtic in 2012.                                FIFTY
7 With your musical talent, you could _____ become a singer.                       EASY
8 Do you like watching sports as a form of _____ ?                                 ENTERTAIN

# 8 Grammar

## 8.1 Can

Χρησιμοποιούμε **can** + **bare infinitive** (γυμνό απαρέμφατο) για:
να μιλήσουμε για γενική ικανότητα στο παρόν και στο μέλλον.
→ She **can climb** the hill easily.
να ζητήσουμε κάτι.
→ **Can I use** your swimming goggles?
να δώσουμε την άδεια για κάτι.
→ Yes, you **can go** to the tournament.

## 8.2 Could

Χρησιμοποιούμε **could** + **bare infinitive** (γυμνό απαρέμφατο) για:
να μιλήσουμε για γενική ικανότητα στο παρελθόν. (Αόριστος του *can*)
→ **Could** you **ride** a bike when you were younger?
να ζητήσουμε κάτι ευγενικά.
→ **Could** you **lend** me your baseball bat?

## 8.3 May

Χρησιμοποιούμε **may** + **bare infinitive** (γυμνό απαρέμφατο) για:
να ζητήσουμε κάτι ευγενικά (με *I* και *we*)
→ **May I sit** here?
να δώσουμε την άδεια για κάτι με ευγενικό τρόπο.
→ You **may use** my bat if you like.

## 8.4 Would

Χρησιμοποιούμε **would** + **bare infinitive** (γυμνό απαρέμφατο) για:
να ζητήσουμε κάτι ευγενικά.
→ **Would** you **take** me to riding lessons?

## 8.5 Shall

Χρησιμοποιούμε **shall** + **bare infinitive** (γυμνό απαρέμφατο) για:
να προσφέρουμε κάτι.
→ **Shall** we **go** surfing tomorrow?
για επιθυμίες.
→ I **shall do** better next time!

## 8.6 Should

Χρησιμοποιούμε **should** + **bare infinitive** (γυμνό απαρέμφατο) για:
να δώσουμε συμβουλή.
→ You **should get** more exercise.
να ζητήσουμε συμβουλή.
→ **Should** I **go** skiing with a group?

## 8.7 Must

Χρησιμοποιούμε **must** + **bare infinitive** (γυμνό απαρέμφατο) για:
να πούμε ότι κάτι είναι απαραίτητο.
→ I **must fix** my bicycle tyres.
να μιλήσουμε για υποχρεώσεις.
→ You **must have** a ticket to enter the stadium.

## 8.8 Mustn't

Χρησιμοποιούμε **mustn't** + **bare infinitive** (γυμνό απαρέμφατο) για να μιλήσουμε για κάτι που δεν επιτρέπεται.
→ You **mustn't use** a flash in the museum.

# 8 Grammar

## 8.9 *Have To*

Χρησιμοποιούμε **have to** για:
να πούμε ότι κάτι είναι απαραίτητο.
→ *You **have to try** hard to win.*
να μιλήσουμε για υποχρέωση.
→ *I **have to be** at the pool at five o'clock for my swimming lesson.*

## 8.10 *Mustn't & Don't Have To*

Υπάρχει μια σημαντική διαφορά ανάμεσα στο **mustn't** και στο **don't have to**. Χρησιμοποιούμε *mustn't* για να δείξουμε ότι κάτι δεν επιτρέπεται, ενώ χρησιμοποιούμε *don't have to* για να δείξουμε ότι δεν υπάρχει υποχρέωση ή αναγκαιότητα.
→ *You **mustn't wear** your outdoor shoes in the gym.*
→ *You **don't have to come** to the gym every day. You can come whenever you want to.*

## 8.11 *Needn't*

Χρησιμοποιούμε **needn't + bare infinitive** (γυμνό απαρέμφατο) για να πούμε ότι κάτι δεν είναι απαραίτητο. Δεν το χρησιμοποιούμε σε καταφατικές προτάσεις.
→ *You **needn't bring** any special equipment. The sports centre has everything.*

**Σημείωση:** Μπορούμε να χρησιμοποιήσουμε το *need* σαν κανονικό ρήμα. Έχει καταφατικό, ερωτηματικό και αρνητικό τύπο, και χρησιμοποιείται συνήθως στον Present Simple και στον Past Simple. Ακολουθείται από full infinitive (απαρέμφατο με to).
→ *She **needs to play** more often.*
→ *You **didn't need to buy** a mountain bike. There are lots of bikes at the outdoor centre.*
→ ***Does** he **need to join** our club to come camping with us?*

# Grammar Exercises

**A** Write questions with a modal verb to match these meanings.

1 Is it possible for us to go riding today?
_____

2 Please lend me a pair of gloves.
_____

3 Was he able to swim when he was two years old?
_____

4 Is it a good idea for me to take riding lessons?
_____

5 I need your permission to go rafting.
_____

6 Is it necessary to bring our own skates?
_____

7 Why don't we go running?
_____

8 Do you want me to fix your tyre?
_____

**B** Choose the correct answers (A, B or C).

1 You ___ look down or you'll feel dizzy when you're abseiling.
   **A** don't have to      **B** don't need to      **C** mustn't

2 People ___ bring their dogs into the park if they keep them under control.
   **A** have to      **B** shall      **C** can

3 We ___ take food on the trip because there will be a free barbecue.
   **A** needn't      **B** didn't need      **C** mustn't

4 You ___ ride that small horse if you like.
   **A** may      **B** must      **C** would

5 You ___ get some sleep because you're leaving early tomorrow.
   **A** have      **B** may      **C** should

6 Uncle William ___ climb mountains easily when he was young.
   **A** can      **B** could      **C** should

7 I ___ do my best to win the race.
   **A** needn't      **B** shall      **C** don't have to

8 ___ you please help me to fix my bike?
   **A** Would      **B** Should      **C** Must

**C** Complete the sentences with *must, mustn't, don't have to* or *doesn't have to*.

1 We _____ leave early to catch the first ferry.
2 You _____ eat or drink on the bus or the driver will get annoyed.
3 I _____ do any homework for tomorrow because I've finished it already.
4 The thief _____ steal a motorbike. The police will catch him.
5 You really _____ practise more to prepare for the marathon.
6 Steve _____ pay to get into the show because he's performing in it.
7 We _____ take the bus to the stadium because it's near our house.
8 Mum _____ bring water for the run; there are lots of drink stations.

# 9 Take a Break

**9.1** **accommodation** (n) /ə,kɒmə'deɪʃn/
a place to stay in • *Our holiday
accommodation wasn't exactly 5 star, but the
room had everything we needed.*
➣ accommodate (v) ❖ κατάλυμα

**9.2** **west** (adj) /west/
on the west; in the direction where the sun
sets • *Corfu is an island off the west coast of
Greece.* ➣ west (n) ❖ Δυτικός

**9.3** **coast** (n) /kəʊst/
the land next to the sea • *From the hotel
window, you can see the boats sailing near the
coast.* ➣ coastal (adj) ❖ ακτή

**9.4** **rainforest** (n) /'reɪnfɒrɪst/
a thick forest or jungle in a place where it rains
a lot • *Farmers shouldn't cut down rainforests
to grow more coffee.* ❖ τροπικό δάσος

# Reading  Pages 110-111

**9.5** **caravan** (n) /'kærəvæn/
a vehicle which you can live inside and you
can pull with a car • *The Wilsons stopped
having camping holidays in a tent and got a
caravan instead.* ❖ τροχόσπιτο

**9.6** **chalet** (n) /'ʃæleɪ/
a traditional wooden house, often built in
mountain areas • *Tom rented a wooden chalet
to stay in when he went skiing in Austria.*
❖ σαλέ

**9.7** **ride** (n) /raɪd/
a trip by bicycle • *Did you enjoy your ride
along the cycle path by the sea?* ➣ ride (v),
rider (n) ❖ βόλτα με ποδήλατο

**9.8** **BBQ** (abbr) /'bɑːbɪkjuː/
short form of the word barbecue • *We're
having a BBQ on Friday. Please come along.*
❖ μπάρμπεκιου

**9.9** **mostly** (adv) /'məʊstli/
mainly • *The island's hotels are mostly close
to the beaches.* ➣ most (adj, n)
❖ κυρίως

**9.10** **all-inclusive** (adj) /ɔːl ɪn'kluːsɪv/
that includes the cost of different things in the
price • *The group went on an all-inclusive tour
of the UNESCO sites in the Peloponnese, so
they didn't have any extra costs to pay.* ❖ όλα-
μέσα, ολ ινκλούσιβ

**9.11** **Barbados** (n) /bɑː'beɪ,dɒs/
❖ Μπαρμπέιντος

**9.12** **city break** (n) /'sɪti breɪk/
a short holiday in a city • *If you don't like
beach holidays, you could take a city break in
Amsterdam.* ❖ σύντομη τουριστική επίσκεψη
σε πόλη

**9.13** **history** (n) /'hɪstri/
the study of things that happened in the
past • *Last week's history lesson was about
Ancient Rome.* ➣ historic (adj), historical (adj),
historically (adv) ❖ Ιστορία

**9.14** **geography** (n) /dʒi'ɒgrəfi/
the study of how the Earth is and where places
and things are on it • *We had to remember the
names of all the rivers and lakes in the country
for our geography test.* ➣ geographical (adj),
geographically (adv) ❖ Γεωγραφία

**9.15** **Iceland** (n) /'aɪslənd/
➣ Icelandic (adj) ❖ Ισλανδία

**9.16** **volcano** (n) /vɒl'keɪnəʊ/
a mountain that has (or had) hot gases and hot
melted rocks coming out of a hole on its top
• *Did you know that the area of Kamchatka
in Russia has over 60 volcanoes?* ➣ volcanic
(adj) ❖ ηφαίστειο

**9.17** **waterfall** (n) /'wɔːtəfɔːl/
a place where a river falls down from high
rocks • *Hundreds of pretty little waterfalls
flow down the steep hills into Loch Lomond in
Scotland.* ❖ καταρράκτης

**9.18** **glacier** (n) /'glæsiə(r)/
a slow-moving mass of ice like a huge frozen
river • *The Earth's glaciers are mostly near the
North and South Poles and they can actually
be hundreds of metres long.* ❖ παγετώνας

**9.19** **awesome** (adj) /'ɔːsəm/
impressive; amazing • *The live volcano in
Sicily was an awesome sight.* ➣ awe (n)
❖ φοβερός

**9.20** **experience** (n) /ɪk'spɪəriəns/
an activity that has an effect on sb • *Skiing
down the slope through the trees was a scary
experience.* ➣ experience (v), experienced
(adj) ❖ εμπειρία, περιπέτεια

## Look!

Χρησιμοποιούμε τη λέξη **experience** σε δύο
περιπτώσεις με διαφορετική σημασία:
*Falling off a horse was one of the worst
experiences I've ever had.* (countable =
εμπειρίες)
*Gordon has had a lot of experience of working
as a travel agent.* (uncountable = πείρα)

**9.21** **it doesn't matter** (phr) /ɪt ˈdʌznt ˈmætə(r)/
it is not important • *It doesn't matter where we go – we just need a short break somewhere.*
❖ δεν πειράζει, δεν έχει σημασία

**9.22** **hot spring** (n) /hɒt sprɪŋ/
a place where hot water comes out of the ground naturally • *Many people enjoy relaxing in the water at the hot springs in Edipsos.*
❖ υδροθερμική πηγή

**9.23** **lagoon** (n) /ləˈguːn/
a lake of salt water that is cut off from the sea
• *The beautiful lagoon was filled with colourful sea birds looking for fish.* ❖ λιμνοθάλασσα

## Word Focus                                    Page 111

**9.24** **the Northern Lights** (n) /ðə ˈnɔːðən laɪts/
coloured lights in the sky that you can see mostly in countries close to the North Pole
• *From the north coast of Scotland, we saw the Northern Lights shining above the sea.*
❖ το Βόρειο Σέλας
✎ Syn: Aurora Borealis

**9.25** **erupt** (v) /ɪˈrʌpt/
When a volcano erupts, it throws out hot rocks and smoke, etc. • *When the volcano on Iceland erupted, the planes had to stop flying for days because of the smoke and ash in the air.* ➢ eruption (n) ❖ εκρήγνυμαι

**9.26** **explode** (v) /ɪkˈspləʊd/
burst loudly and suddenly • *The plane crashed when one of the engines exploded.*
➢ explosion (n), explosive (adj) ❖ εκρήγνυμαι

**9.27** **ash** (n) /æʃ/
grey or black powder from sth that has burnt
• *Our balcony was covered with ashes after the forest fire near our home.* ❖ στάχτη

**9.28** **powder** (n) /ˈpaʊdə(r)/
very small pieces of soft dry material • *The actors were putting powder on their faces before they went on stage.* ➢ powder (v), powdery (adj) ❖ σκόνη

# Reading                        Pages 110-111

**9.29** **sunset** (n) /ˈsʌnset/
the time of day when the sun goes down in the west • *Melinda enjoys taking photos of beautiful sunsets.* ❖ ηλιοβασίλεμα

**9.30** **hole** (n) /həʊl/
an empty space in sth • *There was water pouring out of a hole in the road, so we called the authorities to fix it.* ❖ τρύπα

**9.31** **cliff** (n) /klɪf/
a high area of rock, e.g. at the side of the sea
• *We watched the birds flying near their nests on the rocky cliffs above the beach.* ❖ γκρεμός

**9.32** **cover** (v) /ˈkʌvə(r)/
put sth over sth else so that you can't see it easily • *The snow was covering the garden when we woke up and looked outside.*
➢ cover (n) ❖ καλύπτω

**9.33** **roof** (n) /ruːf/
the top part of a building that covers it • *The rain was coming in through a hole in the roof of the chalet.* ❖ στέγη, οροφή

**9.34** **pretty** (adj) /ˈprɪti/
nice looking • *In the spring, the countryside is full of pretty flowers.* ❖ όμορφος

**9.35** **sunglasses** (n pl) /ˈsʌnglɑːsɪz/
glasses with dark glass to protect your eyes from the sun • *Don't forget to wear your sunglasses and a hat when you go out in the sun.* ❖ γυαλιά ηλίου

**9.36** **seaside** (n) /ˈsiːsaɪd/
an area beside the sea • *Let's go to the seaside for a picnic.* ➢ seaside (adj) ❖ ακτή, παραλία

**9.37** **uncommon** (adj) /ʌnˈkɒmən/
not usual • *It's uncommon to see dolphins from the beach because they don't usually come so close.* ❖ ασυνήθης
✎ Opp: common

**9.38** **average** (adj) /ˈævərɪdʒ/
ordinary; normal • *The average tourist doesn't know much about the history of our country.*
➢ average (n) ❖ κοινός

**9.39** **odd** (adj) /ɒd/
strange • *It's odd to see snow here in summer.*
❖ παράξενος

**9.40** **unnatural** (adj) /ʌnˈnætʃrəl/
not natural • *We saw some unnatural ash on the ground after the fire went out.*
➢ unnaturally (adv) ❖ αφύσικος
✎ Opp: natural

**9.41** **(blog) entry** (n) /blɒg entri/
a piece of writing on a website that gives news or an opinion • *You should write a short but interesting entry on your blog every day to attract more people to your website.*
❖ ανάρτηση, ποστάρισμα (σε μπλογκ)

---

### Nature

| | |
|---|---|
| cliff | landscape |
| continent | rainforest |
| earth | seaside |
| giant tortoise | sunset |
| glacier | the Northern Lights |
| geography | volcano |
| hot spring | waterfall |
| lagoon | |

# Vocabulary Pages 112-113

**9.42 continent** (n) /ˈkɒntɪnənt/
one of the large masses of land on Earth
• *Very few people live on the continent of Antarctica.* ➢ continental (adj) ❖ ήπειρος

**9.43 Asia** (n) /ˈeɪʒə/
➢ Asian (adj, n) ❖ Ασία

**9.44 Africa** (n) /ˈæfrɪkə/
➢ African (adj, n) ❖ Αφρική

**9.45 Oceania** (n) /ˌəʊsiˈɑːniə/
❖ Ωκεανία

**9.46 North America** (n) /nɔːθ əˈmerɪkə/
➢ North American (adj, n) ❖ Βόρειος Αμερική

**9.47 South America** (n) /saʊθ əˈmerɪkə/
➢ South American (adj, n) ❖ Νότιος Αμερική

## Continents

| | |
|---|---|
| Africa | North America |
| Asia | Oceania |
| Europe | South America |

**9.48 population** (n) /ˌpɒpjuˈleɪʃn/
the number of people who live in an area
• *The UK has a population of over 65 million and the number is growing every day.*
➢ populate (v) ❖ πληθυσμός

**9.49 million** (num) /ˈmɪljən/
the number *1,000,000* ❖ εκατομμύριο

**9.50 safari park** (n) /səˈfɑːri pɑːk/
a place where wild animals live and walk around safely while visitors can drive through to watch them from their vehicles • *Don't feed the animals when you drive through the safari park because the wrong food could make them ill.* ❖ πάρκο σαφάρι

**9.51 Inca** (n) /ˈɪŋkə/
one of the native peoples of Peru before the Spanish invasion • *The Incas ruled most of South America in the late fifteenth and early sixteenth centuries.* ➢ Incan (adj) ❖ Ίνκας

**9.52 landscape** (n) /ˈlændskeɪp/
everything you can see around you on the land
• *We were amazed at the colours of the sand and rocks in the desert landscape.* ❖ τοπίο

**9.53 South Korea** (n) /saʊθ kəˈriə/
➢ South Korean (adj, n) ❖ Νότιος Κορέα

**9.54 high tech** (adj) /haɪ tek/
using the latest technology • *Daisy prefers to find her way with a map instead of using a high tech GPS unit.* ❖ υψηλή τεχνολογία
✎ Syn: hi-tech

**9.55 bed and breakfast** (n) /bed ənd ˈbrekfəst/
a place that offers a room that you can rent to sleep in and breakfast • *On our trip across the Highlands, we stayed for a few nights at a lovely bed and breakfast near Loch Ness.*
❖ διαμονή με πρωϊνό (σε πανσιόν)

**9.56 caravan park** (n) /ˈkærəvæn pɑːk/
an area where you can find a space to park a caravan and use any services provided
• *Caravan parks in the UK often have play areas for children as well as games like table tennis.* ❖ χώρος/κάμπιγκ για τροχόσπιτα
✎ Syn: caravan site

**9.57 basic** (adj) /besɪk/
simple; with the things you need most • *Water and food are basic needs for all people and animals.* ➢ basically (adv) ❖ απλός

**9.58 cheap** (adj) /tʃiːp/
not expensive; not costing a lot of money
• *The best campsites aren't so cheap for a family to stay at, but the services are often worth it.* ➢ cheaply (adv) ❖ φτηνός

**9.59 park** (v) /pɑːk/
leave a vehicle in a place for a period of time
• *There were so many cars in the street that Dora couldn't find anywhere to park her car.*
➢ park (n), parking (adj), parked (adj)
❖ παρκάρω

**9.60 toast** (n) /təʊst/
slices of bread that are heated to make them brown on the outside • *I like to have a piece of toast with my egg for breakfast.* ➢ toast (v), toasted (adj) ❖ φρυγανιά

**9.61 uncomfortable** (adj) /ʌnˈkʌmftəbl/
not comfortable to wear or use • *Her helmet felt a bit uncomfortable at first, but she wore it to protect her head while snowboarding.*
➢ uncomfortably (adv) ❖ άβολος
✎ Opp: comfortable

**9.62 tourist information centre** (n) /ˈtʊərɪst ˌɪnfəˈmeɪʃn ˈsentə(r)/
a place where tourists can find out about services and things to do and see in the place they are visiting • *We had to stay for a night at Patra before taking the ferry, so we went to the tourist information centre to ask about hotels.*
❖ κέντρο για τουριστικές πληροφορίες

**9.63 travel agent** (n) /ˈtrævl ˈeɪdʒənt/
sb who makes arrangements for people to travel, e.g. organising tours, tickets, accommodation • *A good travel agent will find you the best rooms at the best prices in the area where you want to go.* ➢ travel agency (n) ❖ ταξιδιωτικός πράκτορας

**9.64 holiday resort** (n) /ˈhɒlədeɪ rɪˈzɔːt/
a place where many people go on holiday
• *The quiet fishing village of Benitses changed completely when it became a popular holiday resort.* ❖ θέρετρο

## Accommodation

| | |
|---|---|
| all-inclusive | caravan park |
| bed and breakfast | chalet |
| campsite | holiday resort |
| caravan | |

**9.65**  **sight** (n) /saɪt/
interesting things that you can see in a place
• *The walking tour included all the famous sights of Edinburgh from the castle to Arthur's Seat.* ❖ αξιοθέατο

**9.66**  **map** (n) /mæp/
a plan that shows the surface of the earth and all the roads, etc. to go somewhere • *Click on the link to see a map of the city.* ❖ χάρτης

**9.67**  **amusement park** (n) /əˈmjuːzmənt pɑːk/
a place where people can pay to go on rides to have fun • *Have you tried a ride on the big wheel at the amusement park? It's so exciting.* ❖ λούνα παρκ

**9.68**  **day trip** (n) /deɪ trɪp/
a short journey to a place and back on the same day • *You can go on a day trip on a boat to some of the islands near the coast.* ❖ ημερήσια εκδρομή

**9.69**  **excursion** (n) /ɪkˈskɜːʃn/
a short journey to a place and back for fun
• *Our class went on an excursion to the West Midland Safari Park and we saw loads of animals.* ❖ εκδρομή

**9.70**  **suitcase** (n) /ˈsuːtkeɪs/
a large bag with flat sides that you can pack clothes in to take for travelling • *Sally packed all her nice summer clothes and swimsuits in her suitcase and took a taxi to the airport.* ❖ βαλίτσα

**9.71**  **wander** (v) /ˈwɒndə(r)/
walk around slowly without going anywhere in particular • *They wandered around London for hours looking at the sights.* ➢ wander (n), wanderer (n) ❖ περιπλανιέμαι

**9.72**  **wonder** (v) /ˈwʌndə(r)/
think about sth to decide what to do, etc.
• *I wonder which is the best place to go for dinner.* ➢ wonder (n), wonderful (adj), wonderfully (adv) ❖ αναρωτιέμαι

**9.73**  **earth** (n) /ɜːθ/
our planet, Earth • *Erica wants to travel to every continent on earth.* ❖ Γη

**9.74**  **Colosseum** (n) /kɒləˈsiːəm/
❖ Κολοσσαίον
✎ Syn: Coliseum

**9.75**  **postcard** (n) /ˈpəʊstkɑːd/
a card with a picture on one side and a space to write a message on the back • *Aunt Jessie sent me a postcard from Madrid when she was on holiday in Spain.* ❖ καρτ-ποστάλ

# Grammar  Pages 114-115

**9.76**  **giant tortoise** (n) /ˈdʒaɪənt ˈtɔːtəs/
a very large reptile with a hard shell on its back • *The largest giant tortoises in the world are from the Galapagos Islands.* ❖ γιγάντια χελώνα

**9.77**  **Galapagos Islands** (n pl) /gəˈlæpəgɒs ˈaɪləndz/
❖ Νησιά Γκαλάπαγκος

**9.78**  **Dubai** (n) /duːˈbaɪ/
❖ Ντουμπάι

**9.79**  **taxi driver** (n) /ˈtæksi ˈdraɪvə(r)/
sb whose job it is to drive a taxi • *Taxi drivers in London have to know all the streets very well.* ❖ οδηγός ταξί

**9.80**  **tram** (n) /træm/
a vehicle that runs on electricity to carry passengers on city streets • *The tram from Edinburgh airport to the city centre is a bit slow.* ❖ τραμ

**9.81**  **sweetly** (adv) /ˈswiːtli/
in a nice way • *She smiled sweetly at the sight of the little cats playing.* ➢ sweeten (v), sweet (adj) ❖ γλυκά

**9.82**  **politely** (adv) /pəˈlaɪtli/
in a polite way • *If you ask Joe politely, he will lend you his bike.* ➢ politeness (v), polite (adj) ❖ ευγενικά
✎ Opp: impolitely

**9.83**  **angrily** (adv) /ˈæŋgrəli/
in an angry way • *Jennifer walked out of the room angrily when her mother told her to stop chatting on Facebook.* ➢ anger (n), angry (adj) ❖ θυμωμένα

**9.84**  **hungrily** (adv) /ˈhʌŋgrəli/
in a hungry way • *The birds ate hungrily when we gave them some bread.* ➢ hunger (v), hungry (adj) ❖ πεινασμένα

**9.85**  **miss** (v) /mɪs/
be too late for sth • *We got to the airport at the last minute and nearly missed our plane.* ❖ χάνω

## Adjectives

| | |
|---|---|
| average | odd |
| awesome | pretty |
| basic | uncomfortable |
| cheap | uncommon |
| empty | unnatural |
| enjoyable | vintage |
| high tech | west |

# Listening Page 116

**9.86**    **take place** (phr v) /teɪk pleɪs/
happen • *When will the concert take place?*
❖ συμβαίνω

# Speaking Page 117

**9.87**    **empty** (adj) /ˈempti/
with nothing/nobody inside • *The village
streets are usually empty in the afternoon
when the local people have their afternoon
sleep.* ➢ empty (v), emptiness (n) ❖ άδειος

**9.88**    **hometown** (n) /ˈhəʊmtaʊn/
the town where you come from • *When Leo
returned to his hometown, it was completely
different from what he remembered as a child.*
❖ γενέτειρα

# Writing Pages 118-119

**9.89**    **social media** (n) /ˈsəʊʃl ˈmiːdɪə/
websites where people connect with each
other to share news and opinion • *Make sure
that information is true before you pass it on
through social media.* ❖ κοινωνικά μέσα

**9.90**    **post** (n) /pəʊst/
a message written on the internet; a part of a
blog • *I never have time to read all the posts
that appear on Twitter every day, so I only read
the most interesting ones.* ➢ post (v)
❖ ποστάρισμα

**9.91**    **flow** (v) /fləʊ/
move easily; sound natural • *The book was
easy to read as the story flowed nicely to the
end.* ➢ flow (n), flowing (adj) ❖ κυλάω, έχω
ροή

**9.92**    **smoothly** (adv) /ˈsmuːðli/
easily, without problems • *Everything went
smoothly as planned during their trip.*
➢ smooth (v, adj) ❖ ομαλά

**9.93**    **avoid** (v) /əˈvɔɪd/
stay away from sth (e.g. that could be bad);
stop sth bad from happening • *You can take
the Underground to avoid traffic jams on the
streets.* ❖ αποφεύγω

**9.94**    **enjoyable** (adj) /ɪnˈdʒɔɪəbl/
that you will enjoy • *The walk around the lake
was an enjoyable experience.* ➢ enjoy (v),
enjoyment (n) ❖ απολαυστικός

**9.95**    **later** (adv) /ˈleɪtə(r)/
at a time in the future • *I'll see you later after
school.* ➢ late (adj) ❖ αργότερα

**9.96**    **Bye** (excl) /baɪ/
short for *Goodbye*; sth you say when you're
leaving or ending a letter, etc. • *Bye for now!
See you soon.* ❖ αντίο, γειά

**9.97**    **vintage** (adj) /ˈvɪntɪdʒ/
very old and typical of a style in the past • *The
museum had a display of vintage clothes from
the 1920s.* ❖ παλαιό, κλασσικό

**9.98**    **contraction** (n) /kənˈtrækʃn/
the shorter form of a verb • *When we write
to friends, we often use contractions like 'I'm'
instead of 'I am'.* ➢ contract (v), contracted
(adj) ❖ συναίρεση

**9.99**    **full stop** (n) /fʊl stɒp/
the mark you write to show the end of a normal
sentence • *Remember to put full stops where
you need them.* ❖ τελεία

**9.100**    **question mark** (n) /ˈkwestʃən mɑːk/
the mark you write to show the end of a
question in English • *Did you know that the
Spanish question mark is like the English one
turned upside down?* ❖ ερωτηματικό

**9.101**    **fall in love** (phr) /fɔːl ɪn lʌv/
have a sudden feeling of liking sb very much
• *Alex decided to move to Glasgow when he
fell in love with Shona and wanted to be close
to her.* ❖ ερωτεύομαι

# Video 9
## The Travelling Photographer
**Page 120**

**9.102** **newspaper** (n) /'njuːzpeɪpə(r)/
a set of pages with news, adverts, articles, etc.
that is made every day or week ● *Which pages
do you read most in the newspaper? News,
sports or adverts?* ❖ εφημερίδα

**9.103** **religion** (n) /rɪ'lɪdʒən/
the belief in a god or gods and activities
related to this ● *Celebrating Easter is part of
the Christian religion.* ➢ religious (adj)
❖ θρησκεία

**9.104** **snake charmer** (n) /sneɪk 'tʃɑːmə(r)/
sb who seems to make snakes move to
the sound of music ● *People like snake
charmers are common on the streets of tourist
destinations in India.* ❖ γητευτής φιδιών

**9.105** **fortune teller** (n) /'fɔːtʃuːn 'telə(r)/
sb who says they can tell you what will happen
in the future ● *The fortune teller said I would
go on a long journey, and guess what! Next
day I was on the plane coming back from our
holiday!* ❖ μάντης

### People

| | |
|---|---|
| fortune teller | taxi driver |
| snake charmer | travel agent |

# Vocabulary Exercises

**A** Match.

| | | | | |
|---|---|---|---|---|
| **1** | day | ☐ | **a** | entry |
| **2** | city | ☐ | **b** | teller |
| **3** | snake | ☐ | **c** | driver |
| **4** | fortune | ☐ | **d** | agent |
| **5** | social | ☐ | **e** | charmer |
| **6** | travel | ☐ | **f** | trip |
| **7** | blog | ☐ | **g** | break |
| **8** | taxi | ☐ | **h** | media |

**B** Complete the sentences with the words from Exercise A.

**1** The _____ sat in the market square and softly played his instrument as the animal began to move.

**2** Ian wrote an interesting _____ about his trip to Iceland.

**3** They asked the _____ to take them to the hotel with their suitcases.

**4** We're going for a four-day _____ in Moscow.

**5** Tomorrow, our class is going on a _____ with our history teacher.

**6** Be careful who you communicate with on _____ websites.

**7** The _____ helped us plan the perfect tour of the islands.

**8** The _____ told my brother he'll be rich and famous one day.

**C** Circle the correct words.

1 I **wander / wonder / wonderfully** where my sunglasses are.
2 You can get on the **map / seaside / tram** to reach the city centre.
3 Which countries in Europe have a bigger **population / repetition / contraction** than the UK?
4 In the ancient Greek **newspaper / excursion / religion**, people believed that Heracles was the son of the god, Zeus.
5 We had some hot **toast / spring / ash** for breakfast before we went hiking.
6 You can **park / explode / avoid** your bike outside the caravan.
7 We stayed in a traditional wooden **hole / BBQ / chalet** in the Alps.
8 When the **glacier / volcano / giant tortoise** began to erupt, everyone ran for their lives.

**D** Complete the sentences with words formed from the words in bold.

1 The rides at the _____ park were cheap enough for us to go on them.          **AMUSE**
2 What type of _____ would you prefer – a campsite or a bed and breakfast?     **ACCOMMODATE**
3 Have you ever taken _____ lessons?                                            **SKI**
4 It's quite _____ to see a glacier at a holiday resort.                        **COMMON**
5 The children had a really _____ day at the seaside.                           **ENJOY**
6 It's _____ to cut down so many trees in the rainforests.                      **NATURE**
7 Toby felt terribly _____ when he tried to sleep in the tent on a rocky beach. **COMFORT**
8 The tourists who come to Jamaica are _____ from North America.                **MOST**

**E Complete the words to match the meanings. Find the hidden word.**

1 the study of how the Earth is and where places and things are on it
2 glasses with dark glass to protect your eyes from the sun
3 a high area of rock, e.g. at the side of the sea
4 one of the large masses of land on Earth
5 a place where a river falls down from high rocks
6 a place where many people go on holiday
7 normal; usual
8 an activity that has an effect on you
9 a set of pages with news, adverts, articles, etc.
10 very old and typical of a style in the past

**The hidden word is** ___ ___ ___ ___ ___ ___ ___ ___ ___ ___.

# 9 Grammar

## 9.1 Relative Pronouns

Χρησιμοποιούμε **relative pronouns** (αναφορικές αντωνυμίες) σε relative clauses που μας δίνουν τις πληροφορίες για να καταλάβουμε σε ποιόν ή σε τί αναφέρεται κάποιος. Όταν η relative pronoun είναι το αντικείμενο του ρήματος, χρησιμοποιούμε **who** ή **that** για να αναφερθούμε σε ανθρώπους και **which** ή **that** για να αναφερθούμε σε πράγματα.
→ *She's the girl **who/that** plays ice hockey.*
→ *Are they the ferries **which/that** go to the island?*

Όταν το *who, which* ή *that* είναι το υποκείμενο του ρήματος σε relative clause, μπορούμε να παραλείψουμε την relative pronoun.
→ *That's the town (**which/that**) we went to.*
→ *He's the travel agent (**who/that**) she bought tickets from.*
Μπορούμε να αντικαταστήσουμε το *who* με *whom* όταν είναι το υποκείμενο του ρήματος, αλλά αυτό είναι πιο επίσημο.
→ *He's the travel agent **whom** she bought tickets from.*

## 9.2 Adverbs

Τα adverbs (επιρρήματα) περιγράφουν τα ρήματα. Για να σχηματίσουμε τα adverbs βάζουμε *-ly* στην κατάληξη των επιθέτων:
*careful* ➣ *carefully, quiet* ➣ *quietly.* Στα επίθετα που τελειώνουν σε *-y*, αλλάζουμε το *-y* σε *-i* και βάζουμε *-ly.*
Μερικά επίθετα που τελειώνουν σε *-e* χάνουν το *-e: true* ➣ truly, *terrible* ➣ terribly.
Όμως κάποια δεν το χάνουν: *sure* ➣ surely.

### Irregular Adverbs

**Σημείωση:** Μερικές λέξεις όπως *hard, late, straight* και *fast* είναι και επίθετα και επιρρήματα. Irregular adverbs (ανώμαλα επιρρήματα) συμπεριλαμβάνουν τη λέξη *well.*
→ *He's a good player. He plays **well**.*
Άλλες λέξεις όπως *friendly, lovely, silly* και *ugly* αν και τελειώνουν σε *-ly*, δεν είναι επιρρήματα αλλά επίθετα.
Με το ρήμα *be* (*είμαι*) χρησιμοποιούμε επίθετα και όχι επιρρήματα.

## Grammar Exercises

**A** Complete the sentences with *who, whom, which* or – .

1 Are they the children _____ went on holiday with you?

2 You're the person _____ I met at camp last year.

3 The man _____ we sat next to on the plane owns the airline.

4 Where are the dogs _____ Amanda feeds every day?

5 Is this the bus _____ goes to Tower Bridge?

6 The woman _____ works at the hotel is very polite.

7 We can take the tram _____ leaves at eight.

8 This is the hotel _____ we stayed at for a week.

**B** Choose the correct answers (A, B or C).

1 That's the photo ___ I took at sunset.

A who        B –        C whom

2 The caravans ___ people park here are mostly from Germany.

A which        B they        C who

3 Is he the tour guide ___ took you around Barbados?

A who        B whom        C which

**4** The woman ___ lives next door is a taxi driver.

**A** that                 **B** which             **C** she

**5** Who was the girl ___ you met in Ireland?

**A** which              **B** –                   **C** her

**6** The employee to ___ you spoke is actually the shop manager.

**A** whom            **B** that               **C** –

**7** Are those the tortoises ___ you saw in the Galapagos islands?

**A** whom            **B** who               **C** that

**8** Tell me about a sight ___ is worth seeing here.

**A** it                    **B** –                   **C** which

**C Complete the sentences with the correct form of these words.**

beautiful   deep   fast   friend   good   hungry   late   love   secure   true

**1** They moved _____ to get away from the erupting volcano.

**2** Henry was _____ involved in the project to save the rainforests.

**3** Kate did very _____ in her geography test.

**4** The local people in the village were _____ and helpful to us.

**5** If you arrive at the airport _____, you'll miss the plane.

**6** People in Hawaii arrange flowers _____ to present them to visitors.

**7** Your new swimsuit is _____ .

**8** We ate _____ after the long walk in the hills.

**9** Make sure you tie the ropes _____ to stop the tents blowing away.

**10** I am _____ sorry to hear about your accident.

## Page121

**10.1** **funicular railway** (n) /fjuːˈnɪkjələ(r) ˈreɪlweɪ/
a railway that goes up and down a steep
hillside on a track by using strong metal ropes
to pull the carriages • *The hill was too steep to
climb quickly, so we went up on the funicular
railway.* ❖ τελεφερίκ

## Reading — Page 122

**10.2** **rickshaw** (n) /ˈrɪkʃɔː/
a two or three-wheeled vehicle pulled by sb
who cycles or runs in front of it, used like a
taxi in some Asian countries • *In the centre
of Hanoi, you can see young boys pedalling
rickshaws to carry passengers.* ❖ χειροκίνητο
ταξί, ρίκσο

**10.3** **reed** (adj) /riːd/
made of thick hard grass (reeds) • *Traditional
rice farmers carry their rice in large reed
baskets.* ➢ reed (n) ❖ καλαμένιος

**10.4** **battery** (n) /ˈbætri/
sth that you put in a machine or device to give
it electricity to make it work • *The TV control
isn't working because it needs new batteries.*
❖ μπαταρία

## Word Focus — Page 122

**10.5** **gear** (n) /ɡɪə(r)/
the equipment and special clothes that you
need to do sth • *We packed all our camping
gear into our rucksacks.* ➢ gear (v)
❖ εξοπλισμός δουλειάς/σπορ

**10.6** **floating market** (n) /ˈfləʊtɪŋ ˈmɑːkɪt/
an area where people sell their products from
flat boats tied up at the side of a river/port
• *The fishermen were selling fresh fish directly
at the floating market at the harbour.* ❖ πλωτή
αγορά

**10.7** **float** (v) /fləʊt/
move freely in water • *The boat began to float
towards the rocks when we stopped rowing.*
➢ floating (adj), float (n) ❖ επιπλέω

**10.8** **waterproof** (adj) /ˈwɔːtəpruːf/
that doesn't let water come through • *You
should wear a waterproof jacket and trousers
to go rafting.* ➢ waterproof (v, n) ❖ αδιάβροχος

## Reading — Pages 122-123

**10.9** **basket** (n) /ˈbɑːskɪt/
a kind of bag for carrying things in • *There's a
basket of fruit on the kitchen table.* ❖ καλάθι

**10.10** **Vietnam** (n) /ˌvjetˈnæm/
➢ Vietnamese (adj, n) ❖ Βιετνάμ

**10.11** **give sb a hand** (phr) /ɡɪv ˈsʌmbədi ə hænd/
help sb to do sth • *I'll give you a hand to move
those boxes.* ❖ βοηθάω κάποιον

**10.12** **fisherman** (n) /ˈfɪʃəmən/
sb who catches fish for food, often as a job
• *The local fishermen can't sail their fishing
boats today because of the bad weather.*
➢ fish (v, n), fishing (n) ❖ ψαράς

**10.13** **on your own** (phr) /ɒn jɔː(r) əʊn/
by yourself; alone • *Do you like listening to
music when you are on your own?* ❖ μόνος
σου

**10.14** **as well** (phr) /əz wel/
also; too • *The tour guide took us to the
temple and the local market as well.* ❖ επίσης

**10.15** **paddle** (n) /ˈpædl/
a pole with a flat end that you use to row a
boat • *Tom's raft got out of control when he
dropped a paddle in the river.* ➢ paddle (v),
❖ κουπί

### Equipment

| | |
|---|---|
| basket | gear |
| battery | paddle |

**10.16** **spot** (n) /spɒt/
a particular place • *They found the perfect
spot to stop for a picnic.* ➢ spot (v) ❖ σημείο

**10.17** **remove** (v) /rɪˈmuːv/
take away • *Terry removed the little fish from
the net and put it back into the sea.* ➢ remove
(v), removal (n) ❖ αφαιρώ

**10.18** **material** (n) /məˈtɪəriəl/
the thing(s) that sth is made of • *What kind of
material do they use to make these bags?*
➢ materialise (v), material (adj) ❖ υλικό

**10.19** **bamboo** (n) /ˌbæmˈbuː/
a tall plant with long stems like hard grass
• *The Chinese often use bamboo to make
furniture.* ➢ bamboo (adj) ❖ μπαμπού

**10.20** **advantage** (n) /ədˈvɑːntɪdʒ/
sth that is good about sth • *The advantage
of using the school bus is that you can chat
with your classmates on the way home from
school.* ➢ advantageous (adj) ❖ πλεονέκτημα
✎ Opp: disadvantage

**10.21** **firstly** (adv) /ˈfɜːstli/
first of all; the first point (is) • *I enjoyed the trip
for two reasons. Firstly, there were so many
activities to do.* ➢ first (adj,n) ❖ πρώτα απ' όλα

**10.22** **secondly** (adv) /ˈsekəndli/
the second point (is) • *Secondly, the
landscape was beautiful, so we took loads of
photos.* ➢ second (adj, n) ❖ δεύτερον, επίσης

**10.23** **wave** (n) /weɪv/
a large mass of water flowing, e.g. in the sea
• *Suddenly, a big wave came and covered the
beach.* ➢ wave (v) ❖ κύμα

**10.24** **change your mind** (phr) /tʃeɪndʒ jɔː(r)
maɪnd/
change your opinion or decision • *Kevin
wanted to go to Alaska, but he changed his
mind when he found out the cost.* ❖ αλλάζω
γνώμη

**10.25** **platform** (n) /ˈplætfɔːm/
the part of a train station where you get on or
off a train • *Which platform does the train to
Edinburgh leave from?* ❖ πλατφόρμα

**10.26** **delay** (v) /dɪˈleɪ/
make sth happen later than planned • *The
snow on the road delayed the traffic.*
➢ delayed (adj), delay (n) ❖ καθυστερώ

**10.27** **heavy** (adj) /ˈhevi/
difficult to lift because of having a lot of weight
• *Could you help me to carry these heavy
bags, please?* ➢ heaviness (n) ❖ βαρύς

**10.28** **gondola** (n) /ˈɡɒndələ/
a traditional kind of long flat boat used in
Venice • *Tourists can enjoy a ride on a
gondola on the canals in Venice.* ❖ γόνδολα

**10.29** **rowing boat** (n) /ˈrəʊɪŋ bəʊt/
a small boat that you move by using paddles
• *We rented a small rowing boat to go around
the island on the lake.* ➢ row (v) ❖ βάρκα με
κουπιά

**10.30** **overhead** (adj) /ˌəʊvəˈhed/
in a place above your head • *I put my suitcase
on the overhead shelf on the train.*
➢ overhead (adv) ❖ πάνω από το κεφάλι

**10.31** **old fashioned** (adj) /əʊld ˈfæʃnd/
not modern; in an old style • *They enjoyed an
old fashioned British meal of fish and chips.*
❖ παλαιομοδίτικος

**10.32** **well-used** (adj) /wel juːst/
that has been used a lot for a long time • *The
well-used café at the station has been there
for years.* ❖ πολυχρησιμοποιημένο

# Vocabulary   Pages 124-125

**10.33** **coach** (n) /kəʊtʃ/
a large bus • *You can take a coach trip to
Olympia for a few days to see the ancient
stadium.* ❖ ταξιδιωτικό λεωφορείο

## Look!

Θυμηθείτε ότι στην Unit 8 είδαμε τη λέξη
**coach** να σημαίνει *προπονητής*. Εδώ όμως
χρησιμοποιούμε την ίδια λεξη για να πούμε
*ταξιδιωτικό λεωφορείο*!
*Our basketball **coach** took us on a **coach**
trip.* (= Ο προπονητής του μπάσκετ μας πήγε
εκδρομή με ταξιδιωτικό λεωφορείο.)

**10.34** **ferry** (n) /ˈferi/
a ship that carries passengers and vehicles
across an area of water • *Keith drove his truck
onto the ferry to travel to Crete.* ➢ ferry (v)
❖ φέρρυ

**10.35** **taxi** (n) /ˈtæksi/
a car with a driver that you pay to take you
somewhere • *There was a long line of taxis
waiting outside the train station.* ➢ taxi (v)
❖ ταξί

**10.36** **protect** (v) /prəˈtekt/
take care of yourself/sth/sb, e.g. to avoid
damage or getting hurt • *Wear a thick jacket
to protect you from the cold wind.* ➢ protective
(adj), protection (n) ❖ προστατεύω

**10.37** **deck** (n) /dek/
a floor on a ship • *Sue and Len sat on the
seats on the top deck of the ferry to watch the
sea gulls flying past.* ❖ κατάστρωμα

**10.38** **captain** (n) /ˈkæptɪn/
sb who is in charge of a ship or plane • *When
the ship moved near the rocks, the captain told
everyone to put on their life jackets.*
❖ καπετάνιος

**10.39** **van** (n) /væn/
a type of big car, usually with no windows on
the sides that you use to carry things or people
• *The Maxwells rented a small van to move
their furniture to their new flat.* ❖ φορτηγάκι,
βαν

**10.40** **airport** (n) /ˈeəpɔːt/
a place where planes arrive and leave from
with areas for passengers to wait, etc. • *We
live near the airport, so there are planes flying
above our house every day.* ❖ αεροδρόμιο

**10.41** **motorway** (n) /ˈməʊtəweɪ/
a wide road where cars can travel very fast
between towns • *There was an accident on
the motorway when a truck tried to drive on the
wrong side of the road.* ❖ αυτοκινητόδρομος

**10.42** **port** (n) /pɔːt/
a place where ships go to let people get on and off, or for sb to move things onto or out of them • *The tourists waved goodbye as the ship was leaving the island port.* ❖ λιμάνι

**10.43** **diploma** (n) /dɪˈpləʊmə/
a paper to show you have finished a course of study, e.g. at a college or school • *Betty studied for her teaching diploma at Dundee University.* ❖ πτυχίο

**10.44** **driving licence** (n) /ˈdraɪvɪŋ ˈlaɪsns/
a paper to show that sb has passed a driving test • *Alison took her test twice before she passed and got her driving licence.*
❖ δίπλωμα οδήγησης

**10.45** **exit** (n) /ˈeksɪt/
a place where cars can drive off a motorway to get on to another road • *When you drive down the motorway from Glasgow, take the first exit to join the road to Lanark.* ➣ exit (v) ❖ έξοδος (από αυτοκινητόδρομο)

**10.46** **journey** (n) /ˈdʒɜːni/
an act of travelling from one place to another • *Yvonne sometimes feels sick when she goes on long bus journeys.* ❖ ταξίδι

**10.47** **fare** (n) /feə(r)/
the amount you pay for a ticket to travel • *How much is the bus fare to Patra from Athens?*
❖ αντίτιμο εισιτηρίου

**10.48** **standard** (adj) /ˈstændəd/
usual; normal • *You can travel at any time with a standard train ticket or pay a cheaper fare to travel at midday only.* ➣ standardise (v), standard (n) ❖ κανονικός

**10.49** **return (ticket)** (n) /rɪˈtɜːn (ˈtɪkɪt)/
a ticket for a two-way journey (to go somewhere and come back) • *It's cheaper to buy a return ticket on the train than to pay for only one way.* ➣ return (v) ❖ εισιτήριο μετ' επιστροφής

**10.50** **packed** (adj) /pækt/
full of people • *The metro is always packed when people go to work in the morning.*
➣ pack (v) ❖ γεμάτος, συνωστισμένος
✎ Syn: crowded

**10.51** **pick sb up** (phr v) /pɪk ˈsʌmbədi ʌp/
collect sb (e.g. to take them with you in your car) • *The taxi will be here to pick us up in half an hour.* ❖ παίρνω κάποιον/κάτι για να μεταφέρω κάπου

**10.52** **get into** (phr v) /get ˈɪntə/
to enter sth (e.g. car, a building) • *The thieves got into a blue van and escaped with the cash.*
❖ εισέρχομαι

**10.53** **drop sb off** (phr v) /drɒp ˈsʌmbədi ɒf/
leave sb somewhere after taking them in a car, taxi, etc. • *My mum can take us in her car and drop us off at the swimming pool.* ➣ drop-off (adj) ❖ αφήνω κάποιον (από Ι.Χ.)

**10.54** **drive off** (phr v) /draɪv ɒf/
leave in a car • *Sam got into his car and drove off quickly.* ❖ αναχωρώ με αυτοκίνητο

**Phrasal Verbs**

| | |
|---|---|
| drive off | get into |
| drop sb off | pick sb up |

**Phrases**

| | |
|---|---|
| change your mind | on foot |
| give sb a hand | on my own |

**10.55** **properly** (adv) /ˈprɒpəli/
correctly; in the right way for the situation • *Ted has a problem with his motorbike because the mechanic hasn't fixed the engine properly.* ➣ proper (adj) ❖ δεόντως, σωστά

**10.56** **pilot** (n) /ˈpaɪlət/
sb who flies a plane • *The pilot welcomed all the passengers when they sat down on the plane.* ➣ pilot (v) ❖ πιλότος, κυβερνήτης

**10.57** **co-pilot** (n) /kəʊ ˈpaɪlət/
a pilot who helps another pilot to fly a plane • *When the pilot took a quick break, the co-pilot was in control of the plane.* ➣ co-pilot (v) ❖ συγκυβερνήτης

**10.58** **public transport** (n) /ˈpʌblɪk ˈtrænspɔːt/
all the ways for people to travel in a country/city that the government provides, e.g. bus, metro • *It's cheap to use public transport in my town, but you have to wait a long time for a bus.* ❖ δημόσια συγκοινωνία, μέσα μαζικής μεταφοράς

**Types of Transport**

| | |
|---|---|
| airline | public transport |
| carriage | rickshaw |
| coach | rowing boat |
| ferry | steam train |
| funicular railway | taxi |
| gondola | van |

# Grammar

Pages 126-127

**10.59** **focus (on)** (v) /ˈfəʊkəs (ɒn)/
give all your attention (to sth) • *I can't go out much this week because I have to focus on studying for my exams.* ➤ focussed (adj), focus (n) ❖ εστιάζω σε

**10.60** **steal** (v) /stiːl/
take sth that belongs to sb else without permission • *Somebody stole Katy's bag when she was on the metro.* ➤ stolen (adj), stealing (n) ❖ κλέβω

**10.61** **change** (n) /tʃeɪndʒ/
money you get back when you give more money than you need to pay for sth • *Make sure you get the correct change when you pay for something at the shop.* ➤ change (v) ❖ ρέστα

**10.62** **airline** (n) /ˈeəlaɪn/
a company that has planes to fly people and things to different places • *Some cheaper airlines don't include the price of food or drinks in the air fare.* ❖ αεροπορική εταιρία

**10.63** **diamond** (n) /ˈdaɪəmənd/
a clear hard stone used for making jewellery and for cutting glass • *The thief stole diamond necklaces and rings from the jewellery shop.* ➤ diamond (adj) ❖ διαμάντι

## Material

| | |
|---|---|
| reed | diamond |
| bamboo | |

**10.64** **Bolivia** (n) /bəˈlɪviə/
➤ Bolivian (adj, n), Bolivia (n) ❖ Βολιβία

**10.65** **mountainous** (adj) /ˈmaʊntənəs/
with a lot of mountains • *The Scottish Highlands are a famous mountainous area which attracts many climbers from around the world.* ➤ mountain (n), mountaineer (n), mountaineering (n) ❖ ορεινός

**10.66** **highlands** (n pl) /ˈhaɪləndz/
an area of land that has a lot of high mountains • *They went skiing in the snowy highlands of Aspen in winter.* ➤ highland (adj), highlander (n) ❖ υψίπεδα

**10.67** **lowlands** (n pl) /ˈləʊləndz/
an area of land that has low hills and flat valleys • *Dylan has a sheep farm in the lowlands of Wales near the English border.* ➤ lowland (adj), lowlander (n) ❖ πεδινά

**10.68** **narrow** (adj) /ˈnærəʊ/
having a short distance between one side and the other • *The bridge was too narrow for two cars to cross at the same time, so they're building a wider one.* ➤ narrow (v) ❖ στενός

**10.69** **death** (n) /deθ/
the state of being dead; the time that sb dies • *After the death of Agamemnon, one of his killers, Aegistheus, became King of Mycenae.* ➤ die (v), dead (adj) ❖ θάνατος

**10.70** **path** (n) /pɑːθ/
a narrow track where people can walk • *We walked up the path right to the top of Ben Nevis.* ❖ μονοπάτι

**10.71** **on foot** (phr) /ɒn fʊt/
by walking • *Our hotel was near the sea, so it was easy to get to the beach on foot.* ❖ πεζός, με τα πόδια

**10.72** **local** (adj) /ˈləʊkl/
connected to one area • *The local bus stops at every village on the island.* ➤ localise (v), local (n) ❖ τοπικός

**10.73** **view** (n) /vjuː/
what you can see from a place (often talking about a beautiful sight) • *We watched the view of the countryside from the window of the train.* ➤ view (v), viewing (adj), viewer (n) ❖ θέα

## Adjectives

| | |
|---|---|
| circular | overhead |
| heavy | packed |
| impressive | popular |
| local | reed |
| mountainous | Vietnamese |
| narrow | waterproof |
| old fashioned | well-used |

# Listening

Page 128

**10.74** **quarter to** (phr) /ˈkwɔːtə(r) tuː/
15 minutes before a particular hour • *I left at quarter to eight this morning and took the eight o'clock bus.* ❖ παρά τέταρτο

**10.75** **a quarter past** (phr) /ə ˈkwɔːtə(r) pɑːst/
15 minutes after a particular hour • *I missed the eight o'clock bus because I reached the bus stop at a quarter past.* ❖ και τέταρτο

**10.76** **noon** (n) /nuːn/
12 o'clock at midday • *They stopped working at noon for a lunch break.* ❖ μεσημβρία, μεσημέρι

**10.77** **end** (v) /end/
to finish • *When the long journey ended, they felt glad to be back home.* ➤ end (n) ❖ φτάνω στο τέλος, τελειώνω

**10.78** **cruise** (n) /kruːz/
a journey by sea, sometimes with accommodation on a ship • *The travel agent offered us tickets for a cruise on the River Seine.* ➤ cruise (v, n) ❖ κρουαζιέρα

**10.79** **circular** (adj) /'sɜːkjələ(r)/
that is round in shape; that moves around in a circle ● *There's a circular route around the city to avoid driving through the centre.*
➣ circle (v, n) ❖ κυκλικός

**10.80** **last** (v) /lɑːst/
to keep going for a certain amount of time ● *I wish my holiday could last forever.*
➣ lasting (adj) ❖ διαρκώ

**Time**

| | |
|---|---|
| end | quarter to |
| last | a quarter past |
| midsummer | rush hour |
| noon | timetable |

# Speaking
**Page 129**

**10.81** **gate** (n) /geɪt/
the part of an airport where you go to get on a plane ● *If you don't have any luggage, you can check in online and go straight to the boarding gate at the airport.* ❖ πύλη

**10.82** **dot** (n) /dɒt/
a full stop; the symbol: . ● *Is there a dot between your names on your email address?*
➣ dot (v), dotted (adj) ❖ τελεία

**10.83** **slash** (n) /slæʃ/
the symbol: / used to separate words, etc. ● *There are two slashes after the letters http: in the web address.* ➣ slash (v) ❖ κάθετος

**10.84** **dash** (n) /dæʃ/
the symbol: – used to separate parts of a sentence, etc. ● *Sometimes we can use dashes instead of commas when we're writing.* ❖ παύλα

**Places**

| | |
|---|---|
| airport | lowlands |
| deck | platform |
| gate | port |
| highlands | terminus |

# Writing
**Pages 130-131**

**10.85** **midsummer** (n) /mɪd'sʌmə(r)/
the middle of summer (in June in the northern countries and December in the southern countries of the world) ● *In the north of Scotland, it only gets dark for a few hours on a midsummer night in June.* ❖ κατακαλόκαιρο

**10.86** **Norway** (n) /'nɔːweɪ/
➣ Norwegian (adj, n) ❖ Νορβηγία

**10.87** **accept** (v) /ək'sept/
take sth that sb offers ● *Michelle accepted her friend's offer of accommodation at her country house for the weekend.* ➣ acceptable (adj), acceptance (n) ❖ δέχομαι

**10.88** **decline** (v) /dɪ'klaɪn/
say 'no' to sth that sb offers ● *I declined the party invitation because I had a bad cold.*
➣ decline (n) ❖ αρνούμαι

**10.89** **splish splash** (phr) /splɪʃ splæʃ/
an expression describing the sound of splashing in water ● *The children were splishing and splashing in the pool.* ❖ πλιτς πλατς

**10.90** **unfortunately** (adv) /ʌn'fɔːtʃənətli/
sadly; unluckily; used to show that you're unhappy about sth that happens or doesn't happen ● *Unfortunately, we had to cancel the barbecue because of the rain.* ➣ unfortunate (adj) ❖ δυστυχώς

**10.91** **wellies** (n pl) /'weliz/
long waterproof boots; Wellington boots ● *It's raining, so put your wellies on to go to school.* ❖ γαλότσες

# Video 10
# Travelling in India
**Page 132**

**10.92** **carriage** (n) /'kærɪdʒ/
the part of a train that passengers sit in ● *Gwyneth got a seat in the first-class carriage of the Trans-Siberian train.* ➣ carry (v) ❖ βαγόνι

**10.93** **rush hour** (n) /rʌʃ 'aʊə(r)/
the busiest times of day on the streets when people are going to or coming home from work ● *It's hard to get a seat on the bus during the rush hour.* ❖ ώρα αιχμής

**10.94** **steam train** (n) /stiːm treɪn/
an old fashioned train whose engine moves using steam ● *We went inside the old steam train at the transport museum.* ❖ τραίνο με ατμομηχανή

**10.95** **track** (n) /træk/
the lines that a train moves along ● *Some country roads cross the railway track and drivers have to be very careful.* ➣ track (v), tracking (adj) ❖ σιδηροδρομική γραμμή

**10.96** **railway** (n) /'reɪlweɪ/
the system of tracks that trains travel on ● *The children were playing with the trains on their model railway.* ➣ railway (adj) ❖ σιδηρόδρομος

**10.97** **impressive** (adj) /ɪmˈpresɪv/
that you admire because it is sth good, well-made, etc. • *The new railway station looks very impressive. It's much bigger and better than the old one.* ➢ impress (v), impression (n) ❖ εντυπωσιακός

**10.98** **employer** (n) /ɪmˈplɔɪə(r)/
a person or company who has others working for them • *Most employers don't pay their workers very well in Greece.* ➢ employ (v), employment (n), employee (n) ❖ εργοδότης

**10.99** **terminus** (n) /ˈtɜːmɪnəs/
the first and/or last stop on the route of a bus or train, etc. • *Get off the bus at the terminus and I'll meet you there.* ❖ τερματικός σταθμός

---

**Types of Road**

| | |
|---|---|
| track | motorway |
| railway | |
| path | |

**People & Jobs**

| | |
|---|---|
| co-pilot | mechanic |
| crowd | pilot |
| employer | reporter |
| fisherman | traveller |

---

# Vocabulary Exercises

**A** Complete the word groups with these words.

bamboo   battery   co-pilot   employer   material   motorway   paddle   platform   rowing boat   spot   track   van

| | | | |
|---|---|---|---|
| **1** captain | fisherman | _____ | _____ |
| **2** gate | terminus | _____ | _____ |
| **3** gondola | steam train | _____ | _____ |
| **4** basket | gear | _____ | _____ |
| **5** railway | path | _____ | _____ |
| **6** diamond | reed | _____ | _____ |

**B** Complete the sentences with the words from Exercise A.

**1** They rented a small _____ to go across the lake to the island.

**2** The bus _____ is in the centre of the town.

**3** We were told to put on our life jackets by the ship's _____ .

**4** The train runs along the _____ next to the road.

**5** Tom put the boxes into the back of his _____ and drove home.

**6** The _____ of fruit was too heavy to carry.

**7** Did you know you can use a _____ to cut a hole in a window?

**8** What kind of _____ are those curtains made of?

**9** The car was racing down the _____ towards the airport.

**10** This is a popular _____ where many tourists stop to take photos of the view.

**C** Circle the correct words.

**1** Welies are useful because they're **waterproof** / **old fashioned** / **heavy**.

**2** The captain stood on the top **port** / **deck** / **ferry** of the ship looking out to sea.

**3** I had to stand on the bus because it was absolutely **popular** / **packed** / **standard**.

**4** Can you give me some **change** / **fare** / **slash** for the ticket machine?

**5** The **narrow** / **well-used** / **local** fisherman offered to take us on a boat trip.

**6** Our ferry was **departed** / **served** / **delayed** because of the bad weather.

**7** Did you travel to the top of the mountain on your **foot** / **own** / **view**?

**8** How long did the boat ride **last** / **end** / **float**?

**D  Read the meanings and complete the words.**

1  a trip by sea, sometimes with a bedroom on a ship          c __ __ __ __ __
2  an act of travelling from one place to another              j __ __ __ __ __ __
3  a large mass of water flowing, e.g. in the sea              w __ __ __
4  somebody who is travelling                                  t __ __ __ __ __ __ __ __
5  the middle part of summer                                   m __ __ __ __ __ __ __ __
6  unluckily; unhappily                                        u __ __ __ __ __ __ __ __ __ __ __ y
7  something that could happen or could be done                p __ __ __ __ __ __ __ __ __ y
8  something said in public to tell people about something     a __ __ __ __ __ __ __ __ __ t

**E  Complete the story with these words.**

accept   change   decline   drive   drop   get   give   focus   pick   steal

It was raining heavily when Pauline went to the car park to ¹ _____ into her car. As she was walking towards it, she saw a boy next to the car. She thought he was trying to ² _____ it, but then she saw that he was crying. He was upset because his dad wasn't there to ³ _____ him up. Pauline offered to ⁴ _____ him off at home. The boy was going to ⁵ _____ at first because he didn't know Pauline. Then he decided to ⁶ _____ his mind because he really needed help. Pauline started driving, but the rain was so heavy that she couldn't ⁷ _____ on the road. Unfortunately, her car broke down on the motorway, but then a man got out of a taxi and offered to ⁸ _____ her a hand. Pauline didn't want to ⁹ _____ his help, but it was the boy's dad who was a mechanic! Soon Pauline was able to ¹⁰ _____ off and everyone got home happily.

# 10 Grammar

## 10.1 The Passive Voice: Tenses

Χρησιμοποιούμε **passive voice** (παθητική φωνή) όταν:
η πράξη είναι πιο σημαντική από αυτόν ή αυτό που ευθύνεται γι' αυτήν (the agent/ποιητικό αίτιο).
→ *The rickshaws were pulled by people on bicycles.*
δεν γνωρίζουμε το ποιητικό αίτιο (the agent), ή δεν είναι σημαντικό, ή εννοείται.
→ *Cars* **are made** *in this factory.*

Μετατρέπουμε μια ενεργητική πρόταση σε παθητική με τον παρακάτω τρόπο:
Το αντικείμενο του ρήματος της ενεργητικής πρότασης γίνεται υποκείμενο του ρήματος της παθητικής πρότασης. Το ρήμα *be* χρησιμοποιείται στον ίδιο χρόνο με το κύριο ρήμα της ενεργητικής πρότασης, μαζί με την παθητική μετοχή (past participle) του κυρίου ρήματος της ενεργητικής πρότασης.
→ *They* **buy** *magazines here.* → *Magazines* **are bought** *here.*
Σε αυτό το παράδειγμα, δεν γνωρίζουμε ή δεν είναι σημαντικό ποιοί αγοράζουν περιοδικά, και έτσι δεν χρησιμοποιούμε τη λέξη *they* στην παθητική πρόταση.

**Σημείωση:** Όταν είναι σημαντικό να αναφέρουμε το ποιητικό αίτιο (agent) στην παθητική πρόταση, χρησιμοποιούμε τη λέξη *by*. Όταν θέλουμε να αναφέρουμε κάποιο εργαλείο ή υλικό στην παθητική πρόταση, χρησιμοποιούμε τη λέξη *with*.
→ *A local fisherman* **caught** *the fish.*
→ *The fish* **was caught by** *a local fisherman.*
→ *The fish* **was caught with** *a net.*

## 10.2 The Passive Voice: Present Simple

Σχηματίζουμε την passive voice με το present simple του ρήματος *be* και past participle (παθητική μετοχή).

| Tense | Active | Passive |
|---|---|---|
| Present Simple | take/takes | am/are/is taken |

## 10.3 The Passive Voice: Past Simple

Σχηματίζουμε την passive voice με τον past simple του ρήματος *be* και past participle (παθητική μετοχή).

| Tense | Active | Passive |
|---|---|---|
| Past Simple | took | was/were taken |

# Grammar Exercises

**A**  Complete the sentences with the present simple passive form of the verbs in brackets.

1  Public transport _____ (use) by many people in the city.
2  Lots of photos _____ (take) here by tourists.
3  Traditional music _____ (play) at this festival.
4  The streets _____ (always/decorate) at Christmas.
5  If you _____ (stop) at passport control, what will you do?
6  I _____ (tell) to tidy my room every week.
7  _____ (you/drive) to school by car?
8  Where _____ (the tickets/sell)?

**B** Rewrite the sentences. Use the passive voice.

1 Somebody drove the coach to the port.

   _____

2 The police caught the car thief.

   _____

3 A mechanic repaired the van quickly.

   _____

4 Did they find the fishing boat?

   _____

5 They gave me the wrong change at the petrol station.

   _____

6 When did they build the new motorway?

   _____

7 Why did they change the bus timetable?

   _____

8 They ate all the food at the barbecue.

   _____

**C** Complete the second sentences with the passive voice. Use *by* or *with* if necessary.

1 My grandma bought my new sunglasses.
   My new sunglasses _____ .

2 Do they serve food on this plane?
   On this plane, _____ ?

3 Someone used a rock to break the shop window.
   The shop window _____ .

4 Somebody stole Andrew's smartphone.
   Andrew's smartphone _____ .

5 The pilot told the noisy passenger to get off the plane.
   The noisy passenger _____ .

6 They used a webcam to take those photos.
   Those photos _____ .

7 The local fishermen catch loads of fish at night.
   Loads of fish _____ .

8 Snow sometimes causes traffic delays.
   Traffic delays _____ .

# 11 It's Raining Cats & Dogs

**11.1** **be raining cats and dogs** (phr) /bi 'reɪnɪŋ kæts ənd dɒgs/
be raining heavily • *We ran home quickly because it was raining cats and dogs.*
❖ βρέχει καρεκλοπόδαρα / κατακλυσμός

**11.2** **stranded** (adj) /'strændəd/
stuck in a place because you have no way to get away from there • *After the plane crash, the passengers were stranded on an island for days before help came.* ➣ strand (v)
❖ απομονωμένος, αποκλεισμένος

**11.3** **tractor** (n) /'træktə(r)/
a heavy vehicle used for pulling equipment or moving sth, often used on a farm • *The farmer was digging his field with his tractor.* ❖ τρακτέρ

**11.4** **flooding** (n) /'flʌdɪŋ/
when a lot of water comes onto a dry area and suddenly covers it • *The heavy rain caused flooding in some fields near the river.* ➣ flood (v, n), flooded (adj) ❖ πλημμύρα

## Reading                                    Page 136

**11.5** **sunshine** (n) /'sʌnʃaɪn/
the light and warmth from the sun • *Let's go out for a walk and enjoy the sunshine.*
➣ sunny (adj) ❖ λιακάδα

**11.6** **bury** (v) /'beri/
put sth in the ground and cover it • *The whole town was buried by rocks and ash when the volcano erupted.* ➣ burial (n), buried (adj)
❖ θάβω

**11.7** **collapse** (v) /kə'læps/
fall down suddenly • *The old wall collapsed when the car crashed into it.* ➣ collapse (n), collapsed (adj) ❖ καταρρέω

**11.8** **injure** (v) /'ɪndʒə(r)/
hurt a part of the body • *Luckily, nobody was injured in the accident.* ➣ injury (n), injured (adj) ❖ τραυματίζω

**11.9** **trap** (v) /træp/
put sth in a place where it's impossible to leave • *The cars were trapped in the snow and couldn't move.* ➣ trap (n) ❖ παγιδεύω

## Word Focus                                 Page 136

**11.10** **sting** (v) /stɪŋ/
touch the skin in a way that hurts and you feel a sudden pain • *Have you ever been stung by a bee?* ➣ sting (n), stinging (adj) ❖ τσιμπάω, κεντρίζω

**11.11** **sharp** (adj) /ʃɑːp/
sudden and painful, like being cut • *Helen felt a sharp pain on her arm when the insect stung her.* ➣ sharpen (v), sharply (adv) ❖ αιχμηρός, μυτερός

**11.12** **somehow** (adv) /'sʌmhaʊ/
in a way that's not known • *We had to find a way to get home somehow.* ❖ κάπως

**11.13** **heater** (n) /'hiːtə(r)/
a machine that gives heat • *I have a small electric heater in my bedroom to keep warm when I'm studying.* ➣ heat (v), hot (adj)
❖ θερμάστρα

## Reading                          Pages 136-137

**11.14** **day out** (n) /deɪ aʊt/
a day trip or visit somewhere • *They had an enjoyable day out at the park.* ❖ ημερήσια έξοδος

**11.15** **such** (det) /sʌtʃ/
used before a noun for emphasis • *There was such a lot of snow last weekend.* ❖ τόσο

**11.16** **impossible** (adj) /ɪm'pɒsəbl/
not possible; that can't happen • *It was almost impossible to find a hotel room in Rome in August, but we finally found a small bed and breakfast.* ➣ impossibility (n), impossibly (adv)
❖ αδύνατον
✎ Opp: possible

**11.17** **go-karting** (n) /'gəʊ kɑːtɪŋ/
racing around a track in a small open car
• *There's a go-karting track near the beach and it's fun to drive around it.* ❖ γκο-καρτ

**11.18** **escape** (v) /ɪ'skeɪp/
get away from an unpleasant place or situation
• *The thieves were caught while they were trying to escape in a stolen car.* ➣ escape (n)
❖ διαφεύγω, δραπετεύω

**11.19** **shoulder** (n) /'ʃəʊldə(r)/
where your arm is connected to the part of your body • *You have to hold the violin on your shoulder and under your chin to play it.*
➣ shoulder (v) ❖ ώμος

**11.20** **expect** (v) /ɪk'spekt/
wait for sth that you think will happen • *I didn't expect to see you at the library. I thought you didn't like reading books.* ➣ expectation (n)
❖ αναμένω

**11.21** **weather forecast** (n) /'weðə fɔːkɑːst/
a description of how sb says the weather will be the next few days • *We should check the weather forecast before we go hiking.*
❖ πρόγνωση καιρού

**11.22** **thunderstorm** (n) /ˈθʌndəstɔːm/
a storm with thunder and lightning • *It was scary travelling by plane to Crete during the thunderstorm.* ❖ καταιγίδα

# Vocabulary   Pages 138-139

**11.23** **fog** (n) /fɒg/
thick clouds that are low down and close to the land • *The drivers went slowly through the fog because they couldn't see the road very well.* ➢ fog (v), foggy (adj) ❖ ομίχλη

**11.24** **storm** (n) /stɔːm/
very bad weather with strong wind and usually rain or snow • *The storm only lasted for an hour, but a lot of trees were damaged by the wind.* ➢ storm (v), stormy (adj) ❖ θύελλα

**11.25** **icy** (adj) /ˈaɪsi/
very cold; covered with ice • *It's dangerous to drive on icy roads.* ➢ ice (v, n), icily (adv) ❖ παγωμένος

**11.26** **snowy** (adj) /ˈsnəʊi/
with a lot of snow • *The snowy hills looked beautiful from the distance.* ➢ snow (v, n) ❖ χιονισμένος

**11.27** **windy** (adj) /ˈwɪndi/
with a strong wind • *It was so windy at the seaside that the beach umbrellas blew away.* ➢ wind (n) ❖ ανεμώδης

**11.28** **away** (adv) /əˈweɪ/
to another place • *My hat blew away off the boat and into the sea.* ❖ μακριά

**11.29** **sink** (v) /sɪŋk/
drop down to the bottom of the sea, lake, river, etc. • *When the boat hit the rock, it began to sink into the river.* ➢ sunken (adj) ❖ βυθίζω

**11.30** **dull** (adj) /dʌl/
not bright; cloudy • *This dull weather is making everybody feel sad; we need some sunshine soon.* ➢ dullness (n) ❖ με χαμηλό φωτισμό

**11.31** **temperature** (n) /ˈtemprətʃə(r)/
how hot or cold sth/sb is • *The temperature in Moscow is very low in winter.* ❖ θερμοκρασία

**11.32** **cool** (adj) /kuːl/
quite cold • *It was very hot at the beach, so we swam in the cool water.* ➢ cool (v), coolly (adv) ❖ δροσερός

**11.33** **degrees Celsius** (phr) /dɪˈgriːs ˈselsiəs/
the measure of temperatures in centigrade • *Water freezes at zero degrees Celsius.* ❖ βαθμοί Κελσίου

**11.34** **What's sb/sth like?** (phr) /wɒts ˈsʌmbədi/ ˈsʌmθɪŋ ˈlaɪk/
used to ask about sb's character, or how sth is • *What's your tennis coach like? Do you recommend her?* ❖ Πώς είναι κάποιος/κάτι; (σαν χαρακτήρας ή εμπειρία, κτλ.)

**11.35** **diary** (n) /ˈdaɪəri/
a book with spaces for each day of the year where you can keep note of things to do or write about what you do or think each day • *It was fascinating to read Grandma's old diary that she wrote as a teenager.* ❖ ημερολόγιο

**11.36** **bush fire** (n) /bʊʃ ˈfaɪə(r)/
a fire that spreads quickly across open countryside • *Some of the farm buildings were burnt in the bush fire that spread all over the area this summer.* ❖ πυρκαγιά στη φύση που σβήνει δύσκολα

**11.37** **lightning** (n) /ˈlaɪtnɪŋ/
a bright flash of light in the sky caused by electricity • *The castle tower fell down when it was struck by lightning.* ❖ αστραπή

**11.38** **thunder** (n) /ˈθʌndə(r)/
a loud noise from the sky after lightning appears • *There was a flash of lightning and then we heard the sound of thunder.* ➢ thunder (v), thunderous (adj) ❖ μπουμπουνητό, κεραυνός

> ## Look!
> Προσέξτε τη διάφορα μεταξή **thunder** και **lightning**.
> *We heard the sound of **thunder** in the distance.* (= τον μπουμπουνητό ήχο)
> *The tree was hit by **lightning**.* (= την αστραπή)

**11.39** **drought** (n) /draʊt/
a long time without rain so the land is very dry • *Farmers in many countries in Africa have problems because of long droughts.* ❖ ξηρασία, λειψυδρία

**11.40** **destroy** (v) /dɪˈstrɔɪ/
damage sth so badly that you can't use it any more • *The farm was destroyed by fire, so the family had to find a new home.* ➢ destruction (n), destructive (adj) ❖ καταστρέφω

**11.41** **brick** (n) /brɪk/
sth like a stone which is man-made for building walls • *Most modern homes in the UK are made from bricks.* ❖ τούβλο

| **Weather Adjectives** | |
| --- | --- |
| clear | icy |
| cool | snowy |
| extreme | southerly |
| foggy | stormy |
| freezing | windy |

# Grammar

**11.42** **climate** (n) /ˈklaɪmət/
the patterns of weather in an area
• *Mediterranean countries have a warm climate.* ❖ κλίμα

**11.43** **southern** (adj) /ˈsʌðən/
in the south part of a country, continent, etc.
• *The weather in southern Australia is a bit cooler than in the northern part.* ❖ Νότιος

**11.44** **clear** (adj) /klɪə(r)/
sunny; without clouds • *It was a clear day, but the temperature wasn't very high.* ➤ clear (v), clearer (adv) ❖ αίθριος

**11.45** **jeep** (n) /dʒiːp/
a vehicle that you can drive off-road across rocky ground • *I'd rather cross the desert in a jeep than by camel.* ❖ τζιπ, 4X4

**11.46** **frightening** (adj) /ˈfraɪtnɪŋ/
that makes you afraid • *It was a frightening experience when our ship nearly sank.*
➤ frighten (v), fright (n), frightened (adj), frighteningly (adv) ❖ τρομακτικός

**11.47** **hurricane** (n) /ˈhʌrɪkən/
a very bad storm with extremely strong winds
• *The hurricane moved across the Atlantic and destroyed many homes in the West Indies.*
❖ τυφώνας

**11.48** **monsoon** (n) /ˌmɒnˈsuːn/
heavy seasonal rains in South Asia • *There was flooding on the railway tracks across Pakistan during the monsoon.* ❖ μουσώνας

**11.49** **heavily** (adv) /ˈhevɪli/
in a large amount • *The snow was falling so heavily that the road was covered in a few minutes.* ➤ heavy (n), heavy (adj) ❖ έντονα

**11.50** **serious** (adj) /ˈsɪəriəs/
with a bad effect; causing problems or danger
• *There was a serious accident on the street and a famous singer was killed.* ➤ seriousness (n), seriously (adv) ❖ σοβαρός

**11.51** **damage** (n) /ˈdæmɪdʒ/
physical harm to an object or building, etc.
• *The damage to his car was terrible and he couldn't drive it again.* ➤ damage (v), damaged (adj) ❖ ζημία

**11.52** **ocean** (n) /ˈəʊʃn/
one of the large areas of water that covers a large amount of the earth • *The Titanic sank when it was on its first voyage across the ocean.* ➤ oceanic (adj) ❖ ωκεανός

**11.53** **conditions** (n pl) /kənˈdɪʃns/
the situation around that has an effect on sth
• *The weather conditions were too bad for us to go sailing.* ➤ condition (v), conditional (adj), conditionally (adv) ❖ συνθήκες

**11.54** **extreme** (adj) /ɪkˈstriːm/
much more than normal • *Temperatures in the desert can go from extreme heat in the daytime to extreme cold at night.* ➤ extreme (n), extremely (adv) ❖ ακραίος

**11.55** **rainstorm** (n) /ˈreɪnstɔːm/
a storm with heavy rain • *The streets were covered in water after the rainstorm.*
❖ νεροποντή

**11.56** **heatwave** (n) /ˈhiːtweɪv/
a period of very hot weather • *It was too hot to go outside at midday during the summer heatwave.* ❖ καύσωνας

## Weather Nouns

| | |
|---|---|
| climate | monsoon |
| conditions | rainstorm |
| flood | snowstorm |
| flooding | storm |
| fog | sunshine |
| heatwave | thunder |
| hurricane | thunderstorm |
| lightning | weather forecast |

## Geography

| Nouns | Adjectives |
|---|---|
| atmosphere | coastal |
| bush fire | southern |
| ocean | deep |
| dust | |

**11.57** **atmosphere** (n) /ˈætməsfɪə(r)/
all the gases in the air around the earth
• *The atmosphere was filled with dust from the desert storm.* ➤ atmospheric (adj), atmospherically (adv) ❖ ατμόσφαιρα

**11.58** **evaporate** (v) /ɪˈvæpəreɪt/
liquid evaporates when it gets hot and turns into steam • *He forgot to switch off the cooker and the water in the spaghetti evaporated.*
➤ evaporation (n), evaporated (adj)
❖ εξατμίζω

**11.59** **record** (n) /ˈrekɔːd/
information that is written down to remember it • *It was the coldest winter on record in Scotland.* ➤ record (v, adj), recording (n)
❖ καταγραφή

**11.60** **occur** (v) /əˈkɜː(r)/
happen • *When the storm occurred, we were sailing in the Caribbean.* ➤ occurrence (n)
❖ συμβαίνει

**11.61** **the Pacific Ocean** (n) /ðə pəˌsɪfɪk ˈəʊʃn/
❖ ο Ειρηνικός Ωκεανός

**11.62**  **face** (v) /feɪs/
meet a situation that could be a problem
• *Simon faced a lot of dangers on his journey
through the jungle.* ➢ face (n) ❖ αντιμετωπίζω

# Listening  Page 142

**11.63**  **cm** (abbr) /ˈsiː em/
centimetre(s) • *There are 100 cm in a metre.*
❖ εκατοστό, cm

**11.64**  **km/h** (abbr) /ˌkeɪ em piː ˈeɪtʃ/
kilometres per hour • *The car was travelling at
200 km/h when it crashed.* ❖ χλμ/ώρα
✎ Syn: kph

**11.65**  **southerly** (adj) /ˈsʌðəli/
(of wind) moving from the south • *A southerly
wind brings warm air from Africa across the
Mediterranean.* ➢ south (n, adj) ❖ νότιος

**11.66**  **m** (abbr) /em/
metre(s) • *A block of ice fell from a roof just a
metre in front of Eric.* ❖ μέτρο

**11.67**  **minus** (adv) /ˈmaɪnəs/
used to talk about temperature below zero
• *The temperature was minus two, but it felt
like minus ten because of the north wind.* ❖
μείον

**11.68**  **distance** (n) /ˈdɪstəns/
how far it is between two places or things
• *They travelled a long distance by coach from
England to Spain.* ➢ distance (v), distant (adj)
❖ απόσταση

**11.69**  **compass** (n) /ˈkʌmpəs/
a device with an arrow that points to north to
show direction • *Before people used GPS,
they found their direction using a map and a
compass.* ❖ πυξίδα

---

**Measurements**

| | |
|---|---|
| compass | record |
| degrees Celsius | temperature |
| distance | cm |
| gallon | m |
| minus | km/h |
| pound | |

---

# Speaking  Page 143

**11.70**  **slightly** (adv) /ˈslaɪtli/
a little bit • *Today the temperature is slightly
colder than yesterday.* ➢ slight (adj)
❖ ελαφρώς

# Writing  Pages 144 -145

**11.71**  **Hyde Park** (n) /haɪd pærk/
a famous large park in London • *Let's relax
and take a walk around the lake in Hyde Park.*
❖ Χάιντ Παρκ

**11.72**  **Empire State Building** (n) /ˈempaɪə(r) steɪt
ˈbɪldɪŋ/
❖ Έμπαϊρ Στέητ Μπίλντιγκ

**11.73**  **exhausted** (adj) /ɪɡˈzɔːstɪd/
very tired • *The exhausted tourists had to stop
for a break at a local restaurant.* ➢ exhaust
(v), exhaustion (n) ❖ εξαντλημένος

**11.74**  **double-decker (bus)** (n) /ˈdʌbl ˈdekə(r) (bʌs)/
a bus that has two floors • *From the top of the
double-decker bus, we had a great view of
the famous buildings in London.* ❖ διώροφο
λεωφορείο

**11.75**  **Big Ben** (n) /ˈbɪg ˌben/
❖ Μπιγκ Μπεν

**11.76**  **Eiffel Tower** (n) /ˈaɪfl ˈtaʊə(r)/
❖ Πύργος του Άιφελ

---

**Vehicles**

| | |
|---|---|
| double-decker bus | jeep |
| go-karting | tractor |

---

**Famous Places & Buildings**

| | |
|---|---|
| Big Ben | Hyde Park |
| Eiffel Tower | the Pacific Ocean |
| Empire State Building | |

---

# Video 11
# Snow on Tigers  Page 146

**11.77**  **have a baby** (phr) /həv ə ˈbeɪbi/
give birth to a child • *My aunt had a baby last
month, so he's my new cousin.* ❖ αποκτώ
μωρό, γεννάω

**11.78**  **snowstorm** (n) /ˈsnəʊstɔːm/
sudden heavy snow with a strong wind
• *We watched the snowstorm outside from the
safety of our home.* ❖ χιονοθύελλα

**11.79**  **extra** (adj) /ˈekstrə/
more than usual • *Take an extra pen and
pencil when you go for the exam.* ➢ extra (n)
❖ επιπλέον

**11.80  earn** (v) /ɜːn/
get sth (usually money) for sth that you have done or made • *Photography is fun, but it's a hard way to earn a living.* ➣ earnings (n)
❖ κερδίζω

**11.81  cub** (n) /kʌb/
a baby tiger (also: baby lion, wolf, fox, bear, etc.) • *A female tiger feeds her cubs and protects them from danger.* ❖ κουτάβι τίγρης

**11.82  chore** (n) /tʃɔː(r)/
a small job that you have to do often • *I like listening to music while I'm doing all the boring chores like dusting.* ❖ αγγαρεία, δουλειά (π.χ. στο σπίτι)

**11.83  deliver** (v) /dɪˈlɪvə(r)/
bring sth to sb • *Brian delivers takeaway food with his small van.* ➣ delivery (n) ❖ παραδίδω

**11.84  pound** (n) /paʊnd/
a unit of weight (about 0.454 kilo) • *Theo bought a pound of cheese and some eggs.* ❖ λίβρα

## Look!

Η λέξη **pound** εδώ αφορά κάποιο βάρος (*λίβρα*) ενώ χρησιμοποιούμε την ίδια λέξη όταν μιλάμε για μια λίρα, το νόμισμα της Μεγάλης Βρετανίας.
*The box **weighs** four **pounds**.* (= λίβρες)
*The box **cost** four **pounds**.* (= λίρες)

**11.85  gallon** (n) /ˈɡælən/
a unit used to measure liquid (about 4.5 litres in the UK, Canada, Australia, etc., about 3.8 litres in the USA) • *Megan stopped at the service station to put a few gallons of petrol in her car.* ❖ γαλόνι

**11.86  simply** (adv) /ˈsɪmpli/
basically • *The heavy rain simply means that drivers have to be extra careful on the road.* ➣ simplify (v), simple (adj), simplicity (n)
❖ απλά, βασικά

### Verbs

| | |
|---|---|
| bury | escape |
| cancel | evaporate |
| cause | expect |
| collapse | face |
| damage | injure |
| deliver | sting |
| destroy | trap |
| earn | |

### Other Adjectives

| | |
|---|---|
| exhausted | serious |
| extra | sharp |
| frightening | stranded |
| impossible | |

### Adverbs

| | |
|---|---|
| heavily | simply |
| seriously | slightly |
| | somehow |

# Vocabulary Exercises

**A  Circle the odd one out.**

| | | | |
|---|---|---|---|
| **1** | bury | earn | trap |
| **2** | heater | jeep | tractor |
| **3** | escape | collapse | sink |
| **4** | hurricane | thunderstorm | atmosphere |
| **5** | sting | deliver | injure |
| **6** | clear | dull | sharp |
| **7** | dust | flood | ocean |
| **8** | extreme | serious | stranded |

**B** **Complete the sentences with words you did not circle in Exercise A.**

1 The cat was trying to _____ the bird to kill it.
2 We heard the sound of the farm _____ working on the field.
3 The passengers jumped into the sea as the ship began to _____ .
4 When the _____ hit the island, hundreds of trees were blown down.
5 Where did the bee _____ you?
6 It happened on a _____ sunny day in June.
7 The furniture on the first floor of our house got wet in the _____ .
8 The storm caused some _____ damage to our roof, so it needs repairs.

**C** **Complete the sentences with both words.**

1 **damaged**      **destroyed**
   Some of the buildings were completely _____ by the storm and many cars were badly _____ .
2 **gallon**        **pound**
   The farmer brought us a _____ of milk and a _____ of butter.
3 **cool**          **freezing**
   Yesterday was slightly _____ , but today it's absolutely _____ .
4 **southern**      **southerly**
   A strong _____ wind will reach the _____ part of the island tomorrow.
5 **climate**       **weather**
   Greece has a warm _____ and the _____ is usually quite dry in summer.
6 **lightning**     **thunder**
   When we saw the _____ across the sea, we counted the seconds before we heard the _____ .

**D** **Complete the sentences with words formed from the words in bold.**

1 Peter fell and broke his arm on the _____ path.                                          ICE
2 It was a bad accident, but nobody was _____ injured.                                      SERIOUS
3 The heavy snow made it _____ for the teams to play the football match.                    POSSIBLE
4 It was so _____ that we couldn't see more than a metre in front of us.                    FOG
5 There will be strong winds around the _____ areas tonight.                                COAST
6 The _____ had to get off his bike and walk home in the storm.                             CYCLE
7 It's unusual to have a _____ in Scotland, but sometimes it can be over 30°C in summer.     HEAT
8 I'm going to the beach to relax and enjoy the _____ .                                     SUN

**E** Find ten words from Unit 11. Then complete the sentences with these words.

| E | M | P | E | R | A | M | D | E | C | R | D |
|---|---|---|---|---|---|---|---|---|---|---|---|
| T | R | C | O | M | P | O | S | S | B | U | O |
| F | L | O | O | D | I | N | G | A | F | D | U |
| O | O | M | O | N | R | S | A | S | O | I | B |
| R | N | P | N | E | D | O | U | T | R | S | L |
| E | G | A | S | D | R | O | U | G | H | T | E |
| C | F | S | E | E | U | N | L | D | E | A | D |
| A | L | S | O | G | H | T | U | R | E | N | E |
| S | O | A | Y | R | T | R | C | A | S | C | C |
| T | E | M | P | E | R | A | T | U | R | E | K |
| D | E | G | R | E | T | E | M | P | C | L | E |
| C | E | L | S | S | H | O | U | L | D | E | R |

1  The weather _____ is for snow tomorrow.
2  There is a serious _____ across central Africa because it hasn't rained for so long.
3  The _____ in Antarctica is too low for people to stay outside.
4  The bus couldn't get to the town because of _____ on the roads near the river.
5  Her _____ was injured when the roof fell in during the storm.
6  Water boils at one hundred _____ Celsius.
7  What's the _____ from London to Edinburgh?
8  We travelled on a _____ bus in London.
9  The _____ showed that we were travelling north.
10  When the _____ rains arrived, half the homes in the village were under water.

# 11 Grammar

## 11.1 Comparative & Superlative Adjectives & Adverbs

Χρησιμοποιούμε **comparative** (συγκριτικό βαθμό) για να συγκρίνουμε δύο πρόσωπα ή πράγματα. Συνήθως σχηματίζουμε το comparative (συγκριτικό βαθμό) προσθέτοντας την κατάληξη *–er* στο επίθετο ή το επίρρημα. Αν το επίθετο ή το επίρρημα έχει περισσότερες από δύο συλλαβές, τότε χρησιμοποιούμε τη λέξη *more*. Συχνά χρησιμοποιούμε τη λέξη *than* μετά από το comparative (συγκριτικό βαθμό).

→ Greek summers are **hotter than** British summers.
→ People should drive **more slowly** on wet roads.

Χρησιμοποιούμε **superlative** (υπερθετικό βαθμό) για να συγκρίνουμε ένα πρόσωπο ή πράγμα με άλλα ομοειδή πρόσωπα ή πράγματα. Συνήθως σχηματίζουμε το superlative (υπερθετικό βαθμό) προσθέτοντας την κατάληξη *–est* στο επίθετο ή το επίρρημα. Αν το επίθετο ή το επίρρημα έχουν περισσότερες από δύο συλλαβές, τότε χρησιμοποιούμε τη λέξη *most*. Χρησιμοποιούμε τη λέξη *the* πριν από το superlative (υπερθετικό βαθμό).

→ Winter is **the coldest** season of the year.
→ The sun shines **the most brightly** at midday.

**Ορθογραφία:** big → bi**gger**/bi**ggest**   large → larg**er**/larg**est**   easy → eas**ier**/eas**iest**
Μερικά επίθετα και επιρρήματα είναι ανώμαλα και σχηματίζουν το comparative και superlative (το συγκριτικό και τον υπερθετικό βαθμό) με διαφορετικούς τρόπους.

| Adjective/Adverb | Comparative | Superlative |
|---|---|---|
| good/well | better | the best |
| bad/badly | worse | the worst |
| many | more | the most |
| much | more | the most |
| little | less | the least |
| far | farther/further | the farthest/ furthest |

**Σημείωση:** Μερικές λέξεις όπως *hard, late, straight* και *fast* είναι και επίθετα και επιρρήματα.
Άλλες λέξεις *friendly, lovely, silly* και *ugly* αν και τελειώνουν με *-ly*, δεν είναι επιρρήματα αλλά είναι επίθετα. Οι λέξεις *hardly (= barely)* και *lately (= recently)* δεν είναι τα επιρρήματα των λέξεων *hard* και *late*.

## 11.2 Other Comparative Structures

Χρησιμοποιούμε *as* + **επίθετο/επίρρημα** + *as* για να δείξουμε ότι δύο πρόσωπα ή πράγματα είναι με κάποιο τρόπο παρόμοια.
→ Italy is **as sunny as** Spain.

Χρησιμοποιούμε *not as/so ... as* για να δείξουμε ότι ένα πρόσωπο ή πράγμα έχει μια ιδιότητα σε μικρότερο βαθμό από ένα άλλο.
→ Today's weather isn'**t as warm as** yesterday's.

# Grammar Exercises

**A** Complete the sentences with the correct comparative form of the words in brackets. Remember to use *than* where necessary.

1 The temperature is _____ (cool) normal for this time of year.

2 Danny got home _____ (quick) usual because his mum picked him up.

3 The clouds seem to be growing _____ (big) every minute.

4 There was _____ (little) sunshine than we hoped for on our holiday.

5 The fog began to clear _____ (fast) when the wind got stronger.

6 The weather forecast is for much _____ (heavy) rain to come tomorrow.

7 I hope the weather will be _____ (good) next week.

8 The roads are always _____ (dangerous) to drive on when they are icy.

**B** Complete the sentences with the correct superlative form of the words in brackets. Remember to use *the*.

1 It was _____ (stormy) night I can remember.

2 I put on _____ (warm) clothes I could find to go snowboarding.

3 We tried _____ (hard) we could to push the car out of the snow.

4 The metro is the type of transport that keeps working _____ (easy) when the weather is bad.

5 Some of _____ (beautiful) islands in the world face terrible hurricanes.

6 The rescue team couldn't reach the people who were _____ (far) out to sea when their boat sank.

7 I read that _____ (hot) temperatures on record are over 50°C.

8 David is the _____ (friendly) person I've ever met.

**C** Complete the sentences with one word in each space.

1 Children in the countryside don't have as many activities to do _____ children in the cities.

2 A jeep is definitely faster _____ a tractor.

3 This is _____ worst winter we've had this century.

4 London is _____ as foggy as it was a few years ago.

5 The snowstorm reached us _____ quickly than we expected and we weren't prepared for it.

6 Skiing is actually _____ difficult than it seems if you have a good coach.

7 Antarctica is the _____ southerly continent on earth.

8 The village wasn't _____ badly damaged by the hurricane as people thought it would be.

# 12 The World Around Us

**Page 147**

**12.1** **surround** (v) /səˈraʊnd/
be all around sth/sb • *The house was surrounded by trees and plants.*
➣ surroundings (n), surrounded (adj)
❖ περιβάλλω

**12.2** **mist** (n) /mɪst/
a thin fog, often above water • *On winter mornings, there's always some mist above the lake.* ➣ misty (adj) ❖ ομίχλη

**12.3** **botanical garden** (n) /bəˈtænɪkl ˈgɑːdn/
an area of a park where different plants and trees are grown, often to study them • *The Auburn Botanical Gardens are popular with visitors who want to enjoy the plants around the lake in Sydney, Australia.* ❖ βοτανικός κήπος

## Reading                                     Page 148

**12.4** **orangutan** (n) /ɔːˌræŋuːˈtæn/
a large animals with long arms and reddish-brown hair that comes from islands in South East Asia • *Orangutans eat mostly fruit, but they also like honey and insects.*
❖ ουρακοτάγκος

**12.5** **panda** (n) /ˈpændə/
a large furry black and white animal like a giant bear • *It seems that pandas can survive longer in captivity than they do in the wild.*
❖ πάντα

**12.6** **sea turtle** (n) /siː ˈtɜːtl/
a large reptile that has a hard shell on its back and lives in the sea • *Some volunteers were looking after injured sea turtles at the rescue centre.* ❖ θαλάσσια χελώνα

**12.7** **polar bear** (n) /ˈpəʊlə(r) beə(r)/
a large white bear from the area around the North Pole • *Polar bears are the biggest bears on earth and weigh up to 720 kilos.* ❖ πολική αρκούδα

**12.8** **cute** (adj) /kjuːt/
attractive or sweet • *Puppies and kittens always look so cute when they're playing.*
➣ cuteness (n) ❖ χαριτωμένος

**12.9** **furry** (adj) /ˈfɜːri/
covered with soft hair • *I saw a furry animal in the back garden eating the nuts from our tree.*
➣ fur (n) ❖ γούνινος

**12.10** **aggressive** (adj) /əˈgresɪv/
that can get angry and attack sb • *Polar bears can be aggressive, so don't get too close.*
➣ aggression (n) ❖ επιθετικός

**12.11** **extinct** (adj) /ɪkˈstɪŋkt/
not existing any more • *Pandas could soon become extinct if we don't protect them.*
➣ extinction (n) ❖ εξαφανισμένος, εξαλειμμένος

**12.12** **massive** (adj) /ˈmæsɪv/
very large • *Female turtles lay a massive number of eggs, but not many survive.*
➣ massiveness (n) ❖ ογκώδης, τεράστιος

**12.13** **nest** (n) /nest/
a place that an animal, especially a bird, builds to have its babies • *There's a bird's nest at the top of the tree in our garden.* ➣ nest (v), nested (adj) ❖ φωλιά

## Word Focus                                 Page 148

**12.14** **environment** (n) /ɪnˈvaɪrənmənt/
the air, water, land around us • *We must stop polluting the environment and keep our beaches clean.* ➣ environmental (adj), environmentally (adv) ❖ περιβάλλον

**12.15** **volunteer** (n) /ˌvɒlənˈtɪə(r)/
sb who does a job because they want to and not for money • *A group of volunteers were planting new trees where the forest fire occurred last year.* ➣ volunteer (v), volunteering (adj) ❖ εθελοντής

**12.16** **moonlight** (n) /ˈmuːnlaɪt/
the light from the moon • *We watched the moonlight shining on the sea.* ➣ moonlit (adj) ❖ σεληνόφως

**12.17** **cage** (n) /keɪdʒ/
sth made of metal bars to keep sb/sth inside • *I hate seeing birds that have to live in a cage.* ➣ cage (v), caged (adj) ❖ κλουβί

**12.18** **bars** (n) /bɑː(r)s/
metal poles that are used to stop sb/sth going into or out of a place • *The thief used a special tool to cut through the bars and break the window.* ➣ barred (adj) ❖ κάγκελα, μπάρες

## Reading                                 Pages 148-149

**12.19** **loggerhead turtle** (n) /ˈlɒgəhed ˈtɜːtl/
a type of sea turtle that has a large beak ad a reddish-brown shell • *Loggerhead turtles can live for almost 70 years.* ❖ είδος θαλάσσιας χελώνας

**12.20** **disappear** (v) /ˌdɪsəˈpɪə(r)/
stop existing; be lost • *Many types of plants and animals are disappearing because of pollution around the world.* ➣ disappearance (n), disappearing (adj) ❖ εξαφανίζομαι

**12.21**  **trick** (v) /trɪk/
confuse sb; make sb/sth think that sth is true
• *The heat in the desert can fool travellers into*
*believing they can see things far away.* ➣ trick
(n) ❖ κόλπο, τέχνασμα

**12.22**  **count** (v) /kaʊnt/
check how many or how much there is of sth
• *We counted four sea turtles in the sea on*
*our way to Santorini.* ➣ count (n) ❖ μετράω

**12.23**  **feel like** (phr) /fiːl laɪk/
have a particular feeling • *She felt like*
*touching the cute looking bear, but she knew it*
*was dangerous.* ❖ νιώθω σαν

**12.24**  **die out** (phr v) /daɪ aʊt/
become extinct • *Pandas have almost died out*
*because people are destroying their natural*
*environment.* ❖ εξαφανίζομαι (σαν είδος)

**12.25**  **go back** (phr v) /gaʊ bæk/
return • *Before sunset, the birds went back to*
*their nests.* ❖ επιστρέφω

# Vocabulary  Pages 150-151

**12.26**  **the Sahara Desert** (n) /ðə səˈhɑːˌrə ˈdezət/
❖ η Έρημος Σαχάρα

**12.27**  **the River Nile** (n) /ðə ˈrɪvə(r) naɪl/
❖ ο Ποταμός Νείλος

**12.28**  **Tahiti** (n) /tɑːˈhiːti/
❖ Ταϊτή

**12.29**  **tropical** (adj) /ˈtrɒpɪkl/
in or from the areas not far from the equator
• *Would you like to spend a holiday on a*
*tropical island?* ➣ Tropics (n), tropically (adv)
❖ τροπικός

**12.30**  **Lake Como** (n) /leɪk ˈkaʊməʊ/
❖ Λίμνη Κόμο

**12.31**  **cut down** (phr v) /kʌt daʊn/
make sth, e.g. a tree, fall by cutting it at the
bottom • *Ian cut down the tall trees around*
*his garden to make it brighter.* ❖ κόβω,
εκχερσώνω

**12.32**  **dry up** (phr v) /draɪ ʌp/
become dry • *The lake has dried up*
*completely because of the drought.*
❖ στεγνώνω, αποξηραίνω

**12.33**  **go down** (phr v) /gaʊ daʊn/
become less • *The number of visitors to the*
*island has gone down since the two big hotels*
*closed.* ❖ μειώνομαι

**12.34**  **bring up** (phr v) /brɪŋ ʌp/
raise (a child) • *Daniel was brought up in the*
*countryside, so he knows a lot about farming.*
➣ upbringing (n) ❖ τρέφω, μεγαλώνω (ένα
παιδί)

**12.35**  **use up** (phr v) /juːz ʌp/
use all that there is of sth • *We wanted to stay*
*at the campsite for two weeks, but we had to*
*come home early because we used up all our*
*food in the first week.* ❖ εξαντλώ

**12.36**  **deal with** (phr v) /diːl wɪð/
pay attention to sth and do sth about it
• *Governments are talking about ways to deal*
*with pollution.* ❖ ασχολούμαι με

**12.37**  **turn off** (phr v) /tɜːn ɒf/
stop sth working by moving sth or pressing
a switch • *We always turn off the water and*
*electricity at home before we go on holiday.*
❖ σβήνω, απενεργοποιώ

**12.38**  **at risk** (phr) /ət rɪsk/
in danger • *Don't put yourself at risk by going*
*sailing in dangerous weather conditions.*
➣ risk (n), risky (adj) ❖ σε κίνδυνο

**12.39**  **penguin** (n) /ˈpeŋgwɪn/
a large black and white bird that comes from
Antarctica • *Penguins have short wings that*
*they use to swim, but they can't fly.*
❖ πιγκουίνος

**12.40**  **at most** (phr) /ət maʊst/
not more than • *Many insects only live for a*
*few days at most.* ➣ most (n), mostly (adv)
❖ το πολύ

**12.41**  **in danger** (phr) /ɪn ˈdeɪndʒə(r)/
facing the risk of dying out • *Elephants are*
*in danger of becoming extinct.* ➣ danger (n),
dangerous (adj) ❖ σε κίνδυνο

---

### Phrasal Verbs

| | |
|---|---|
| bring up | dry up |
| cut down | go back |
| deal with | turn off |
| die out | use up |

### Phrases

| | |
|---|---|
| at most | feel like |
| at risk | in danger |

---

**12.42**  **species** (n) /ˈspiːʃiːz/
type of living thing (e.g. animals, plants) • *We*
*saw different species of tropical plants at the*
*flower show.* ❖ είδος

**12.43**  **plant** (v) /plɑːnt/
put sth into the ground so it can grow • *Nick*
*planted an apple tree in his garden.* ➣ plant
(n) ❖ φυτεύω

**12.44** **seed** (n) /siːd/
the small hard part inside a plant or fruit that
new plants can grow from • *The farmer was
planting seeds in his field to grow cabbages.*
❖ σπόρος

**12.45** **water** (v) /ˈwɔːtə(r)/
put water on an area of ground, etc. • *Mrs
Jackson offered to water the garden while we
were on holiday.* ➣ water (n) ❖ ποτίζω

**12.46** **wet** (v) /wet/
make sth wet • *The rain wet the chairs on our
patio.* ➣ wetness (n), wet (adj) ❖ βρέχω

**12.47** **branch** (n) /braːntʃ/
one of the parts of a tree that grows out of the
main part and leaves and flowers grown on
• *We tied a rope on a high branch of the tree
and used it to play on.* ❖ κλαδί

**12.48** **sunlight** (n) /ˈsʌnlaɪt/
the light from the sun • *The sunlight shone
through the bedroom window and woke me
up.* ➣ sunlit (adj) ❖ ηλιακό φως

**12.49** **creature** (n) /ˈkriːtʃə(r)/
any animal (including insects, fish, people)
• *The sea turtle is a strange looking creature.*
➣ create (v) ❖ πλάσμα

**12.50** **butterfly** (n) /ˈbʌtəflaɪ/
a type of insect with big coloured wings • *A
beautiful butterfly flew onto one of the flowers
in the garden.* ❖ πεταλούδα

**12.51** **hamster** (n) /ˈhæmstə(r)/
a small animal like a large mouse with a short
tail and large cheeks • *Ken has a furry little
hamster as a pet which he keeps in a cage.*
❖ χάμστερ

**12.52** **guinea pig** (n) /ˈgɪni pɪg/
a small animal (bigger than a hamster) with
short ears and no tail • *Did you know that
guinea pigs, like the ones people keep in
cages as pets, actually live in the wild in South
America?* ❖ ινδικό χοιρίδιο

**12.53** **goldfish** (n) /ˈgəʊldfɪʃ/
a small yellow, orange or red fish that people
sometimes have as a pet • *The small lake in
the park is full of goldfish that grew too big for
their fish bowls.* ❖ χρυσόψαρο

**12.54** **canary** (n) /kəˈneəri/
a small (usually yellow) bird that sounds
beautiful when it sings • *My granny used to
have two canaries that sang beautifully and
she let them fly around her living room every
day.* ❖ καναρίνι

**12.55** **hutch** (n) /hʌtʃ/
a box made of wood or plastic and metal for
keeping pet rabbits in • *Eileen's rabbit lives
in a hutch on the balcony, but he comes out
to run around and play for a couple of hours
every day.* ❖ φωλιά κουνελιού

**12.56** **lettuce** (n) /ˈletɪs/
a leafy green vegetable that is often used in
salads • *Our rabbit loves to eat lettuce and
carrots.* ❖ μαρούλι

**12.57** **cabbage** (n) /ˈkæbɪdʒ/
a vegetable with thick green, white or purple
leaves that is often cooked or served in salads
• *Christine is cooking some cabbage that she
grew in her garden to have with the dinner.*
❖ λάχανο

### Plant Life

| Nouns | Verbs |
|---|---|
| botanical garden | plant |
| branch | water |
| cabbage | wet |
| lettuce | |
| living roof | |
| seed | |
| species | |

### Animals

| | |
|---|---|
| butterfly | loggerhead turtle |
| canary | orangutan |
| creature | panda |
| dolphin | penguin |
| goldfish | polar bear |
| guinea pig | sea turtle |
| hamster | species |

# Grammar  Pages 152-153

**12.58** **rectangular** (adj) /rekˈtæŋgjələ(r)/
in a box shape that has two long sides and
two short sides • *Our pet fish are in a large
rectangular tank.* ➣ rectangle (n)
❖ ορθογώνιος

**12.59** **litter bin** (n) /ˈlɪtə(r) bɪn/
a bin for small pieces of rubbish inside a
building or outside in public areas • *We
collected the rubbish in the park and put it in
the litter bins.* ❖ κάδος απορριμάτων

**12.60** **documentary** (n) /ˌdɒkjuˈmentri/
a film or TV programme, etc. that gives
detailed information about sth/sb • *There are
interesting wildlife documentaries on this TV
channel every evening.* ❖ ντοκυμανταίρ

**12.61** **dolphin** (n) /ˈdɒlfɪn/
a sea animal like a large fish with a round
nose • *Dolphins are very clever and they
communicate with each other using sounds.*
❖ δελφίνι

**12.62** **tiring** (adj) /ˈtaɪərɪŋ/
that makes you feel tired ● *It was a long tiring journey across the country by bus.* ➢ tire (v), tired (adj), tiredness (n), tiringly (adv)
❖ κουραστικός

**12.63** **sign** (v) /saɪn/
write your name on sth to show you wrote it (or read it) ● *Remember to sign the form before you post it to the company.* ➢ signature (n)
❖ υπογράφω

**People**

| | |
|---|---|
| explorer | volunteer |
| hunter | |

# Listening
**Page 154**

**Page 154**

**12.64** **safety** (n) /ˈseɪfti/
the state of being safe; a place that is safe from dangers ● *When he saw the bear, he climbed up the branches of a tree for safety.*
➢ safe (adj), safely (adv) ❖ ασφάλεια

**12.65** **height** (n) /haɪt/
the measure of how high or tall sth/sb is
● *What's the height of the world's tallest tree?*
➢ heightened (adj) ❖ ύψος

**12.66** **a.m.** (abbr) /ˌeɪ ˈem/
before noon ● *Our school begins at 8.30 a.m.*
❖ π.μ.

**12.67** **p.m.** (abbr) /ˌpiː ˈem/
after noon ● *We get home from school at 3.45 p.m.* ❖ μ.μ.

**12.68** **weigh** (v) /weɪ/
measure sth/sb to see how heavy it is ● *How many kilos does an adult elephant weigh?*
➢ weight (n) ❖ ζυγίζω

**12.69** **(my) own** (adj) /(maɪ) əʊn/
belonging to me ● *I'd like to have my own car when I am older.* ➢ own (v), owner (n) ❖ δικός μου

**Look!**

Θυμηθείτε ότι στην Unit 10 είδαμε την έκφραση **on my own** που σημαίνει *μόνος μου*. Εδώ είναι διαφορετικά επειδή χρησιμοποιούμε τη λεξη *own* σαν επίθετο πριν από κάποιο ουσιαστικό με την σημασία *δικός μου*.
*I enjoy painting **on my own**.* (= μόνος μου)
*These are **my own** paintings.* (= δικές μου)

**Containers & Animal Homes**

| | |
|---|---|
| bars | nest |
| cage | tank |
| litter bin | |

# Speaking
**Page 155**

**Page 155**

**12.70** **overfishing** (n) /ˌəʊvəˈfɪʃɪŋ/
taking too many fish out of the sea so that there are not many left ● *If overfishing doesn't stop, many species of fish will die out.*
➢ overfish (v) ❖ υπεραλιεία / υπεραλίευση

**12.71** **effect** (n) /ɪˈfekt/
the change that sth makes to sth/sb else; a result ● *The weather often has an effect on how we feel.* ➢ affect (v), effective (adj), effectively (adv) ❖ αποτέλεσμα

**12.72** **issue** (n) /ˈɪʃuː/
a subject; a problem ● *We discussed our opinions on the issue of hunting.* ❖ ζήτημα

**12.73** **animal welfare** (n) /ˈænɪml ˈwelfeə(r)/
protection of animals to keep them healthy and safe ● *The RSPA is an animal welfare organisation in the UK which looks after lost or injured animals.* ❖ καλή διαβίωση των ζώων, φιλοζωική

**12.74** **food mile** (n) /fuːd maɪl/
how far food is moved from where it was grown/made to the people who eat it, and how much petrol is needed to move it ● *The best way to save on food miles is to eat things that grow in the local area.* ❖ τροφο-μίλια, ποσότητα τροφής επί την απόσταση που μεταφέρθηκε

**12.75** **chemical** (n) /ˈkemɪkl/
sth made using a scientific process ● *Some of the chemicals used to kill insects on farms can be bad for our health.* ➢ chemical (adj)
❖ χημικά

**12.76** **waste** (v) /weɪst/
throw away sth that you don't want which could still be useful ● *If we stop wasting energy, we could help the environment and save money.* ➢ waste (n), wasteful (adj), wastefully (adv) ❖ σπαταλάω

**12.77** **formulate** (v) /ˈfɔːmjuleɪt/
create sth in a planned way ● *Let's formulate a plan to make our environment cleaner.*
➢ formulation (n) ❖ διατυπώνω

**12.78** **tonne** (n) /tʌn/
a weight of 1,000 kilos ● *It's awful to think how many tonnes of food are wasted every day.*
❖ τόνος (1,000 κιλά)

## Environment

| | |
|---|---|
| chemical | organisation |
| documentary | overfishing |
| energy | questionnaire |
| food mile | safety |
| height | sunlight |
| mist | waste |
| moonlight | |

## Verbs

| | |
|---|---|
| amaze | recommend |
| bore | shop |
| count | sign |
| disappear | surround |
| excite | tire |
| experience | trick |
| formulate | waste |
| frighten | weigh |
| interest | |

# Writing
**Pages 156-157**

**12.79**  **introduction** (n) /ˌɪntrə'dʌkʃn/
the first part of a piece of writing that tells
you about the idea • *In your introduction, you
should explain why you're writing.* ➣ introduce
(v), introductive (adj) ❖ εισαγωγή

**12.80**  **findings** (n pl) /'faɪndɪŋz/
what sb has found out • *The report described
the findings from the scientist's research into
climate change.* ➣ find (v), finder (n)
❖ ευρήματα

**12.81**  **conclusion** (n) /kən'kluːʒn/
the end of a piece of writing • *In your
conclusion, write what you think should
happen next.* ➣ conclude (v), conclusive (adj)
❖ συμπέρασμα

**12.82**  **recommendation** (n) /ˌrekəmen'deɪʃn/
a suggestion about what to do • *The
environmental group made a recommendation
that the new road should not be built through
the wildlife park.* ➣ recommend (v) ❖ σύσταση

**12.83**  **questionnaire** (n) /ˌkwestʃə'neə(r)/
a list of questions that many people are asked
so answers can be compared • *We made a
class questionnaire to see what most people
do to help the environment.* ❖ ερωτηματολόγιο

**12.84**  **reusable** (adj) /riː'juːzəbl/
that can be used again • *Glass jars are
reusable because you can clean them and
keep other things in them.* ➣ reuse (v)
❖ που μπορεί να χρησιμοποιηθεί ξανά

**12.85**  **purpose** (n) /'pɜːpəs/
the result sb plans to get; why sb is doing sth
• *The purpose of the article was to ask for
help from local people.* ➣ purposeful (adj),
purposely (adv) ❖ σκοπός

**12.86**  **based (on)** (adj) /beɪst (ɒn)/
that came from another main idea • *The
results of the report are based on the answers
from our questionnaire.* ➣ base (n), base (v)
❖ βασισμένος σε

**12.87**  **however** (adv) /haʊ'evə(r)/
used to start saying sth that is the opposite or
different from what was said before • *I'd love
to help your organisation. However, I don't
have any extra time or money right now.*
❖ ωστόσο

**12.88**  **energy** (n) /'enədʒi/
the type of power used to make sth work
• *Why don't all homes use solar energy to
produce electricity?* ➣ energise (v), energetic
(adj) ❖ ενέργεια

**12.89**  **perfect** (adj) /'pɜːfɪkt/
ideal; the best, without any faults • *The perfect
home would use only green energy that
doesn't damage the environment.* ➣ perfection
(n), perfect (v), perfectly (adv) ❖ τέλειος

# Video 12
# Mega Green Museum
**Page 158**

**12.90**  **living roof** (n) /lɪvɪŋ ruːf/
a roof with lots of plants growing on it
• *Some buildings in the city now have living
roofs where plants grow to create a better
atmosphere.* ❖ πράσινη οροφή
✎ Syn: green roof

**12.91**  **flying carpet** (n) /'flaɪɪŋ 'kaːpɪt/
a magic carpet that can fly • *Where would you
like to travel if you had a magic flying carpet?*
(adv) ❖ ιπτάμενο χαλί
✎ Syn: magic carpet

**12.92**  **impact** (n) /'ɪmpækt/
a strong effect on sth • *A better public
transport system would have a positive
environmental impact on the city.* ➣ impact (v)
❖ επιρροή

**12.93**  **complicated** (adj) /'kɒmplɪkeɪtɪd/
not simple; hard to understand or explain
• *Making our environment better to live in
shouldn't need complicated plans. It's so
simple.* ➣ complication (n), complicate (v)
❖ περίπλοκος

**12.94**  **recycled** (adj) /ˌriː'saɪkld/
made from sth that was used before • *These
notebooks were made from recycled paper.*
➣ recycling (n), recycle (v) ❖ ανακυκλωμένος

## Adjectives

| | |
|---|---|
| aggressive | furry |
| attractive | massive |
| based (on) | perfect |
| complicated | rectangular |
| cute | recycled |
| environmental | reusable |
| extinct | simple |
| frightened | tiring |

# Vocabulary Exercises

## A Match.

| | | | | |
|---|---|---|---|---|
| 1 | animal | ☐ | a | carpet |
| 2 | food | ☐ | b | roof |
| 3 | botanical | ☐ | c | turtle |
| 4 | polar | ☐ | d | bin |
| 5 | sea | ☐ | e | mile |
| 6 | litter | ☐ | f | welfare |
| 7 | flying | ☐ | g | bear |
| 8 | living | ☐ | h | garden |

## B Circle the correct words.

1 When the goldfish got too big for their **tank / cage**, Terry made a pool for them in his garden.

2 The **cabbage / hamster** looked funny with its cheeks full of nuts.

3 The white tiger is in danger of becoming **extinct / tropical** if we don't protect it.

4 The long drought had a terrible **effect / issue** on the lives of local farmers.

5 As they walked through the forest, they heard the sound of a wild **orangutan / canary** that sang above them.

6 Simon got involved in the organisation when he read the article that **bored / interested** him.

7 We shouldn't let so much food go to **safety / waste** when many people are hungry.

8 Our health is at **risk / most** from air pollution, especially in cities.

## C Complete the phrasal verbs with *down, out, off, up* or *with*.

1 Please turn _____ the tap when you've finished watering the plants.

2 A whole forest was cut _____ to build new houses near the motorway.

3 The organisation was formed to deal _____ local environmental issues.

4 The river began to dry _____ during the hot summer.

5 The number of pandas in the wild has gone _____ so much that they're almost extinct.

6 Some species of turtle might die _____ in the near future.

7 We used _____ all the wood we had collected for the camp fire and it was too dark to look for more.

8 Frank and Betty believe it will be better to bring _____ their children in the countryside.

**D** **Complete the sentences with words formed from the words in bold.**

1   We saw a small _____ moving in the sand and realised it was a sea turtle.           **CREATE**

2   What was the government's _____ to stop sea pollution?           **RECOMMEND**

3   The main _____ of the report were that we must stop using so much plastic.           **FIND**

4   Would you like to join an _____ group to plant more trees on the mountain?           **ENVIRONMENT**

5   Do you know the _____ of the tallest animal in the world?           **HIGH**

6   People should take _____ bags for shopping instead of using more plastic ones.           **REUSE**

7   The new species of snake was found by an _____ who was walking through the Amazon rainforest.           **EXPLORE**

8   The police caught the _____ who were trying to kill the tigers.           **HUNT**

## E  Do the crossword.

**Across**

4  somebody who does a job because they want to and not for money
5  a type of insect with big colourful wings
8  a kind of box that a pet rabbit lives in
9  a type of living thing (e.g. animal or plant)
10  a vegetable with thin green leaves that you eat in salads
11  a place where birds put their eggs

**Down**

1  a situation in which something or somebody is at risk
2  taking too many fish out of the sea so that there are not many left
3  the natural light that shines from the moon at night
5  one of the parts of a tree that the leaves and flowers grow from
6  thin fog
7  a large black and white bird that comes from Antarctica

# 12 Grammar

## 12.1 Ordering Adjectives

Μερικές φορές χρησιμοποιούμε περισσότερα επίθετα μπροστά από ουσιαστικά.
→ It's a **small, furry** animal.
→ They own an **old, black, French** car.

## Opinion Adjectives

Μερικά επίθετα δίνουν μια γενική γνώμη, που θα μπορούσε να περιγράψει ο,τιδήποτε.
→ It's **nice** weather.
→ He's a **fantastic** singer.
→ We had a **lovely** meal.
Άλλα επίθετα δίνουν μια συγκεκριμένη γνώμη για να περιγράψουν συγκεκριμένα ουσιαστικά.
→ a **tasty** snack
→ a **smart** lion cub
→ a **silly** turtle

Συνήθως χρησιμοποιούμε ένα επίθετο μιας πιο γενικής γνώμης πριν από μια πιο συγκεκριμένη γνώμη.
→ a **tasty** snack
→ an **amazing, smart** lion cub
→ a **surprising, silly** turtle

Όταν χρησιμοποιούμε δύο ή περισσότερα επίθετα μπροστά από ένα ουσιαστικό για να περιγράψουμε κάτι ή κάποιον, συνήθως τα βάζουμε με αυτή τη σειρά.

| general opinion | great | beautiful |
|---|---|---|
| age | old | new |
| size | little | long |
| shape | square | rectangular |
| colour | red | white |
| nationality | Chinese | Egyptian |
| material | wooden | cotton |
| noun as adjective | music | bath |
| NOUN | box | towel |

Γενικά, βάζουμε τα επίθετα που έχουν την ισχυρότερη σχέση με το ουσιαστικό πιο κοντά στο ουσιαστικό από τα επίθετα με πιο αδύνατες σχέσεις (αφορά γνώμη και όχι γεγονότα). Φυσικά, συνήθως δεν χρησιμοποιούμε περισσότερα από δύο ή τρία επίθετα μπροστά στο ουσιαστικό.
→ They visited the **fascinating, famous London Natural History Museum** on a **horrible, rainy day**.
→ They put their **old, brown paper** boxes into the **ugly, huge, blue, plastic recycling bin**.

## 12.2 Adjectives ending in *-ing* and *-ed*

Τα επίθετα με την κατάληξη –ed περιγράφουν πώς νιώθει κάποιος.
Αυτά έχουν μια παθητική σημασία.
→ The animals **were frightened** by the storm. The animals **were frightened**. The **frightened** animals hid in the farm building.
Τα επίθετα με την κατάληξη –ing περιγράφουν την συνέπεια κάποιου πράγματος.
Αυτά έχουν μια ενεργητική σημασία.
→ The storm **frightens** the animals. The storm was **frightening**. They brought the animals inside during the **frightening** storm.

**Θυμηθείτε**
Δεν λέμε *I am boring*. επειδή σημαίνει ότι αυτός που το λέει κάνει τους άλλους να βαριούνται, είναι δηλαδή ο ίδιος βαρετός!
→ The lesson was **boring**.
→ The students were **bored**.

# Grammar Exercises

**A** Circle the correct words.

1 I can't take another day of **horrible wet / wet horrible** weather.

2 We had a really **Indian tasty / tasty Indian** takeaway last night.

3 They sat at one of the **square small / small square** coffee tables next to the window.

4 She wrote a book of **fascinating short / short fascinating** stories about animals in danger.

5 The ship sank in a **dangerous tropical / tropical dangerous** thunderstorm in the Caribbean.

6 We need to think of more **new clever / clever new** ideas to save the tigers.

7 There was a **scary blue / blue scary** tree frog in a glass tank at the zoo.

8 Don't go out in the rain without your **rubber waterproof / waterproof rubber** wellies.

**B** Complete the sentences with the adjectives in the correct order.

1 cheap • mobile • Chinese
Ivan ordered a _____ phone on the internet.

2 white • wooden • rectangular
In the kitchen, there was a _____ table.

3 little • cute • furry
In the cage, a _____ hamster was running inside its wheel.

4 caravan • French • large
They spent two weeks at a _____ .

5 Swiss • perfect • round
We used a _____ compass to find our direction on the map.

6 aggressive • polar • angry
The explorers were shocked to see the _____ bear coming towards them.

7 impressive • environmental • new
Would you like to join this _____ organisation?

8 old fashioned • noisy • steam
The _____ train moved slowly out of the station.

**C** Complete the sentences with the correct adjective form of the words in brackets.

1 After a _____ (tire) day cleaning the beach, the volunteers had a cool swim to unwind.

2 The children were getting _____ (excite) about going to the wildlife park.

3 Gordon was so _____ (frighten) when he got lost in the centre of the city.

4 I know it's important, but I get _____ (bore) reading so many articles about recycling.

5 We saw an _____ (amaze) building that creates its own electricity.

6 The report gave some _____ (interest) facts about food production.

7 The _____ (exhaust) climbers reached the top of the mountain at last.

8 When they found out that the natural history museum was closed, the _____ (disappoint) travellers complained to the tour guide.

# Alphabetical Word List

An alphabetical list of all the words that appear in the companion follows. The number next to the entry shows where the word appears.

## A

abseil   8.82
a bit   2.150
a quarter past   10.75
a.m.   12.66
ability   7.17
Aboriginal Australian   2.8
absolutely   7.66
accept   10.87
accident   7.97
accommodation   9.1
according to   2.55
accuracy   1.177
action   1.144
activity   1.5
actually   7.67
address   1.182
administrator   6.126
admission   8.5
adult   5.71
advantage   10.20
adventure   8.115
advert   7.11
advice   4.71
aerobics   8.45
Africa   9.44
afterlife   3.128
aggressive   12.10
ago   2.27
agree   2.114
air   6.56
air conditioner   5.4
airline   10.62
airport   10.40
Alaska   3.3
Albania   1.89
alive   7.46
all-inclusive   9.10
allow   6.29
alone   1.218
alpha pair   1.212
also   1.45
altogether   1.111
always   1.47
amazing   1.56
Americano   4.93
amount   4.75
amusement park   9.67
ancient   3.130
angrily   9.83
animal skin   5.8
animal welfare   12.73

announce   1.205
annoyance   2.92
answer the phone   1.151
anywhere   7.92
apartment   1.171
app   6.88
appearance   2.133
application   1.184
April   1.91
Arabic   1.142
architect   6.131
area   1.20
around   1.53
arrangement   3.98
arrive   2.153
artist   1.30
as well   10.14
ash   9.27
Asia   9.43
ask about   3.54
assistance   8.51
at most   12.40
at risk   12.38
athlete   4.16
atmosphere   11.57
attachment   3.69
attempt   7.3
attractive   2.60
audience   7.70
August   1.77
Aussie   3.15
Australia   1.42
authorities   8.27
average   9.38
avoid   9.93
away   11.28
awesome   9.19
awful   4.99

## B

back   1.214
background   2.117
backpack   4.62
backyard   3.16
baking   7.7
ballet   3.147
bamboo   10.19
bang   6.17
bank   3.20
banquet hall   6.15
bar   4.56, 12.18
Barbados   9.11

barbecue   3.41
baseball   8.21
based (on)   12.86
basic   9.57
basket   10.59
bat   8.57
battery   10.4
BBQ   9.8
be into   7.12
be raining cats and dogs   11.1
be worth   7.57
beard   2.78
beat   8.69
beauty   2.93
bed and breakfast   9.55
beef   4.115
before   7.91
begin   1.166
believe   2.166
believe in   6.33
best friend   1.160
better   1.62
Big Ben   11.75
bill   6.68
biscuit   4.68
blanket   5.17
blinds   5.52
blog   8.102
blond/blonde hair   2.74
blow   2.14
board   3.111
board game   7.62
boarding pass   3.112
boiling   4.9
Bolivia   10.64
book   4.92
bookshelf   5.83
bored   2.5
borrow   4.42
botanical garden   12.3
bounce   8.66
boyfriend   3.142
braces   2.71
branch   12.47
brave   7.83
Brazil   2.52
break   1.137
break down   6.51
break-dance   3.145
breathe   6.70
brick   11.41
bride   2.1
brilliant   1.28

bring up   12.34
British   3.18
brochure   8.19
brown eyes   2.65
brown hair   2.64
brush   7.30
bucket   6.101
building   6.4
bull   8.30
bulldog   1.97
bullfighting   8.28
bury   11.6
bus stop   1.149
bush fire   11.36
business   2.22
business class   3.104
busy   1.34, 1.61
butterfly   12.50
button   8.50
by herself   6.28
Bye   9.96

## C

cabbage   12.57
cafeteria   4.14
cage   12.17
call   2.104
call back   3.57
call off   3.58
camel   5.19
camp   5.96
can   4.57
Canadian   1.135
canary   12.54
cancel   5.88
candle   3.43
capital   4.4
cappuccino   4.78
captain   10.38
car park   5.68
caravan   9.5
caravan park   9.56
care   2.94
Carnival   3.148
carpet   4.25
carriage   10.92
cart   5.95
carton   4.53
cash   4.51
cashier   4.46
catch up   8.74
cause   5.89

caution 6.32
celebrate 3.11
centre 5.97
ceremony 8.114
certainly 2.110
chalet 9.6
champion 2.29
Champions League 3.8
change 5.65, 10.61
change your mind 10.24
changing room 8.48
chat 1.152
cheap 9.58
check 3.90
cheerful 2.83
chemical 12.75
chess 7.39
childhood 6.115
Chile 5.62
chill out 5.13
Chinese 1.92
chocolate brownie 4.85
choice 2.48
chore 11.82
Christian 3.157
Christmas 3.139
circular 10.79
circus 2.160
city break 9.12
classical 7.24
classmate 1.138
clear 11.44
click 3.87
cliff 9.31
climate 11.42
close 1.33
club 1.170
cm 11.63
coach 8.68, 10.33
coast 9.3
coconut 3.30
collapse 11.7
colleague 3.118
collect 6.100
colony 8.23
Colosseum 9.74
colourful 1.57
column 6.90
come down with 6.53
come from 1.134
comfortable 4.80
communicate 3.84
company 3.95, 5.64
compass 11.69
competitive 7.65
complete 1.178
complicated 12.93
computer geek 1.195
concentration 8.125
concert 3.135

conclusion 12.81
conditions 11.53
confetti 3.44
confidence 7.18
congee 4.11
Congratulations! 2.4
connected 5.100
contact 3.85
continent 9.42
continue 6.73
contraction 9.98
contrast 6.84
controller 7.31
conversation 3.34
convert 5.1
cooking 1.197
cool 1.162, 11.32
co-pilot 10.57
corner shop 6.35
correctly 7.52
cost 1.167
cozy 5.22
costume 3.7
cottage 5.31
count 12.22
country 1.13
course 1.169, 7.4
court 8.54
cover 9.32
crash 2.102
crazy (about sth) 7.42
crazy 6.19
creative 1.63
creature 12.49
creek 8.2
cricket 1.7
crossroads 6.119
crowded 1.49
cruise 10.78
cry 1.126
cub 11.81
cuckoo clock 1.98
culture 2.17
curly hair 2.77
curtain 5.51
customer 4.47
cut down 12.31
cute 12.8
cycle 1.120
Cyprus 1.115

## D

daily 4.119
damage 11.51
dancer 1.95
dangerous 6.63
darling 5.87
dash 10.84
date 1.64
date of birth 1.181

daughter 1.219
day out 11.14
day trip 9.68
dead 3.127
deal with 12.36
death 10.69
December 1.75
decide 2.49
deck 10.37
decline 10.88
decorate 3.153
deeply 5.99
degrees Celsius 11.33
delay 10.26
delete 3.63
delicious 3.37
deliver 11.83
Denmark 6.138
departure 3.110
describe 2.141
desert 7.85
design 2.25
desktop (computer) 3.82
despite 5.85
dessert 4.84
destroy 11.40
device 3.70
diamond 10.63
diary 11.35
dictionary 7.50
didgeridoo 2.11
die out 12.24
different 2.41
difficult 3.38
digital 3.71
dining table 5.46
diploma 10.43
directions 6.75
disagree 2.138
disappear 12.20
disappointed 8.113
disaster 8.111
disco 3.137
discount 8.100
discuss 2.139
dislikes 2.143
display 3.129
distance 11.68
DJ 7.77
do the laundry 5.91
do the washing up 4.26
documentary 12.60
dollar 4.69
dolphin 12.61
dot 10.82
double-decker (bus) 11.74
download 3.100
dragon 1.93
drama club 7.81
drawer 5.79

dream come true 8.110
dress 2.3
drill 8.7
drink station 8.88
drive off 10.54
driver 2.158
driving licence 10.44
drop out 8.73
drop sb off 10.53
drought 11.39
drums 7.64
dry 4.30
dry up 12.32
Dubai 9.78
due to 8.40
dull 11.30
during 4.15
dust 4.23
Dutch 1.99

## E

each one 2.40
each other 2.136
early 2.30
earn 11.80
earth 9.73
easily 8.105
Easter 3.154
economy class 3.105
edge 6.134
effect 12.71
Egyptian 3.120
Eiffel Tower 11.76
eightieth 8.95
elbow pad 8.18
electric 8.103
electricity 5.26
emotion 8.108
Empire State Building 11.72
employer 10.98
empty 9.87
encounter 4.105
end 10.77
endurance 8.123
energy 12.88
engineer 6.137
England 1.41
enjoyable 9.94
enter 6.6
enter a competition 1.187
entertainment 8.29
(blog) entry 9.41
environment 12.14
epic 1.202
equal 8.75
equipment 4.73
erupt 9.25
escape 11.18
especially 1.194
espresso 4.77

serious 11.50
service 6.60
session 7.20
settler 3.12
seventieth 8.94
shady 5.40
share 1.172
shark 2.33
sharp 11.11
shave 2.80
shed 5.36
shelf 4.48
shin guard 8.17
shine 2.119
shock 2.96
shopping 2.147
shopping centre 6.39
short hair 2.62
shoulder 11.19
shoulder pad 8.16
shy 2.84
Sicily 6.106
sight 9.65
sightseeing 6.91
sign 12.63
sign off 4.104
signal 6.98
signature 1.189
silly 2.86
silver 1.213
similar 2.135
simply 11.86
since 5.60
singer 2.103
sink 11.29
situation 1.147
sixtieth 8.93
skateboarding 7.53
skates 8.14
ski 3.91
ski slope 8.119
skill 7.6
skin 2.70
skyscraper 6.130
slash 10.83
sleeping bag 7.33
sleepover 3.5
slightly 11.70
smart 2.39
smartphone 3.74
smell 5.41
smile 2.91
smoothly 9.92
snack 2.18
snail 3.80
snake charmer 9.104
snowboarding 7.54
snowstorm 11.78
snowy 11.26
so 2.34

sociable 2.85
social media 9.89
social network 3.96
solar panel 5.25
solve 7.29
somehow 11.12
someone 6.26
sometimes 1.127
somewhere 6.14
son 1.221
soon 1.139
sound 2.23
South Africa 1.40
South America 9.47
South Korea 9.53
southerly 11.65
southern 11.43
souvenir 1.24
space 5.81
spaghetti 1.94
Spain 1.82
sparkler 3.45
sparkling water 4.87
species 12.42
specific 1.132
spectacular 3.14
spend 4.38
spend time 1.35
splish splash 10.89
spooky 6.25
sport 1.37
spot 10.16
sprinkles 3.28
square 3.29
stadium 6.40
staff 4.107
stage 7.69
stamp 6.67
stamp collecting 7.80
stand 8.9
stand on your hands 8.58
standard 10.48
starter 4.82
stay in 3.52
stay up 3.53
steak 4.65
steal 10.60
steam train 10.94
steamed 4.7
steep 7.96
still 2.53
still water 4.89
sting 11.10
storm 11.24
straight hair 2.63
straight on 6.83
stranded 11.2
strange 1.201
strawberry 4.74
streamer 3.46

street market 1.23
strength 8.118
stressed 7.51
structure 6.122
student 1.27
subject 1.175
successful 2.43
such 11.15
suddenly 2.120
suggestion 7.74
suitcase 9.70
summer 1.36
sunbathe 4.98
suncream 2.76
sunglasses 9.35
sunlight 12.48
sunset 9.29
sunshine 11.5
support 2.149
sure 2.163
surf the net 3.92
surfer 2.26
surname 1.109
surprised 2.6
surround 12.1
survive 5.73
swap 2.140
sweep 4.27
sweetly 9.81
swimming 1.9
swimming costume 2.115
swimsuit 8.81
switch on 5.56
Switzerland 1.88
symbol 1.96
synonym 8.38

## T

table tennis 7.41
Tahiti 12.28
Taiwan 7.5
take a break 1.150
take part in 2.28
take photos 1.163
take place 9.86
take sb out 3.56
take sb away 3.55
take up 6.44
takeaway 4.95
talent 7.61
tall 2.124
tan 2.67
tank 6.42
tap 5.7
task 4.108
tasty 2.19
taxi 10.35
taxi driver 9.79
teach 1.168
team 1.208

technology 3.73
teddy 6.114
tell jokes 2.89
temperature 11.31
temple 6.89
temporary 1.146
tent 4.61
terminus 10.99
terrible 2.100
text 3.75
Thailand 4.59
that's a pity 3.35
that's a shame 7.28
the Aegean 8.59
the Alps 6.95
the Caribbean 8.36
the Highlands 7.37
the Himalayas 6.105
the Mediterranean 6.104
the Netherlands 1.100
the Northern Lights 9.24
the Pacific Ocean 11.61
the rest 5.29
the River Nile 12.27
the Sahara Desert 12.26
the United States 6.108
the West Indies 8.32
theatre 6.41
thief 8.43
thirtieth 8.90
thirty-second 8.97
thirty-third 8.98
thrilled 8.109
thumb 1.3
thunder 11.38
thunderstorm 11.22
tidy 4.34
till 4.45
time out 7.1
timetable 8.46
tin 4.55
tip 4.91
tiramisu 4.90
tiring 12.62
title 1.180
toast 9.60
toilet 5.5
tomb 3.123
tonne 12.78
too 1.46
tool 5.37
touch 8.107
tour guide 6.13
tourist 1.50
tourist information centre 9.62
tournament 8.64
towards 2.121
towel 5.76
tower 6.2
track 10.95